Sir Walter Ralegh

Twayne's English Authors Series

Arthur F. Kinney, Editor

University of Massachusetts, Amherst

TEAS 469

Sir Walter Ralegh in a 1588 portrait attributed to "H."
National Portrait Gallery, London

Sir Walter Ralegh

by Steven W. May

Georgetown College

Twayne Publishers
A Division of G. K. Hall & Co. • Boston

Sir Walter Ralegh
Steven W. May

Copyright 1989 by G. K. Hall & Co.
All rights reserved.
Published by Twayne Publishers
A Division of G. K. Hall & Co.
70 Lincoln Street
Boston, Massachusetts 02111

Copyediting supervised by Barbara Sutton
Book production by Gabrielle B. McDonald
Book design by Barbara Anderson

Typeset in 11 pt. Garamond
by Compositors Corporation, Cedar Rapids, Iowa

Printed on permanent/durable acid-free paper
and bound in the United States of America

Library of Congress Cataloging-in-Publication Data
May, Steven W.
    Sir Walter Ralegh / by Steven W. May.
        p.   cm. — (Twayne's English authors series ; TEAS 469)
    Bibliography: p.
    Includes index.
    ISBN 0-8057-6983-8
    1. Raleigh, Walter, Sir, 1551?–1618—Criticism and interpretation.
I. Title.   II. Series.
PR2335.M3   1989
828'.309—dc20   89-33454
                                                              CIP

For my Mother and Father

Contents

Editor's Note

Drawing on considerable manuscript and documentary evidence, some of it new, Steven W. May provides at last an authoritative canon of Sir Walter Ralegh's work, a brief but definitive biography of Ralegh's puzzling and controversial life, and a fresh review of all his literary, historical, and occasional prose and poetry. What emerges here is a man dedicated to religious principle and committed to certain political beliefs who learns how to flatter, avoid, or write directly to Elizabeth I and James I as well as for Prince Henry and numerous political and literary patrons. The extended treatment given to the courtier's poetry, the *Ocean to Cynthia*, the exploration pamphlets, and the magisterial (and highly political) *History of the World* are detailed and exemplary. What Professor May has provided us is, quite simply, the most reliable guide we now have to Ralegh as man and poet. This book deserves to be the basic guide for scholar and student alike.

Arthur F. Kinney

About the Author

Steven W. May received his higher education at Rockford College and the University of Chicago, and has served as professor of English at Georgetown College, Georgetown, Kentucky, since 1969. His professional interests include the study of Renaissance manuscripts, textual criticism, and literature at the Elizabethan court. He edited *The Poems of Edward, Seventeenth Earl of Oxford and of Robert, Second Earl of Essex* for the 1980 Texts and Studies issue of *Studies in Philology*. His edition of Cambridge University Library MS. Dd.5.75 was published in 1988 as *Henry Stanford's Anthology*. He has published articles on Ralegh, Shakespeare, William Hunnis, George Cavendish, and other Tudor authors.

Preface

Definitive assessment of Sir Walter Ralegh's achievement as a writer necessarily awaits a definitive edition of his works. Although generations of scholars have tried to determine exactly what he wrote in verse and prose, the received editions of his works continue to fall short of the highest standards of twentieth-century editing. This is not altogether the fault of Ralegh's editors, for his canon presents one of the most complicated problems in English Renaissance literature. Against five poems set forth in his own handwriting we find scores of lyrics attributed to him in late Renaissance books and manuscripts, each of which must be evaluated individually. Both before and after the English Civil War a number of prose tracts were ascribed to Ralegh because they expressed unorthodox or antiestablishment views of the type that became associated with his posthumous reputation. And even the prose works that he published during his lifetime, such as his *Guiana* tract and the *History of the World*, may be contaminated with passages by such protégés and associates as Thomas Harriot, Richard Hakluyt, or Ben Jonson.

In light of these problems it is little wonder that, overall, the upgrading of Ralegh's canon has proceeded slowly since the publication of his collected *Works* in 1829. In the twentieth century, the prose canon has been defined within acceptable limits, particularly through the efforts of Ernest A. Strathmann and Pierre Lefranc, albeit the textual work needed to produce critical editions of the prose has scarcely begun. Lefranc's *Sir Walter Ralegh Écrivain* (Paris, 1968) is the single most valuable and comprehensive contribution to Ralegh studies since Edward Edwards's two-volume *Life of Sir Walter Ralegh* (London, 1868). Lefranc's treatment of the poetry, however, is weakened by his reliance on the inflated canon in Agnes M.C. Latham's *Poems of Sir Walter Ralegh* (London, 1951). Similarly, Strathmann's *Sir Walter Ralegh. a Study in Elizabethan Skepticism* (New York, 1951) offers penetrating analysis of Ralegh's intellectual disposition, yet it too must be qualified to the extent that it deals with spurious works and omits titles subsequently added to the canon. While the present study is less ambitious than those of Strathmann and Lefranc, it examines Ralegh's contribution to English letters with reference to a more authentic canon than has been previously established for him.

The canon and texts of Ralegh's works evaluated here are listed in the Bibliography under Primary Works. A critical text of Poem 6, "Fortune hath taken thee away," is printed here for the first time, and the text of Poem 21, "My daye's delight," is provided in chapter 6. The remaining texts of Ralegh's poems follow Michael Rudick's unpublished doctoral dissertation, "The Poems of Sir Walter Ralegh" (Chicago, 1970). The poems are enumerated in the Bibliography by their abbreviated first lines, with Rudick's numbering aligned with that of Agnes Latham's in *The Poems of Sir Walter Ralegh*. I omit the first lines of Ralegh's translated verses in *The History of the World*, which are reprinted by both Rudick and Latham. Where short titles are used in my narrative for Ralegh's prose works, these appear first in parentheses in the Bibliography, followed by the full title and edition used. References to Ralegh's letters follow Edwards's *Life of Sir Walter Ralegh*, vol.2, unless otherwise noted. The exclusion of poems from the canon has been guided by Rudick's introduction, chapter 3, his "The 'Ralegh Group' in *The Phoenix Nest*," *Studies in Bibliography* 24 (1971):131–37, and Philip Edwards's "Who Wrote 'The Passionate Man's Pilgrimage?'" *English Literary Renaissance* 4 (1974):83–97. My formulation of Ralegh's canon and text in verse and prose is indebted throughout to Peter Beal's *Index of English Literary Manuscripts* (London, 1980), vol. 1, part 2:365–445.

In an appendix to his *Sir Walter Raleigh* (Princeton, 1959), Willard M. Wallace noted that "From June 9, 1584 until his death, [Ralegh's] signature on all correspondence was Ralegh, the name that also appears in his books" (319). Although he did sign "W Raleighe" to a letter calendared in the State Papers, Addenda, 1587–88 (SP 15/30, ff. 283–84), this lone exception should not override Sir Walter's clear preference for the spelling Ralegh.

I am grateful to Professor Michael Rudick for permission to base my study of the canon and texts of Ralegh's poetry upon his doctoral dissertation (University of Chicago, 1970), and to Professors Pierre Lefranc and Jerry Leath Mills for reading and commenting upon various chapters of the book in progress.

Steven W. May

Georgetown College

Chronology

1554 Walter Ralegh born at Hayes, Devonshire, the son of Walter and Katherine Champernown Ralegh, widow of Otho Gilbert.

1568?–1571 In France fighting in support of the Huguenot forces.

1572–1574 In residence at Oriel College, Oxford.

1575 27 February, transfers membership from Lyon's Inn to the Middle Temple.

1576 Commendatory verses for Gascoigne's *The Steele Glas* mark Ralegh's first appearance in print.

1578 Captain of the *Falcon* on Sir Humphrey Gilbert's voyage, November–May 1579.

1580 July, departs for military service in Ireland. December–early February 1581, returns to London with captured letters.

1581 Resumes military service in Ireland; returns to London by late December.

1582 February, accompanies the Duke of Anjou to Antwerp in train of the Earl of Leicester.

1583 Receives patent for licensing wine sales.

1584 25 March, receives patent for the discovery of foreign lands; confirmed by the House of Commons 18 December. March, receives lease to customs of woolen cloth exports. April, sponsors first voyage to North America. November–March 1585, sits in his first Parliament.

1585 6 January, knighted by Queen Elizabeth. Makes first attempt to establish an English colony in North America. August, appointed steward of the Duchy of Cornwall and lord warden of the Stanneries.

1586 Gets land grant in Munster, Ireland. Sits second term in Parliament.

1587 Is appointed lieutenant of Cornwall by 1587. May, sponsors second colonizing voyage to Virginia.

1588   February?, marries Elizabeth Throckmorton. July, serves in
        the Channel against the Spanish Armada.

1589   March, transfers his Virginia colony to syndicated owner-
        ship. August–December, in Ireland. December, brings
        Edmund Spenser to court.

1591   May, prepares a fleet to resist expected Spanish invasion.
        September, Spanish squadron captures the *Revenge*, com-
        manded by Sir Richard Grenville; Ralegh publishes the *Re-
        venge* tract.

1592   January, Queen Elizabeth bestows Sherborne on Ralegh.
        February, commissioned for a privateering voyage against
        Spain; sails in May, but is recalled to London. 26 March,
        Damerei, Ralegh's son by Elizabeth Throckmorton Ralegh,
        born. July, loss of royal favor; Ralegh and his wife sent to the
        Tower. September, released from the Tower to supervise un-
        loading of the *Madre de Dios* treasure at Dartmouth.

1593   February–April, attends his third Parliament. March, com-
        mission investigates Ralegh's religious orthodoxy. 1 Novem-
        ber, son, Walter, baptized.

1594   December, receives letters of marque authorizing his priva-
        teering ventures against Spain.

1595   February–September, makes Guiana voyage.

1596   June–July, sails with Essex and Lord Admiral Howard on
        the "Cadiz" raid.

1597   June, reconciled with the queen and resumes his duties as
        captain of the Guard. July–September, commands one of
        four squadrons in the "Islands" voyage.

1598   January, is a prominent speaker in Parliament.

1600   August, appointed governor of Jersey.

1601   February, helps to suppress the Essex rebellion. October–
        December, attends his last session of Parliament.

1602   Sends two expeditions to Virginia.

1603   24 March, Queen Elizabeth dies. Ralegh speaks with King
        James in May; loses his wine-licensing patent and offices of
        captain of the Guard, lieutenant of Cornwall, and governor
        of Jersey; ordered to vacate Durham House. July, arrested

on suspicion of plotting with Lord Cobham to overthrow King James. 17 November, convicted of high treason. 9 December, James commutes the death sentence to imprisonment during pleasure.

1603–1616 Ralegh confined in the Tower of London.

1606 15 February, second son, Carew, baptized.

1608 James begins the process of acquiring Sherborne for Sir Robert Carr.

1609–1610 Ralegh invests in two authorized expeditions to Guiana.

1612 6 November, Prince Henry dies.

1614 December, publication of *The History of the World* suppressed by the king.

1615 February, Ralegh reported to be dangerously ill.

1616 19 March, warrant issued for Ralegh's release from the Tower to prepare for the voyage to Guiana.

1617 12 June–21 June 1618, makes second voyage to Guiana.

1618 9 August, attempts to escape to France. 29 October, is beheaded in the yard of the old Palace of Westminster.

1628 *Prerogative of Parliaments* published; the *History* reaches a fourth edition.

1632 "Instructions to his Son" published; seven editions follow by 1636.

Chapter One
Ralegh's Life

Ascent to Royal Favor, 1554–81

The Renaissance ideal of the active life in military and political service to one's country came readily, almost easily, to Walter Ralegh. As a captain in Ireland he survived a murderous ambush, as he survived during the "Cadiz" raid of 1596 a wound to the thigh of the kind that had proven fatal to Sir Philip Sidney a decade earlier. And where Sidney yearned in vain for a significant role in his country's affairs, Ralegh enjoyed office at court as captain of the queen's Guard, administrative responsibility on the national level as lieutenant of Cornwall and warden of the West Country tin industry, the Stannaries, and as governor of Jersey. Although his ambition to be sworn to the Privy Council eluded him, he was nevertheless regularly consulted by the queen and her councillors, who respected his knowledge of military strategy, Irish affairs, and West Country politics. Above all, he maintained for nearly twenty years his sovereign's considered esteem, and with it the advantages of wealth and influence such as few favorites enjoyed in the course of her long reign.

Indeed, nothing less than royal favor could have elevated plain Walter to the heights of prosperity and public responsibility that he achieved in the 1580s and 1590s. He was born into an ancient but only moderately prosperous Devonshire family, the youngest son of Walter Ralegh of Budleigh. By his first wife, Joan Drake, the elder Ralegh had sired his heir, George, and another son, John. His second wife, Katherine Champernown Gilbert, was herself the mother of three sons and one daughter by her first husband, Otho Gilbert. Thus Walter, the future poet, courtier, and soldier, was the youngest son of both his parents; he would rise by his own merits if he were to rise very far at all.

The intertwined families of Ralegh, Gilbert, Champernown, and Drake provided Ralegh with an enduring base of West Country support; they were, moreover, allied by marriage with other families who had risen to office and influence in London and at court. Through his mother Ralegh was related to Katherine Astley, Queen Elizabeth's most trusted lady-in-waiting until her death in 1565. Two great-uncles, Sir Gawain and George Carew, were also prominent at court, the latter as dean of the queen's Chapel. Elizabeth no doubt alluded to these family ties when she wrote on Walter's behalf in 1582, "in respecte of his kyndred, that have served us some of them (as you knowe) neer aboute our Parson."[1] At a similar remove Ralegh could claim kinship with Sir Thomas Gorges, groom of the privy chamber and an intimate royal servant. He was more nearly allied to Sir William Gorges, one of the queen's gentleman pensioners and the father of Walter's second cousin and lifelong friend, Sir Arthur Gorges. Thus a number of his relatives had gained access to the highest levels of patronage, although none of these ties was so immediate as to guarantee Ralegh's advancement.

In the absence of documentary evidence Walter's youth and education can be only vaguely reconstructed. He was undoubtedly nurtured in a strongly Protestant home, for both his parents had publicly demonstrated their commitment to the reformed religion. Ralegh's grammar school education must be deduced (as must Shakespeare's) from evidence that surfaced later in his career. He could not have studied at Oriel College, Oxford, for example, without a significant background in the classics, for he was reputed "the ornament of the juniors, . . . proficient in oratory and philosophy."[2] His university studies lasted only a few years, from 1572 through 1574 at the latest, yet his writings reveal the benefit of typical university training in logic and rhetoric in their concise, organized style, use of telling examples, and the habit of anticipating counterarguments. Meanwhile, he had gained a firsthand knowledge of France through his Champernown relatives, who were deeply involved with the Huguenot cause. Indeed, a Champernown cousin married the daughter of Gabriel, count of Montgomery, a prominent commander of the Huguenot forces. Ralegh was in France as early as May 1569 and presumably joined the English volunteers under Henry Champernown when they arrived in October. Years later Richard Hakluyt affirmed in dedicating to Ralegh his translation of a French tract that his patron understood French better than he did.[3]

Ralegh matriculated at Oriel soon after returning from France, and in 1574 he entered Lyon's Inn, one of the Inns of Chancery in London. In February of the following year, and despite Lyon's connection with the Inner Temple, Ralegh entered the Middle Temple, one of the four Inns of Court and one whose membership was dominated by gentlemen from southern and western counties.[4] His association with these institutions offered Ralegh ample opportunity to prepare for a legal career, although he protested at his trial in 1603 that he had never studied law. The London Inns of Court were, after all, fashionable social clubs as well as law schools and thus proper addresses for gentlemen in search of patronage and career openings at court or in the state at large. If Walter declined the study of law as a Templar, he nevertheless broadened his humanist education, including the cultivation of poetry. His earliest datable verse, the commendatory stanzas for George Gascoigne's *The Steele Glas*, appeared in 1576 and reveal his association with England's foremost poet between Surrey and Spenser. By this date Arthur Gorges was also in London pursuing service at court and writing lyric verse. Ralegh was no doubt acquainted as well with the poet George Whetstone and with Henry Noel, who had collaborated in penning the verse tragedy *Tancred and Ghismond* in 1567. Both Noel and Whetstone sailed as did Ralegh on Sir Humphrey Gilbert's voyage of 1578–79, while Noel's name is linked with Ralegh's throughout the 1580s when both were established courtiers.[5]

During the winter of 1578–79 Ralegh held a responsible command with Gilbert as captain of the *Falcon* in Sir Humphrey's voyage in search of the Northwest Passage. The expedition became sidetracked by privateering interests, however, in which the *Falcon*'s encounter with a Spanish warship gave Ralegh his earliest recorded experience with naval combat, and no doubt his first experience as a military commander. The voyage itself was in every respect a failure, and Ralegh returned to London to search for other means of advancement.

His interest in exploration and poetry may have recommended him to Edward DeVere, the seventeenth earl of Oxford, a poet who also invested in several voyages of discovery. Ralegh belonged to Oxford's circle during at least a few months of 1579, for just after DeVere's infamous quarrel on the tennis court with Philip Sidney, Ralegh and Charles Arundel delivered the earl's challenge to Philip. By this time, however, DeVere had been secretly reconciled with the Catholic church, and Ralegh's enduring opposition to Catholicism may well explain the sudden antagonism that grew up between them. Arundel even charged that Oxford plotted to murder Ralegh when he left for Ireland the following summer. Some years later Ralegh used his influence with the queen to restore DeVere to royal favor, although he compared his errand to one who would "laye the sarpente before the fire" where, should he recover, "myself may be moste in danger of his poyson and stinge."[6]

DeVere may have been Ralegh's first patron, but he seems not to have secured any tangible rewards for Ralegh, least of all the military command in Ireland, which was the kind of appointment the earl was never able to gain for himself. Ralegh's experience as a teenager in the wars in France even coupled with his command on Gilbert's abortive expedition scarcely made him the obvious choice for an infantry appointment, yet in the summer of 1580

Ralegh took charge of a company of one hundred foot soldiers and twelve horse under Lord Grey, the newly appointed lord deputy of Ireland. Ralegh never referred to Grey as to a patron, but he did write to the earl of Leicester as one of his "poore followers" to whom Grey had offered so little opportunity that, were he not "on[e] of yours, I would disdayn it as mich as to keap sheepe." Apparently then, and perhaps not long after Oxford had clashed with Sidney, Ralegh had transferred his allegiance to Sidney's uncle, the earl of Leicester.[7] Within a few months his new patron had secured his post in the Irish wars, while Oxford was so furious at this desertion to the opposite camp that he plotted Ralegh's assassination.

What began clearly enough as the entree to a military career became, surprisingly, Ralegh's means of establishing himself at court. His duties began ignominiously enough, however, at the siege of Smerwick where his troops, at Lord Grey's command, slaughtered the disarmed Spanish and Italian garrison. In sorting through their belongings Ralegh discovered a quantity of correspondence that revealed "some matters of secrecy"; it was judged sufficiently important that he was sent to London with these documents in December. Ralegh was apparently still in England on 3 February following when he testified on Gilbert's behalf in a Chancery suit.[8]

This heretofore unrecorded journey home was no doubt a critical step in his rise to prominence at court. The captured papers brought him into personal contact with members of the Privy Council. His earliest letters to men of this rank are those written to Secretary Walsingham and to Lord Treasurer Burghley upon his return to Ireland in late February. Through their influence he may well have received his appointment as "esquire for the body extraordinary," a title he invoked for the first time at his deposition that same month.[9] Although Ralegh had styled himself "de curia" as early as December 1577, the title of esquire is the earliest evidence that he had succeeded in gaining a foothold, or at least a toehold, at court. Esquires in ordinary, those with regular duties and salaries, held trusted positions in the royal household. Esquires extraordinary, however, held unpaid, essentially honorary posts. They could call themselves her majesty's servants and claim to be "of the court," yet their sinecures bestowed no demonstrable right of access to Elizabeth herself, and thus no direct tie with the preeminent source of patronage.

Upon resuming his duties in Ireland, Ralegh's conduct was honorable to the point of heroism. He faced down an ambush by Irish forces much superior to his own, and he captured and led back to Munster the rebel Lord Roche and his Lady by deftly infiltrating their well-defended castle and marching with them through miles of hostile countryside. Edmund Spenser worked an allegorized version of the thwarted ambush into book 3 of the

Faerie Queene[10] and, as Lord Grey's secretary, he had also been present at the Smerwick massacre. Spenser and Ralegh could have met at this time or before going to Ireland through their common ties with the earl of Leicester, but there is no evidence for such an acquaintance. Extant official correspondence in Spenser's handwriting proves that his position with Lord Grey was no sinecure, while Ralegh was occupied with his troops in the field. The opportunities for casual socializing between the two were probably minimal, and Spenser was not dependent on Ralegh for the account of his Irish exploits. They were readily available in print in John Hooker's "Irish Chronicle" that appeared with the 1587 edition of Holinshed's *Chronicles*. Spenser's allusions to Ralegh in book 3 are more likely a tribute to a new patron than the acknowledgment of an old friendship.

Throughout Elizabeth's reign aspiring gentlemen found that active service abroad tended to swallow careers at court and sometimes lives as well. Sidney died in battle, Sir Humphrey Gilbert perished at sea, and neither Gilbert nor Sidney's father, Sir Henry, were rewarded by the Crown for their years of rigorous duty in Ireland. The most notable Elizabethan exceptions to this dismal pattern of overseas failure are Francis Drake and Walter Ralegh. The former became a royal favorite and national hero when he returned, laden with Spanish treasure, from his circumnavigation of the globe. Ralegh, within a few months of his return from Ireland late in 1581, entered the second major phase of his career by becoming Elizabeth's chief favorite.

Ralegh had probably been at court for days or even weeks by 29 December when Walsingham signed the warrant reimbursing him for his expenses on the journey home. By 1 January of the new year Ralegh had consulted with the queen personally concerning Irish affairs; he soon became an indispensable member of her innermost circle of courtiers. Thus his ascent to favor, so puzzling to his biographers, was a gradual process initiated by his discovery of enemy documents at Smerwick. The find put him in contact with important privy councillors during the winter of 1580–81 when he established himself as an expert on Irish affairs. This reputation in turn explains his audience with the queen upon his subsequent return to London. Ralegh's steps to preferment agree in general with the account of Sir Robert Naunton, who came to know Ralegh personally. Naunton errs in supposing that Ralegh and Lord Grey debated policy matters before the Privy Council; Grey instead wrote from Ireland to protest Ralegh's suggestions. But Naunton is surely correct in stating "that the Queen and the lords took no slight notice of him and his parts, for from thence he came to be known and to have access to the Queen and the lords, and then we are not to doubt how such a man could comply and learn the way to progression . . . she began to be taken with his elocution and loved to hear his reasons to her demands."[11] Here the emphasis on Ralegh's speaking ability tallies with the informed, persuasive discourse that characterizes his letters and prose tracts. It also shows that Elizabeth did not know Ralegh as an individual before his second return from Ireland, for royal favor followed almost at once in the wake of their personal acquaintance.

Naunton's relatively contemporary account of Ralegh's success with the queen is far more plausible than Thomas Fuller's tale of the cloak across the puddle, an anecdote that did not surface until the mid-seventeenth century. Fuller's version is further compromised by the fact that it presupposes what it attempts to explain. Elizabeth did not wander among her subjects in hopeful expectation of such spontaneous and gallant gestures. One of her immediate courtier attendants might have spread his cloak before her—Ralegh himself might have done so, but after rather than before he gained Elizabeth's favor. The threat of assassination plus the tendency of her loving subjects to surround her in stifling crowds forced the queen to travel in public variously attended by her footmen, the well-armed yeomen of the guard, the gentlemen pensioners, and the royal waymaker, who was charged with helping her avoid the kind of obstacle that figures in the cloak anecdote. And even under less formal circumstances it would have been difficult for anyone outside the queen's immediate circle of courtiers to approach her so closely as to spread a cloak before her.

Prosperity and Promotion, 1582–92

In all, Ralegh enjoyed some two decades as a prominent courtier and participant in his country's affairs, an era of prosperity tempered only by the disgrace of 1592–97. He was perhaps a recognized courtier as early as February 1582, when he accompanied the Duke of Anjou from England to Antwerp in the train of the Earl of Leicester. Ralegh claimed that the Prince of Orange gave him a personal message for Elizabeth at that time, something he would scarcely have entrusted to a mere underling. By April, at latest, Ralegh was well-established in the queen's favor. As she informed Lord Grey, Captain Ralegh was, of course, to further his military career in Ireland but, she continued, he is for the time being licensed to remain here with his company commanded by his lieutenant.[12] It would be seven years before she allowed Walter to return to Ireland or to be long absent from her side for any reason.

With royal favor came rewards, both financial and social. Within the year Ralegh had Crown leases to sell for ready cash and a patent to license retail wine sellers at the rate of one pound yearly to the patentee. Early in 1584 the queen granted him the customs duties on exports of overlength woolen cloths, a gift that proved to be even more lucrative than the wine patent. He sat in his first parliament in 1584, was knighted by the queen in 1585, and gained important offices that same year, as vice-admiral for Devon and Cornwall, steward of the Duchy of Cornwall, and warden of the Stannaries, the southwestern tin-mining enterprise that employed some ten to twelve thousand men. By 1587 he was also lieutenant of Cornwall.[13] Through these appointments Ralegh exercised the principal Crown authority in all matters civil and military in southwestern England. Elizabeth also secured prestigious lodgings for Ralegh at Durham House in London, and in 1587 or shortly thereafter he gained official standing at court as captain of the queen's Guard.

This latter office became open to Ralegh when Elizabeth appointed the incumbent, Sir Christopher Hatton, to the lord chancellorship. Hatton's career as favorite resembles Ralegh's more closely than any other during Elizabeth's reign, for both, as mere gentlemen from modest families, reaped extraordinary benefits after becoming courtiers. Hatton, however, was content to pursue a rather docile career in the royal service void of military or diplomatic ambitions. Ralegh, by contrast, used his new resources to develop and pursue with fervor a unified policy of national as well as personal aggrandizement. His plan countered the threat of Spain's global hegemony with the vigorous use of English sea power, in colonization and for direct confrontation through piracy and raids on Spanish territories. Elizabeth supplied Ralegh with the means to enact this plan, yet his status as her favorite prevented him from carrying it out in person. He became therefore a manager, devising and financing his various enterprises, while leaving their execution to others.

Ralegh's earliest such venture was the continuation of Gilbert's maritime expeditions after Sir Humphrey was lost at sea in the summer of 1583. With Gilbert's brother, Adrian, Ralegh drew up an expansionist proposal entitled "The Colleagues of the discovery of the Northwest passage," the provisions of which show that its main thrust was English colonization abroad. Letters patent authorized the project in March 1584, and these were confirmed by the House of Commons in December.[14] Ralegh dispatched expeditions to North America every year from 1584 through 1587. The land he tried to colonize along the present coast of North Carolina he named Virginia, and he was styled its "Lord and Governor" in subsequent official documents.

Ralegh fully intended to profit from whatever trade could be established by the venture; he was guaranteed, for example, an exemption from import customs and a monopoly on trade with the newly discovered lands. On the other hand, it is impossible to doubt his sincere dedication to the founding of an English colonial empire that would rival Spain's. He was among the first of his countrymen to see that England's future as a world power depended upon overseas colonization and trade, and the voyages he sponsored in 1585 and 1587 were the first serious efforts to found English colonies in the New World. Meanwhile, he promoted his colony at home by popularizing the smoking of tobacco, introducing two American Indians to the queen and her court, and by employing Thomas Harriot and Richard Hakluyt to set forth detailed, illustrated accounts of the "New Found Land." In 1589 Ralegh relinquished his interest in Virginia to a syndicate, but maintained his right to found colonies elsewhere, nor did he abandon the "Lost Colony" of settlers he had sent to Virginia in 1587. As late as 1602 he sent ships to America to find them; as he wrote Sir Robert Cecil in that year, "it were pitty to overthrowe the enterprize for I shall yet live to see it an inglish nation."[15]

At the same time that he recruited West Country settlers to colonize Virginia, Ralegh was dispatching others to a parallel colonial enterprise in Ireland. Some half-million acres in southern Ireland were laid waste by the English campaign that crushed the Desmond rebellion in 1583. Ralegh attempted to repopulate many thousands of acres in counties Cork and Waterford as part of an overall goal to make Ireland a secure and prosperous English satellite. He spent years, for example, trying to establish there an export trade in pipestaves, the wooden pieces from which casks were made. His Irish holdings failed to become profitable, however, and by 1602 he had liquidated them all except for a single castle.

The work of building an English colonial empire was interrupted in 1588 by the sailing of the Spanish Armada. Indeed, the mustering of English ships throughout the year to meet this challenge kept Ralegh from sending supplies to his Virginia colonists. The Armada did, however, allow him to test the preparations he had made for direct conflict with Spain. He had launched in 1587 the *Ark Ralegh*, a warship constructed with a "new invention of Castles" designed to counter the Spanish tactic of boarding enemy vessels from their high-built galleons. Lord Admiral Howard praised Ralegh's creation as the ideal fighting ship and chose it as his flagship in repelling the Spanish attack.[16]

Ralegh's biographers have cast doubt upon his involvement in the fight, for it appears that he came up to London only after the Armada had sailed east as far as Gravelines, and that he was then merely sent to the coast with instructions for the Lord Admiral. When the Armada first entered the Channel, Ralegh's military offices required him to be on watch in Cornwall and Devon to resist a Spanish landing. After this threat had passed, he returned to London, and he did sail against the Armada according to a contemporary account in verse of the principal gentlemen who joined battle with the Spaniards.[17]

The English victory of 1588, far from ending the threat from Spain, launched an all-out war between the two countries that lasted until the accession of King James. Ralegh joined the direct assault on Spain by stepping up his privateering enterprises. By the mid-1580s he and his closest associates including his brother, Carew, and Sir Richard Grenville had assembled a small fleet that preyed on enemy shipping. Ralegh's vessels included the *Bark Ralegh, Roebuck, Mary Spark, Dorothy, Pilgrim,* and the *Serpent.* He was often obliged to defend the captains under his command for seizing neutral or even friendly French and Dutch ships when complaints from both nations flowed in to the Privy Council and the Admiralty Court. Ralegh protested that their cargoes were destined for Spanish ports or that contraband had been discovered below deck; meanwhile, those cargoes were sold and the profits distributed among Ralegh and his associates.[18] It was the one wholly profitable aspect of his anti-Spanish policy, although the profits would have been much reduced had his ships restricted their forays to enemy vessels alone.

Beyond doubt Ralegh wore his newly acquired wealth and status with a haughty swagger that infuriated his fellow courtiers and lesser countrymen alike. His first decade as the queen's favorite established his reputation as the proudest man in England. Intermittent friction in the early 1580s with such rival favorites as Hatton and Leicester gave way to prolonged quarreling with the earl of Essex as that young nobleman effectively replaced Ralegh as Elizabeth's chief favorite in 1587. Noble birth insulated Essex from the resentment that accompanied Ralegh's success with the queen. Every hanger-on at court aspired to the dazzling preferment that Ralegh enjoyed. But his success violated an ancient cultural standard still widely accepted during the Renaissance. Centuries of religious and philosophical teaching held that such drastic elevations in status disrupted the order of things, an order ultimately established and blessed by God himself. A contemporary anthologist summed up the popular attitude in the couplet, "A Lewder wretche ther lyves not under skye, / Then clown that climes from base estate to hie."[19] This conservative, medieval tradition opposed the pressures that favored individualism and social mobility, pressures that increased throughout Elizabeth's reign.

It is nevertheless misleading to suppose that Ralegh attended to his affairs beneath an umbrella of royal protection, despised and resented by nearly everyone. On the contrary, he used his influence as a courtier and officeholder to benefit his relatives, friends, and constituents, especially those in the West

Country and in Ireland. His correspondence is full of letters on behalf of others, in addition to which there is concrete evidence that his words were often effective. As Warden of the Stannaries he increased the income of the tin workers from two shillings to four shillings per week. He procured a land grant for Lady Anne Gilbert, Sir Humphrey's widow, and was instrumental in saving from execution the Puritan clergyman John Udall. Lest this be taken as evidence of his own religious leanings, Ralegh also arranged a stay of prosecution against a Cornish couple charged with recusancy. He secured pardons for three men accused of manslaughter, and in a letter of February 1588 ordering Sir John Gilbert to enforce a Privy Council restraint on shipping to Newfoundland he added the postscript, "Such as I acquaynted you withall to whom I haue geuen leue yow may lett them steale away."[20] Sir Walter nurtured his resources of patronage with the result that he could count on widespread support in men, money, and supplies for his various expeditions, private or official. Sir Robert Cecil reported in 1592 that when Ralegh arrived at Dartmouth he was greeted so joyfully by "his poor servants, to the number of 140 goodly men, and all the mariners," that Cecil "never saw a man more troubled to quiet them."[21] And Sir Lewis Stukely, who betrayed Ralegh's attempt to save his life in 1618 by escaping to France, found himself widely condemned by the nickname Sir Judas Stukely, and so hounded by recriminations that he exiled himself to a coastal island where he died insane in 1620.

After 1587 Ralegh's enemies found a stable rallying point in the career of Robert Devereux, second earl of Essex. Indeed, the Essex faction actively opposed Ralegh long after the earl was brought to the scaffold for treason in 1601. Both men incited passionate outbursts that disrupted the court and wrought ironic harm to their careers. Elizabeth intervened personally to reconcile them in August 1587 after Essex quarreled with Ralegh and boxed his ears. In December of the following year Devereux challenged Sir Walter to a duel, which was averted through the strenuous efforts of other courtiers. Although they cooperated in the expeditions against Spain in 1596 and 1597, their relations were always volatile and distrustful. Ralegh never accepted the fact that the younger man had displaced him as Elizabeth's primary favorite, while Essex fumed that she nevertheless held Ralegh in high esteem. Yet these men were natural allies, for both advocated taking the war to Spain and its colonies, in opposition to the Privy Council faction headed by Lord Treasurer Burghley and his son, Sir Robert Cecil, who favored peace with Spain.

A quite minor episode in the struggle between these rivals led in 1589 to momentous consequences for English literary history. In August it was rumored that Essex had "chased Mr. Ralegh from the court, and confined him into Ireland."[22] What actually happened was probably akin to Devereux's attempt to flee the country two years before when he found that he could not force the queen to denounce Ralegh; Essex got as far as the coast before being recalled to court.[23] Ralegh was certainly in the queen's good graces earlier in the year, for she gave him a gold chain as a special sign of favor, and in May a grant of the customs on five thousand broadcloths.[24]

The rift with Elizabeth could hardly have been substantial, but it sent Ralegh to Ireland for a few months where he apparently first became acquainted with Edmund Spenser. Spenser too had benefited from the dispersal of the earl of Desmond's lands. His seat at Kilcolman Castle stood within thirty miles of Ralegh's Irish holdings, so that it was quite natural that the two would meet as countrymen faced with the task of developing their neighboring estates. Given Ralegh's enduring fondness for poetry, there is no reason to doubt Spenser's account in *Colin Clouts Come Home Againe* that their friendship was grounded upon this common interest, to which was added a strong commitment to the Protestant cause and Spain's overthrow. Ralegh appreciated the significance of Spenser's *Faerie Queene* and encouraged the author to return to England under his patronage to present the work at court. The success of this plan demonstrates that Ralegh had indeed maintained his favor with Elizabeth, else he could not have helped Spenser, for as Gascoigne, John Lyly, and George Peele among others had already learned, poetic talent alone offered scant hope of royal preferment.

Both Spenser and his great poem, however, were well received at court that winter. After Spenser had returned to Ireland that spring, it was surely Ralegh's persistent support of his friend's interests that culminated in the substantial fifty-pound pension granted to Spenser in February 1591. Unfortunately, he never secured another patron with Ralegh's dedication and influence, so that when Sir Walter's sway with the queen ended abruptly in mid-1592, his protégé was likewise cut off from further rewards or office.

At the very time that Spenser's grant was being readied for Elizabeth's signature, Ralegh was busy organizing a naval expedition in which he was to be directly involved. Essex's ascendancy with the queen had not seriously eclipsed Ralegh's status at court, but it did mean that he could be spared for active service abroad. In January 1591 he obtained joint command with Lord Thomas Howard of the warships assembled to intercept the Spanish treasure fleet that was soon to leave the West Indies with a two years' supply of gold and silver bullion. Elizabeth prevented Ralegh from sailing with Howard not because she refused to risk him at sea but because he was needed to withstand a more immediate threat at home. King Philip had prepared a fleet of fifty-three warships to convoy his plate fleet safely home, although

English intelligence had it that some or all of this force might invade England while her best ships were at sea with Howard. Thus Ralegh was dispatched to the west in May to prepare both the land forces and an English navy to confront the Spaniards while also seeing to it that Howard received needed supplies.[25]

In the event, the invasion never materialized; instead the English squadron was surprised at the Azores by the Spanish fleet. Most of the English ships got safely away, but the captain of the *Revenge*, Ralegh's kinsman, Sir Richard Grenville, chose to fight. After a long and valiant battle Grenville was forced to surrender to overwhelming odds; his surviving crewmen and what was left of the ship fell into enemy hands. This was not only the first time that Spanish ships had overpowered an English fighting ship of any consequence, but it meant the loss by Ralegh's own later estimate of one of only thirteen capital ships of the royal navy ("Invention of Ships," 328). Ralegh countered the disaster with his first prose work, the anonymously published "Revenge" tract.

The new year began happily enough for Ralegh with the acquisition of the manor of Sherborne, an estate belonging to the see of Salisbury, now leased to Ralegh at an advantageous rent. Ralegh cherished Sherborne, his "fortune's fold," where he planned to found an enduring county family. As early as 1583 his regard for the Ralegh family caused him to have his pedigree drawn up by the heralds. Another genealogy prepared in 1601 from papers in his own possession traced his family back to the days of King John. In 1584 he attempted to purchase his father's home at Hayes where, as he explained to the then owner, "being borne in that house, I had rather seate my sealf there then any where els."[26] Sherborne was a much grander estate in northern Dorsetshire, less than forty miles from his birthplace. Ralegh obtained it just in time for on 29 March his wife, Elizabeth Throckmorton Ralegh, gave birth to his first son. The child, who died in infancy, was christened Damerei, an unusual name that again shows Ralegh's concern with his ancestry, for in dedicating to Ralegh the "Irish Chronicle" of 1587, Hooker had traced his family's alliance with a French nobleman, Sir Roger D'amerei or de Amerei.[27]

Ralegh's wife was the daughter of Sir Nicholas Throckmorton, who had served the queen as ambassador to both France and Scotland before his death in 1571. The historian William Camden termed Elizabeth "*honoraria Reginae virgine*," but she was not one of the queen's six maids of honor. The maids can be identified from the time Mistress Throckmorton came to court in 1584 until as late as November 1590. Her name is never mentioned, although it does appear regularly on the New Year's gift lists among the ladies and gentlewomen who attended the queen in the privy chamber.[28] Ralegh's bride could have become a maid of honor between 1590 and early 1592, yet such a transition from the privy chamber would have been quite unprecedented, and it is rendered even more unlikely if Ralegh had indeed married Elizabeth in 1588 as the only contemporary documentation suggests.[29] The Raleghs would only have compounded the crime of their secret marriage by the further deceit of representing Elizabeth as a maid of honor. Instead, she returned to the privy chamber in April without any acknowledgment of her marriage or its consequence.

In response, the queen sent Ralegh and his wife to the Tower. The only mystery here concerns why she waited until the end of July to do so. A similar scandal erupted two years later when another privy chamber attendant, Lady Bridget Manners, eloped with Robert Tyrwhit, a gentleman without connections with the queen or court of any kind; the newlyweds were likewise committed to the Tower.[30] Elizabeth felt personally betrayed when her servants married without her consent whether or not they were maids of honor, and she punished them accordingly.

Disgrace and Exile from Court, 1592–97

The disgrace of the Throckmorton marriage damaged Ralegh's status and prestige more than his ability to function in national or even international affairs. True, he could no longer prefer suits to the queen, for all personal access was denied him. He expressed his poignant sense of this loss in his longest and most important poetic work, the "Cynthia" poems. But he retained Sherborne, his patents of monopoly, and his major offices including even the captainship of the Guard, which was exercised by a deputy during his exclusion from court. Elizabeth could have crushed Ralegh; instead, she left him free to serve her and the realm with the added incentive that through some notable exploit he might regain his sovereign's favor.

Ralegh had scarcely completed his first month in prison when Elizabeth discovered anew just how valuable his services could be. The expedition he had organized that spring returned to Dartmouth with the greatest maritime prize ever taken by the Elizabethan seadogs, the *Madre de Dios* or "Great Carrack." It was estimated to hold jewels, cloth, spices, and other treasures from the East Indies worth half a million pounds. Once in port, however, the dispersal of so much booty by sailors and merchants proved impossible to control, whereupon Ralegh was released from the Tower and sent to Dartmouth to restore order. There his credit with his own captains and mariners thrived in spite of Elizabeth's displeasure, enabling him to help save what belonged to himself, the queen, and the London merchants who were among the primary investors in the voyage. It was a wonderful bonanza from which Elizabeth profited immensely, but it could not gloss over her sense of being doubly betrayed. Ralegh was sent back to the Tower with his share in the treasure reduced to a net loss on his investment.

By early 1593 Ralegh had progressed from royal captive to member of Parliament, and in this his third session in the House of Commons he exerted unusual influence for someone so notoriously out of favor. He strongly supported the bill that would grant Elizabeth an unusually large subsidy. Of course, he was trying to ingratiate himself with the queen, yet his arguments were wholly sincere, for the subsidy would be devoted primarily to the war with Spain. Ralegh argued strongly for the necessity of taking the conflict to Spanish territory and for making it a declared war so that all questions of the legality of seizing enemy ships might be laid to rest. He was appointed to the committee that drafted the bill and in the end Parliament granted the queen a triple subsidy to be collected in record time. National policy, at least, was running very much in Ralegh's favor.

Both in and out of Parliament Ralegh dealt with a number of touchy religious issues at this time, although it seems doubtful that they tell us much if anything about his own religious convictions. He spoke against a bill that would have imposed severe punishments on the extremist Protestant sect known as the Brownists. His objections concerned the practicality of the act itself, for he affirmed that "the Brownists are worthy to be rooted out of a Commonwealth." He asked, however, who was to pay for transporting them out of the country, and who would support their wives and children left behind?[31]

It was with a similar pragmatic spirit that Ralegh argued with Reverend Ralph Ironside about the nature of God and the soul. The occasion was a dinner party in the summer of 1593 at the home of the deputy-lieutenant of Dorset, Sir George Trenchard. Nothing in Ralegh's remarks challenged orthodox Christian belief in God, the soul, or the authority of Scripture; he objected instead to the faulty logic with which Ironside defended these doctrines. Local gossip, however, accused Sir Walter of heresy. Early in 1594 a commission was appointed to investigate the matter. The fact that the commissioners dismissed the case without a single charge against the queen's former favorite reveals that nothing he had said to Ironside or in later testimony smacked of heresy. Instead, he was writing to Cecil in April with the happy news that a Jesuit had been apprehended and would be examined by Ralegh, Trenchard, and another guest who had also attended the much-acclaimed dinner party.[32] Clearly, religious orthodoxy was well under control in Dorsetshire.

By mid-1594 Ralegh was absorbed in a major project to which the Ironside investigation was only a minor distraction. He had studied for years the possibility of establishing an English presence in Guiana, a part of modern Venezuela. The expedition he organized for this purpose was launched under a much broader franchise as revealed in the royal warrant authorizing it. In December Elizabeth signed letters of marque giving Ralegh blanket rights to attack possessions of the king of Spain. He and his associates in the venture were promised full amnesty for whatever they accomplished toward that end, and everyone down to the mariners was charged to obey Sir Walter "as they will answer at their uttermost peril."[33] The warrant reveals both the predatory nature of the expedition itself and the degree to which Elizabeth was ready to assist her outcast favorite.

On Ralegh's part, the shift from North America to the Caribbean was dictated first by his desire to take the war to Spanish soil and, second, to enrich himself to a degree that, clearly, the laborious colonization of Virginia could not readily accomplish. He needed another great prize such as the carrack of 1592, and the little fleet that set sail in February 1595 was as opportunistic in its lesser capacity as the royal squadrons that regularly tried to intercept Spain's entire plate fleet. Guiana was the main target because, while a succession of Spanish conquistadors had attempted to settle the area, none of their efforts had met with success. Thus England might manage to found a colony plump in the midst of the Spanish Main. Ralegh believed, moreover, that the land contained fabulous wealth, that it was indeed the source of much of the gold the Spaniards had taken from the Inca Empire.

Unfortunately, Ralegh returned to England with neither gold nor Spanish prizes. Although he penetrated the Orinoco River for several hundred miles, he reached, as he thought, only the border of Guiana itself. Farther inland was its capital, El Dorado, a city richer in precious metals than any that Spain had yet seized in the New World. As in Virginia, and now under his personal supervision, Ralegh's party treated the natives well and laid the foundation for successful English colonization. The *Guiana* tract he published in 1596 described the rich potential of the colony, yet his lack of tangible results led to considerable scoffing. From skepticism about the oysters Ralegh described growing on trees, to the headless men and the Amazon women, the doubters extended their ridicule to the idea that gold, pearls, and diamonds would be found there. The Guiana project did attract private investors, but without government support no serious effort at colonization could be made. Its sponsor remained an exile from the court.

Ralegh did send his trusted associate Lawrence Keymis back to Guiana in 1596 while he was himself busied with an official expedition. He received a subordinate command under Essex and Lord Admiral Howard in the voyage that sailed in June to harass Spain and if possible seize the plate fleet. In July the English force attacked the mainland Spanish port of Cadiz, some twenty-five miles north of the Strait of Gibraltar on the Atlantic side. Ralegh's account of the battle with the Spanish fleet inside the harbor is corroborated by other sources, which also give him credit for dissuading Essex from a disastrous troop landing with small boats in rough seas. Instead, Ralegh led the English warships under the fort's defensive guns to attack the Spanish fleet in the harbor, after which the soldiers safely disembarked to attempt the city itself. It was a major blow to Spain's pride as well as to its shipping. Ralegh's impetuous action was risky, even ill-advised, yet it led to the only important success of the voyage.

The forces returned home to heroes' welcomes amid great public rejoicing; still, the plate fleet had eluded them while most of the plunder from Cadiz remained with the individual plunderers. Investors in the voyage, the queen included, reaped scant returns. Ralegh complained that Elizabeth showed no appreciation for his services and he vowed to "goe to the plough, and never harken after imploiements any more."[34]

His resolve did not last long. By early spring he was commissioned to recruit and supply six thousand men for another attack on Spain. It was clear, furthermore, that rapprochement with Elizabeth was at hand. By May he was regularly coming to court, very much in company with Essex and Secretary Cecil. He was reconciled with the queen in June and resumed his duties as captain of her Guard.

The Last Years of Favor, 1597–1603

When the fleet sailed a month later on the "Islands" voyage, Ralegh held a principal command as rear admiral. The appointment served him well in the aftermath of the only noteworthy success of the venture. While separated from the rest of the squadron in the Azores, Ralegh ordered his troops to seize the island of Fayal. He led the landing in person and risked his life under heavy fire while battling for the forts that controlled the town of Villa Dorta. When Essex found that all this had been accomplished without his orders, he attempted to pass sentence of death on Ralegh through a court martial. This was prevented only because Ralegh claimed, and his fellow officers agreed, that his command in the expedition justified his action—so much for friendly cooperation in a patriotic cause. Again, the plate fleet evaded the

English dragnet and the expedition straggled home with little to boast of beyond Ralegh's signal victory.

The "Islands" voyage marked Ralegh's last major adventure during Elizabeth's reign. Although he continued to sponsor expeditions to the Americas as well as the usual privateering, his only active service involved a brief setting to sea when another Spanish invasion was expected in August 1599.[35] Poor health apparently contributed to his inactivity. He was too ill to attend the first few weeks of the Parliament of 1597, and reports of his bad health crop up frequently thereafter. In an effort to consolidate his position at court he tried during these years to gain a seat on the Privy Council and the vice-chamberlainship of the royal household. Neither effort succeeded, despite his continuing close ties with Essex and Cecil. In September 1600 he settled instead for the governorship of Jersey, no minor reward, but one that would necessarily keep him from the center of power at court.

By the time Ralegh gained his governorship the structure of power at court had been realigned following the disgrace of the earl of Essex. Devereux had been sent to Ireland with the largest Elizabethan army ever assembled, but he failed to end or even curtail the earl of Tyrone's rebellion. He compounded his failure by returning to court without leave in September 1599. Now it was Essex's turn to suffer exile, in addition to which Elizabeth deprived him of the income from his various offices plus the sweet wines monopoly that served as a major source of his income. Writing privately to Cecil, Ralegh urged him to crush their rival now that he was vulnerable, for without the queen's favor, Sir Walter argued, this "tyrant" would again become only a common person.[36]

The scheming secretary hardly needed such advice. Essex remained cut off from the queen and the means to pay his considerable debts. By early 1601 he was desperate, and surrounded by gentlemen and noblemen who counseled immediate action, beginning with the assassination of his foremost enemies, Ralegh and Cecil. In February Essex and a company of armed retainers marched into London seeking support for their plan to seize the court on the excuse that Ralegh and his friend, Lord Cobham, were plotting to assassinate him. By nightfall the coup had collapsed. Its leaders retreated to Essex House, which was then besieged by forces loyal to the Crown, including Ralegh. Sir Walter testified at the earl's trial and was present at his execution in the Tower of London. Thus ended one of the bitterest and longest court rivalries of the Tudor age. For Ralegh, the consequence was neither reward nor office but a lingering resentment in many quarters that he had somehow caused the earl's downfall and prevented Elizabeth from pardoning him.

Ralegh was again in ill health by the fall of 1601, but took his seat in Parliament where he spoke forcefully on two of his favorite themes. He argued for the granting of another subsidy so that the Crown could press the war against Spain, now that Spanish troops had landed in Ireland. He likewise supported a ban on the export of iron ordnance, that is, ships' cannon, for through export of superior English arms Spanish galleons had gradually become an even match for English warships. The subsidy bill passed while that against export of cannon failed, no doubt because licenses for such exports were very profitable to a small but influential group of merchants and courtiers.

In this same Parliament Elizabeth delivered her "golden speech," an emotional affirmation of her devotion to her people and their welfare. It was clear to most of her subjects, however, that her reign was drawing to a close. Ralegh prepared for the worst by conveying Sherborne to his son, Wat. On New Year's Day 1603 he exchanged gifts with the queen, this being the only occasion when his name appears on the extant gift rolls. On 24 March Elizabeth died. Ralegh walked in her funeral procession with the rest of her guard, and while it has been supposed that Elizabeth never forgave Lady Ralegh, she too appeared at the funeral among the ladies of the privy chamber and bedchamber.[37] Both husband and wife had more reason to mourn than they could well anticipate.

James I and the Tower, 1603–16

Elizabeth's successor, King James of Scotland, was a poet, author, and theologian, yet he was Ralegh's opposite in taste and temperament. Moreover, he had long ago been turned against Ralegh by the relentless efforts of his English correspondents, some of whom Ralegh counted as his closest friends. Secretary Cecil, whose son "Will" played with Wat during lengthy visits at Sherborne, informed King James that Sir Walter was "a person whom most religious men do hold anathema." Another courtier who maintained a secret correspondence with the future king of England was Henry Percy, earl of Northumberland, one of Ralegh's oldest friends at court. Yet Northumberland assured James that his friend of sixteen years was "insolent, extremely hated," and one whom the earl befriended rather "out of constancy than pollicy."[38] And this was the best that James heard about the captain of the Guard; much worse flowed from the venomous pen of Lord Henry Howard. Nor was James immune to the charges that Ralegh had conspired in the downfall of Essex, whose death James greatly lamented. Small wonder that within a few months of the king's accession Ralegh had been deprived of his wine-licensing patent, replaced as Captain of the Guard, and ordered to vacate Durham House.

For his part, Ralegh approached his new sovereign with characteristic but self-defeating boldness. When James visited the home of Lady Ralegh's uncle, Ralegh encouraged him to pursue the war with Spain, even offering to supply him with a discourse on strategies for conducting such a war. To James the pacifist, a man tolerant of Catholicism and deathly afraid of weapons and warfare alike, Ralegh's enthusiastic belligerency shattered any hope of friendly rapport between them. James distanced himself from Sir Walter while he moved ahead with negotiations that led to a formal peace treaty with Spain in 1604.

By then, of course, Ralegh had been convicted of high treason. His crime was probably nothing more than listening to some foolish schemes proposed by his friend Henry Brooke, Lord Cobham. Cobham may have seriously considered arranging for a Spanish-financed coup that would topple the alien Stuart regime and give outcasts such as himself their due place in state affairs. Certainly his brother, George Brooke, was genuinely involved in a Catholic plot to assassinate the royal family. As the government began to unravel this clumsy conspiracy, it questioned Ralegh about Cobham, and Cobham, supposing that he had been betrayed, charged Ralegh with inciting him to treason.

Ralegh was lodged in the Tower in July 1603. The trial took place at Winchester on 17 November, with Ralegh's conviction a foregone conclusion for several reasons. Above all, the prosecution, justices, and jury found in it an opportunity to prove their loyalty to their new sovereign by condemning a person who was notoriously non grata. Secretary Cecil, a commissioner at the trial, had been a key figure in moving James to strip Ralegh of his offices and in summoning him before the Privy Council to answer questions about the alleged plot. The charges against Ralegh and Cobham are suspiciously similar to those set forth in a letter written by the earl of Essex that Cecil had acquired at the time of Essex's death. The letter affirmed that Ralegh and Cobham were already at work to prevent King James's accession. They planned instead to put the king of Spain's daughter on the throne after Elizabeth's death, and they had good means for doing so since Cobham as Lord Warden of the Cinque Ports controlled the southeastern coast while Ralegh controlled the southwest and Jersey. How easily might these two admit a foreign army into "the Imperiall citie of this realme." It was exactly the sort of conspiracy that Cecil's close associate in the new government, Lord Henry Howard, had urged Cecil to fabricate on behalf of Ralegh and Cobham.[39] Lord Cobham, perhaps, did entertain some such scheme, but the charge is absurd when applied to Ralegh, for it ignores his lifelong struggle against Catholicism and Spain, a struggle rooted in his deepest convictions. In preparation for the trial Ralegh assembled two strong lines of defense. Consulting the lawbooks he had neglected as a Middle Templar, he found that the charge of treason could not be proved in court with fewer than two witnesses, and only the desperate Cobham had accused him. Second, he managed a secret exchange of letters with his former friend and obtained a complete repudiation of the charges in Cobham's own handwriting. Almost half a century later Ralegh's son Carew claimed that the original letter was still in his possession.[40] Thus the government's case against Ralegh rested on the testimony of a single wavering and uncertain witness.

In court, the prosecution could do no better than to resort to bluster, irrelevant ad hominem attacks, and circular arguments. The king's attorney, Sir Edward Coke, would become one of England's greatest jurists, but on this occasion he disgraced himself and the principles of English justice by his furious attacks upon the prisoner. Ralegh, he exclaimed, had "an English face, but a Spanish heart."[41] The bench declined Ralegh's repeated requests that Cobham be brought to testify before him. He was told that the statute requiring two witnesses had been superseded, and finally, that Cobham had reaffirmed all of his accusations against Ralegh in spite of the letter he had previously sent to him. The court ignored the dubious reliability of their lone, vacillating witness and dismissed the jury to ponder its verdict. Within twenty minutes Ralegh was pronounced guilty of high treason. With Cobham and two other conspirators, he was sentenced to be hanged, drawn, and quartered on 9 December. Then, in a self-serving display of royal mercy, James arranged for the prisoners to be marched one by one to the scaffold and prepared for death, whereupon they were told that the king had commuted their sentences to imprisonment during pleasure. Ralegh was soon back in the Tower, a condemned traitor who literally did not exist in the eyes of the law.

Sir Walter was now fifty years old, a veteran of court intrigues, warfare on land and sea, and the organization and setting forth of both colonies and voyages of exploration. The studious and necessarily reclusive life that James imposed on Ralegh was the Renaissance counterpart to the active life of public service that he had pursued under Queen Elizabeth. Such retirement, however, if properly spent, might hold virtues of its own, and these were widely celebrated in contemporary pastoral and devotional literature. Ralegh used his thirteen years of enforced leisure to pursue his interests in science, navigation, geography, and international politics. Despite his avid pursuit of gold,

Ralegh confined his chemical experiments to metallurgy; he smelted ores but did not attempt to change base metals into gold. He also experimented with what would today be called pharmacology. He was allowed to operate a small distillery in the Tower, and here he concocted his "Balsam of Guiana" and the ingredients for his "Great Cordial." His medicinal interests went back to at least 1596 when John Hester dedicated to him a translation of various experiments and cures by Paracelsus. Ralegh's related interest in plants, stimulated no doubt by discoveries of new species in Virginia and Guiana, is also reflected in John Gerard's dedication to him of a catalog of indigenous and exotic plants in 1599.[42] From a literary standpoint, moreover, his years in the Tower were the most productive of his career, for he turned out a handful of poems and at least nine prose works including his monumental *History of the World*.

Ralegh probably composed the "Instructions to his Son" between the time of his arrest in 1603 and the birth of Carew Ralegh, his second son, early in 1605. He wrote commendatory verses for Sir Arthur Gorges's translation of Lucan's *Pharsalia* (1614), and may have collaborated with Gorges in writing his "Observations . . . Concerning the Royal Navy." Ralegh fretted, of course, at his imprisonment, and many of his works were designed to win favor and eventual freedom. He gained the sympathy of Queen Anne and, through her, perhaps as early as 1607, he became acquainted with Prince Henry, then in his early teens. In addition to the *History*, Ralegh probably wrote especially for the prince's eye his "Art of War by Sea," "On the Seat of Government," the "Jesuit" dialogue, and possibly the "Match" and "Marriage" tracts. After Henry's death in 1612 Ralegh composed the "Prerogative of Parliaments in England," an attack on Jacobean domestic policy, which saw wide circulation in manuscript, and the discourse on the "Cause of War" and the "Invention of Ships."

In support of these wide-ranging projects, Ralegh assembled in his quarters in the Tower a library of over five hundred volumes. He was allowed to plant a small garden and to build a furnace for his experiments with ores in addition to the distillery. He kept at least three servants and played host to a steady stream of visitors, from the wife of the French ambassador to the playwright Ben Jonson, as well as his own family and friends.

The Tower years cost Ralegh more than his freedom. In 1605 he apparently suffered a stroke, which was followed by another in 1615.[43] His most grievous setback, however, was the loss of Sherborne. Early in 1607 James took a sudden fancy to a young Scotsman named Robert Carr. Cecil, now earl of Salisbury, advised his master that Sherborne would be a suitable gift for the new minion. The papers that had conveyed Sherborne to Ralegh's son

Walter were found to lack a crucial phrase, so Cecil turned the matter over to Sir John Popham who had served as Lord Chief Justice at Ralegh's trial. Popham informed Cecil that by law no transfer of land had taken place so that Sherborne was legally forfeit to the king by virtue of Ralegh's attainder.[44] Ralegh and his wife used what influence remained to them to save their home, but James relented only so far as to compensate them with £8,000 cash and a £400 annuity for Lady Ralegh. Before James could deliver the spoils to Carr, however, Prince Henry demanded Sherborne for himself. Henry would no doubt have conveyed the manor to Ralegh had he lived; Carr enjoyed it briefly before his own fall and imprisonment, but it was lost forever to Ralegh and his heirs.

The Last Voyage

As early as 1607 Ralegh had proposed to the king that a great deal of wealth could be easily obtained in Guiana.[45] The government authorized voyages to the area in 1609 and 1610, with Ralegh an investor in both expeditions. He pressed his suit with peers, statesmen, and anyone else who would listen, pleading to be released from the Tower in order to serve king and country by establishing a working gold mine in Guiana. James, whose inability to compromise with Parliament deprived him of the subsidies that Elizabeth had so readily obtained, found himself many hundreds of thousands of pounds in debt by 1614. Any promise of aid sounded attractive to him, and in that year the staunchly anti-Catholic Sir Ralph Winwood became first secretary. Ralegh's offer now had some hope of acceptance, but it took months of political maneuvering and at least one handsome bribe before the project met with royal approval. On 19 March 1616 Ralegh left the Tower to prepare for his second expedition to Guiana.

Ralegh named the ship he commissioned for the voyage the *Destiny*, in memory no doubt of Prince Henry, who had learned to sail on the Thames in a smaller ship of the same name built for him by the same shipwright.[46] Preparations for the voyage took more than a year, during which time James virtually guaranteed its failure by secretly supplying its itinerary to the Spanish ambassador, Gondomar. Ralegh's men found a copy of their plans when they seized Santo Tomé de Guayana, the settlement founded by the Spaniards not long after Ralegh's departure from Guiana in 1596. Although Queen Anne continued to support Ralegh, he found no ally in Henry's younger brother, Prince Charles. Within a few years Charles would be seeking a Spanish bride for himself; he so opposed Ralegh's venture that he prevented his mother from visiting his ship before it left the Thames.[47]

The fleet of some thirteen ships and one thousand men left England 12 June 1617, but bad weather, sickness, and desertions kept them from reaching the coast of Guiana until mid-November. Ralegh himself spent most of October stricken with fever and confined to his cabin. He was far too weak to attempt the journey upriver so he appointed Keymis, a veteran of the Guiana voyages, to lead the search for the mine. As the English force of several hundred men neared Santo Tomé they were ambushed by Spanish soldiers. Keymis had little choice but to disobey Ralegh's orders and fight off his attackers; he was able to seize the town, but Ralegh's son Walter was killed upon the first assault. After a few weeks of aimless wandering amid continuing ambushes by the Spaniards who had fled Santo Tomé, Keymis returned down the Orinoco to announce the failure of his efforts to his appalled leader.

On the voyage home Ralegh faced more desertions and outright mutiny. The *Destiny* entered Plymouth Harbor alone on 21 June 1618. Not only was the mission a failure, but Secretary Winwood had died in Ralegh's absence, being replaced by Sir Robert Naunton, who favored neither Ralegh nor his policies. Sir Lewis Stukely was charged with bringing Sir Walter to London, although Ralegh feigned illness at Salisbury where he managed to write his "Apology" for the Guiana fiasco. He had kept his vows to his friends and the king by returning to England. In London he was allowed to rest in his own house for several days before going back to the Tower. The French ambassador used this occasion to assure Ralegh that he would find welcome and refuge in France. Ralegh decided to escape if he could but he unwisely revealed his plans to Stukely, who told all to the Privy Council. On the night of 9 August Ralegh set out in a skiff on the Thames but was intercepted and sent at once to the Tower.

Not until 28 October was he summoned to court at the King's Bench to learn that, all pleading aside, he would be executed on the following morning. The government found it awkward to charge new offenses to someone who, legally, did not exist, so Ralegh was condemned to suffer for the old conviction of 1603. The death sentence was no doubt motivated by James's personal dislike but it was also to be a token of appeasement toward Spain. Family and friends visited Ralegh in the Gatehouse at Westminster that night. He spent some of his final hours inscribing in his Bible the verses that begin "Even such is tyme" and writing a protestation of his Christian faith that he meant for Lady Ralegh to circulate after his death in case he was not allowed to speak from the scaffold.[48]

Sir Walter Ralegh was led to execution before eight the next morning through a large crowd of onlookers. At least a half dozen peers were there along with Thomas Harriot, who took brief notes on his patron's last words.

Numerous complete accounts of the proceedings have also survived. Ralegh spent half an hour justifying his actions, from his treatment of Keymis and Stukely to his innocence of any negotiations with the French other than to save his life, even to denying that he "pufft Tobacco out in disdayne" as Essex went to the block.[49]

Eyewitnesses concurred that Sir Walter went to his death in a composed and cheerful frame of mind. This was an act of sheer will, for he was still subject to attacks of fever as a result of his voyage. He had lost his eldest son as well as nearly all the worldly possessions he might have left for the support of his wife and surviving son. He died a convicted traitor in order to placate Spain, whose interests he had opposed and thwarted in so many ways. The execution was an immoderate and unjust punishment. It immediately focused popular disillusionment with the Stuart regime upon Ralegh as a heroic victim of its excesses. As one contemporary put it, "he hath purchased here in the opinion of men such honour and reputation, as it is thought his greatest enemies are they that are most sorrowful for his death, which they see is like to turn so much to his advantage."[50] A legendary Ralegh arose from the block as from a martyrdom. His political writings, including the *History* and those that circulated only in manuscript, enjoyed enormous popularity, above all with Puritan and antiroyalist factions. His condemnation of bad rulers was distorted into an opposition to monarchy in general. There can be little doubt that this legacy, in part a myth embellished with attributions to him of works he did not even write, contributed nevertheless its due weight to the forces that in 1649 caused Charles I to suffer a fate identical to Ralegh's own.

Chapter Two

The Courtier's Pen

Early Verse

"Swete were the sauce," "Sweete ar the thoughtes."   According to John Aubrey, Ralegh "was sometimes a Poet, not often," while a contemporary said of his last verses that they marked "his farewell of Poetrie wherin he had ben a pidler even from his youth."[1] Both assessments appear to be essentially correct provided we do not underestimate Ralegh's continuous use of poetry in the promotion of his own interests or his sincere appreciation of it as an enjoyable art form. The earliest identifiable influences upon Ralegh's development as a poet are the works of George Gascoigne, George Whetstone, Arthur Gorges, and the earl of Oxford. For Gascoigne Ralegh composed the commendatory verses published in 1575 (Poem 1). The first stanza of Poem 2 echoes that of a lyric published by Whetstone in 1576, although it is not clear that Ralegh imitated Whetstone. The reverse is possible, or their poems may have resulted from a joint exercise, a verse-writing competition.[2] Ralegh's cousin Gorges apparently began writing poetry by imitating the work of George Turberville, one of the most ambitious and talented of the early Elizabethan poets. Gorges also translated or adapted lyrics by a number of French Pleiade poets, including Du Bartas and Ronsard. Finally, by the late 1570s Ralegh was in contact with the earl of Oxford, a practicing courtier poet. Whether or not Oxford shared any of his writings with Ralegh, Ralegh had access to eight of them that appeared in 1576 in a popular verse anthology, the *Paradise of Dainty Devices*.

Ralegh's earliest poems display the usual characteristics of the mid-century "drab" or "plain" style.[3] During the first half of the sixteenth century metrical uncertainties disrupted the rhythms of virtually every English poet, from Stephen Hawes to Sir Thomas Wyatt. These problems were solved in the generation after Surrey as poets rediscovered accentual-syllabic verse. Gascoigne's "Certayne notes of Instruction" (1575) teaches the reader how to alternate stressed and unstressed syllables to produce regular iambic lines. Ralegh's first two poems are written in well-defined iambic pentameters; the regularity of his meter is underscored by the end-stopped lines and the caesuras, natural pauses in syntax, after the second foot in each line which are frequently marked by commas in the original texts:

> But what for that? this medcine may suffyse,
> To scorne the rest, and seke to please the wise.
>   (1.5–6)
> Dainty the lyfe, nurst still in Fortune's lappe,
> Much is the ease, wher troubled mindes finde reste.
>   (2.3–4)

From a technical standpoint, truly pleasing English verse had been impossible until such metrical regularity was reestablished, for the jolting, arhythmic passages in early Tudor verse necessarily distracted the reader's attention. Yet the overly regular meters of the mid-century style are also distracting for such heavy, unalleviated alternations of weak and strong accents produce doggerel. Gradually, the Elizabethan poets, Ralegh among them, learned to vary their rhythms as they discovered how enjambment and the placement of syllables poised between stressed and unstressed pronunciation created more delightful poetic effects. To this end, the initial trochaic feet in both of Ralegh's earliest poems, and indeed in the first five lines of "Sweet ar the thoughtes" ("Great ar," "Dainty," "Much is," "These ar"), mark a beginning. Similar substitute feet are rare, however, with "worthiest" and "envious" in 1.9–10 being the chief exceptions. Technically then, these poems fall into the same singsong rhythms that characterize most of the verse by Gascoigne, Whetstone, Turberville, and other early Elizabethan writers.

The rhetoric of these poems is also of a kind characterized by a poverty of devices, the repetition of a limited array of tropes (figures of speech), and schemes (devices that appeal to the ear). Aside from rhyme, the principal rhetorical figure in this verse tradition is another scheme, alliteration, as in 1.8 and 2.7 where different sounds combine on each side of the caesura: "Yet worthiest wights, yelde prayse for every payne," "Thus Hope bringes Hap but to the worthy wight." In 1.17 two alliterative patterns are worked into the second half of the line: "who list like trade to trye." Where these poems are not emphatically alliterative, the ear responds to such repeated sounds as "valure doth advaunce" and "cankred stomackes placte." The anaphora of "Thus Hope . . . Thus Pleasure, . . . Thus Fortune" (2.6–9) is likewise a device common to the mid-century style, although Ralegh's poems lack two other typical devices, similes and mythological allusions.

Ralegh's approach and tone, however, create verse very similar to most of that written during the 1570s. Poetic ability was largely measured by the

sounds that resulted from these obtrusively heavy rhythms, rhyme, alliteration, anaphora, assonance, and consonance. Both of his poems are also sententious, detached from their subjects, and lacking in concrete imagery. As a
result, his praise of Gascoigne's *Steele Glas* is so general that it might be applied to almost anything. To paraphrase its second stanza, for instance, "although works are variously interpreted by individuals, the worthiest people
praise every effort while envious ones refuse to acknowledge achievements
that exceed their own abilities: whoever excels will be hated." The reader
could hardly guess from this that Gascoigne's book was a significant contribution to Tudor verse satire.

The abstract treatment of hope, dread, pleasure, and fortune in "Sweete ar
the thoughtes" creates a similarly objective tone, and only the last line reveals
that this is not merely a philosophical meditation but a species of love lyric.
"And lyve to serve, in hope of your goodwyll" portrays the poet-lover as servant in the courtly love tradition; the lady's favor, her "goodwyll," is the reward of true service. The poem is a fine example of the love poetry that Sir
Philip Sidney criticized in his *Defence of Poetry*. These writers, he observed,
were primarily concerned with "certain swelling phrases which hang together" to produce verses that "if I were a mistress, would never persuade me
they were in love . . . so coldly they apply fiery speeches."[4] Granted, most of
the amorous verse by Gascoigne, Whetstone, and Turberville as well as
Ralegh's poem imparts none of the emotion and sense of personal involvement that Sidney felt was the hallmark of true poetry. Subsequent taste and
critical judgment have confirmed his view. Yet Ralegh and his contemporaries should not be faulted for missing goals they never tried to hit. Their creative efforts were centered upon the highly rhetorical presentation of
platitudinous content. Their verse conveyed general truths in a predictable
fashion through unmistakable rhythms and simple, readily apprehended or-
naments of style. By these criteria Ralegh's efforts are as proficient as the
works of nearly all his contemporaries.

Poems 3–11, Possible Poem i.   Both Gascoigne and Whetstone
followed careers as soldiers and widely published authors, while Ralegh undertook a military career without ever attempting to establish himself as a
writer. In 1582 he came to court as an expert in Irish affairs, but possessed
as well with a practicing commitment to poetry, and this he used to advantage in creating his own style as courtier and royal favorite. If his approach
to the art changed little at first, its social context and import were substan-
tially altered.

"Farewell falce Love" (Poem 4, ca. 1582–85) is simply an extended, negative definition of love that emphasizes the Renaissance commonplace of

love's irrationality. It lists examples of love's harmful and contradictory nature, and ends by rejecting love outright: "False love, desire, and bewtye frayle adewe, / Dead is the roote from whence such fancy grewe."[5] A few images, such as the "poysoned serpent covered all with flowers," help bring this definition to life, and indeed the series of metaphors used to define love creates more imaginative appeal than is typical of mid-century verse. Yet the end-stopped lines, fixed caesuras, alliteration, and anaphora place this poem firmly in that tradition.

The exact circumstances of composition for Poem 4 are unknown, although it seems clear that Ralegh allowed it to circulate widely under his name. It survives in six contemporary manuscripts and was set to music in William Byrd's *Psalmes, Sonets, and Songs* of 1588. A rival courtier and established favorite, Sir Thomas Heneage, countered with answering verses that praised love in phrasing that was carefully aligned with Ralegh's own. This suggests that, quite early in his career at court, Ralegh used his poetic skills as part of his courtiership so successfully that Heneage was moved to reply in kind. The exchange of poetic rebuses between Ralegh and Henry Noel (Poem 5) probably dates from the same period and suggests a similarly public use of verse in the service of courtiership. In this case, however, we know that despite the insulting content of these couplets their authors were friends of long standing.

Ralegh's claim to "Lady farewell, whome I in Sylence serve" is doubtful, yet the manner of its dissemination, "put into my Lady Laitons Pocket by Sir W. Rawleigh," fits the aggressive use of poetry he seems to have employed at court. As a love lyric, Poem i is far more direct and immediate than "Sweet ar the thoughtes." It tells the lady outright, "wold god thou knewste the depth of my desire" (line 2), and even in the process of abandoning his suit he affirms that "I thynke I Love thee Beste." These personal touches aside, the style here remains essentially "drab." Alliteration is often employed flagrantly as in line 14, "The wynde of woe hath torne my Tree of Truste," and the proverbial "spare to speake doth often spare to speed" (line 6) is another plain-style convention that undercuts the sincerity of other passages in this lyric.

Whoever wrote the poem, its recipient was probably Elizabeth Leighton, a lady of the privy chamber. In 1578 she had married, with the queen's blessing, Captain Thomas Leighton, and she continued to serve in the privy chamber until the end of the reign; Elizabeth Throckmorton, Ralegh's future bride, joined her there in 1584. It is hard to believe that Ralegh would have risked his standing with the queen through pursuit of a married woman among her closest personal attendants. The poem was more likely meant to compliment Lady Leighton as part of a courtly game, but in the absence of known ties between the Leightons and Ralegh this and the poem's authenticity remain conjectural.

"Callinge to minde," Poem 3, is a canonical work that also belongs to the early or mid-1580s, although its Petrarchan manner differentiates it from the rest of Ralegh's early verse. In content it resembles Gorges's Poem 6 and may be translated or adapted from a French source as was Gorges's lyric.[6] Here the emphasis is on the development of thought within a markedly fictional context as the lover seeks to blame his restless state first on his eye, then on his heart, and finally upon his entire being. The lyric's rising structure is punctuated by the responses of the eye and heart in the last lines of stanzas 1 and 2. The pattern builds to its capping reversal in the final couplet, "Yet when I saw myself to yow was trew, / I lovde myself, bicause miself lovde yow." This progression follows the normal course of falling in love in the courtly love tradition, from the vision of the beloved striking the eye to loss of the heart to loss of the entire self. Equally conventional is the metaphor of love as a war in stanza 2 and the heart as a fortress controlled by Love/Cupid. The poem's force as a love lyric is generated by the excuses that end each stanza: the vision of "my mystris face" sufficiently excuses the eye; the heart protests "That he was yours, and had forgon me cleane"; and the poet's true love for the lady turns out to be a worthy devotion, thus resolving the problem that initiated the poem in the first place. The lady is praised as the lover confirms his devotion at each step leading up to the resolution.

"Callinge to minde" (Poem 3) employs some alliteration plus an interlocking array of assonance, consonance, and internal rhyme in the last three lines, yet these rhetorical devices are unobtrusive compared with their deployment in Ralegh's other poems from the same era. Here ornament is subordinated to meaning; it is not allowed to detract from the relatively concise development of the lyric's three-part structure. Ralegh's iambic pentameter sixains are technically identical to his commendatory verses for Gascoigne's book, but he handles them far differently in Poem 3. Not only does he use more substitute feet (in the opening trochaics of lines 1, 3, 5, and 11, for example), but the iambic rhythms are so modulated as to reduce our awareness of meter, as illustrated by a natural reading of lines 13–15:

> At length when I perceivde both eye and hearte
> Excuse themselves, as guiltles of mine ill,
> I found my self the cause of all my smarte.

In line 13 "I" receives less emphasis than "length," "eye," or "hearte," while the sense requires that "self" in line 15 is its most strongly accented syllable.

Far greater contrasts between alternating stressed and unstressed syllables characterize Ralegh's earlier verse:

> This Glasse of Steele, unpartially doth shewe,
> Abuses all, to such as in it looke,
> From prince to poore, from high estate to lowe.
> (Poem 1.14–16)

Here the stressed syllables of "unpartially" and "as in it looke" receive varied weights, yet the range from accented to unaccented syllables is generally much wider, especially in the last line, so that the rhythm moves toward doggerel. "Callinge to minde" shows Ralegh growing more sensitive to the effect of slightly irregular alternations of stressed and unstressed syllables and how they could be combined to create more pleasing verse rhythms as these variations played against the form rather than pounding it out to a staccato beat.

Ralegh's most ambitious poem before 1592 was his elegy for Sir Philip Sidney, which belongs to the years between 1587 and 1591. Its formal exposition has often been criticized for a lack of true feeling, an impression underscored by the fact that lines 45–48 are adapted from an anonymous verse epitaph placed above Sidney's tomb in St. Paul's Cathedral.[7] Still, the sincere first-person introduction and the dignity imparted to Sidney's career thereafter make this a true elegy rather than a poetic exercise. Its three-part structure begins with Ralegh's apology for writing the poem (lines 1–12), summarizes Sir Philip's career with emphasis upon his final service in the Netherlands (lines 13–40), and ends with a combination of praise for his achievements and lament for his premature death (lines 41–60).

The style of Poem 7, more varied and complex than in any of Ralegh's earlier works, is directed to the portrayal of Sidney's worth instead of calling attention to itself. In the ninth stanza, for example, Ralegh portrays Sidney vanquishing a host of personified misfortunes, and then employs two metaphors that stress his triumphant departure from this world:

> There didst thou vanquish shame and tedious age,
> Grief, sorow, sicknes, and base fortunes might:
> Thy rising day, saw never wofull night,
> But past with praise, from of[f] this worldly stage.
> (lines 33–36)

Thus Sidney's career is made to resemble a day that never declined into darkness, himself the hero-actor who exits undefeated and admired by all. The metaphor offers consolation by suggesting that Sidney, like an actor leaving the stage, proceeds to some new reality, an idea given concrete expression in line 52, "Thy soul and spright enrich the heavens above."

Ralegh and Sidney were fellow courtiers with similar interests, including poetry, yet they never became friends as far as is known. They shared a policy of active resistance to Spain and advocacy of overseas colonization; Sidney sat on the parliamentry committee of 1584, for example, that confirmed Ralegh's patent to found English colonies abroad. Ralegh admits in the elegy, however, that "envie in thy life supprest" his love for Sir Philip to the extent that he "Did onely praise thy vertues in my thought" (lines 7, 10). Why then did he commemorate Sidney's death with this sixty-line elegy while he is not known to have written anything similar upon the deaths of much closer friends such as Gilbert, and later Queen Elizabeth and Prince Henry? The answer probably lies in his connections with Sidney's brother, Sir Robert, and sister Mary, countess of Pembroke.

In September 1584 Robert Sidney married Sir Walter's distant relative Barbara Gamage.[8] Thereafter, warm social ties between the two families were established; Ralegh visited the Sidney home on several occasions in 1595 shortly after returning from his voyage to Guiana, and in 1599 he and his wife were among those being considered as godparents for the Sidneys' newborn daughter.[9] Ralegh's ties with the countess of Pembroke are more difficult to trace, yet they must have been of long standing for Mary did her best to secure a full pardon for him after the commutation of his death sentence in 1603. It was said that "she is to be commended for doing her best in showing *veteris vestigia flammae*."[10] The Latin quotation hints at some former romantic attachment between Ralegh and the countess, yet she had married the earl of Pembroke in 1577, before Ralegh had been admitted to the court circle. Her attempt to save him could still be termed commendable, however, if it were on behalf of an old family friend, as is adduced by Ralegh's known ties with Barbara and Robert Sidney. Accordingly, the Sidney elegy was written as much from respect for these living family members as for their departed brother.

The Rivalry with Essex, 1587–91. After 1586 nearly all of Ralegh's poems reflect in some way his bitter struggle with the earl of Essex for the queen's affections. Devereux had supplanted Ralegh as principal favorite by the spring of 1587, and it was no doubt in that year that Ralegh addressed the following lines (Poem 6) to her:

A sonnett

Fortune hath taken thee away, my Love,
My live's Joy and my sowle's heaven above;
Fortune hath taken thee away my princess,
My world's delight and my true fancy's mistris.

Fortune hath taken all away from me,   [5
Fortune hath taken all by takinge thee;
Ded to all Joyes, I onlie Live to woe,
So Fortune now becomes my fancie's foe.

In vaine mine eyes, in vaine you wast your tears,
In vaine my sighes, the smokes of my despairs,   [10
In vaine you serch the earth and heavens above,
In vaine you serch, for fortune keepes my love.

Then will I leave my Love in fortune's hands,
Then will I leave my love in worthlesse bands,
And onlie love the sorrowe Due to me,   [15
Sorrowe hencefourth that shall my princess bee.

And onlie Joy that fortune conquers kings,
Fortune that rules on earth and earthlie things
Hath ta'ne my Love in spite of vertue's might,
So blind a goddesse did never vertue right.   [20

With wisdome's eyes had but blind fortune seen,
Then had my love my love for ever bin;
But Love farewell, though fortune conquer thee,
No fortune base shall ever alter me.[11]

We may suspect that "Farewell falce Love" and "Callinge to minde" grew out
of Ralegh's relationship with the queen, but if so, their circumstances cannot
be reconstructed. Poem 6, however, was undoubtedly presented to Elizabeth,
who replied to it with verses of her own that urge, "Mourne not my Wat, nor
be thou so dismaid."[12]

The sonnet beginning "Like truthless dreames, so are my joyes expired"
(Poem 8) incorporates wording and themes that parallel those of "Fortune."
That it too was meant for the queen's eyes is revealed by Ralegh's later allusion in one of his "Cynthia" poems to the sonnet's refrain: "of all which past
the sorrow only stayes, / So wrate I once and my mishapp fortolde"
(14.123–24). The "Cynthia" verses were designed to elicit royal forgiveness

for the Throckmorton marriage. To this end, Ralegh would not have cited his earlier refrain unless he thought that the queen would be sure to recognize it.

Poems 6 and 8 probably belong to the years from 1587 through 1589. Both are amorous complaints that depict a man who is "Ded to all Joyes" (6.8); "so are my joyes expired" (8.1). In Poem 6 his love has been seized by fortune and clasped "in worthlesse bands" (line 14), whereas she is simply "misled" in the sonnet. The poet has resigned his life to "fortunes hand" in Poem 8, while fortune has become his "fancie's foe" in Poem 6, that is, an enemy victorious over his affection for his mistress, just as his fancy has "quite retired" in Poem 8.

These correspondences aside, the poems pursue rather different strategies for influencing the queen. In Poem 6 Ralegh and his love are victims of fortune. Here "love" refers unambiguously to Elizabeth while "fortune" is both the blind goddess of line 20 and her personification in the earl of Essex, who owes his wealth and status to the merely fortuitous accident of his birth. He also represents fortune in the sense of this worldly prosperity, something the queen enhanced by showering gifts of office and land on her new favorite. Ralegh plays on these ambiguities to associate his rival with all the negative qualities of blind fortune. He repeats in four of the poem's first six lines that fortune "hath taken thee"; the affinity with a rape of the virgin queen is developed further by assertions that "fortune Keepes my love," that she languishes "in fortune's hands," and that she has been utterly conquered by fortune (lines 17, 13, 23). Ralegh's symbolic treatment of the rivalry plays on Elizabeth's sense of her own sovereignty, implying that she can preserve it only by resisting her seducer. Overtly, she is flattered throughout the poem as a loss of inestimable value to the poet, yet in the final couplet he places himself above her (and incidentally provides an example for her to follow) by asserting that "No fortune base shall ever alter me." The poem's structure moves from woeful lament to this firm resolve not to submit to the degrading force that has overwhelmed the queen. It is a strong appeal for her likewise to free herself from bondage to Fortune/Essex.

Poem 8, "Like truthless dreams," plays on Elizabeth's emotions in a somewhat different fashion. Ralegh describes the anguish of his loss and loneliness in each quatrain and in the refrain that concludes each of them. The poem opens with the simile comparing his past joy to fleeting, truthless dreams. In stanza 3 a second simile develops the sense of loneliness and exile, then moves in the last two lines to the metaphor of his life as the passage of the seasons: the "sweete spring spent" and "sommer well nie don" leave him only "age and winter colde" in the final couplet where he introduces an unexpected reversal. Now the sense of alienation that was treated as an affliction in the quatrains is transformed into a desirable course of action. His losses warn him "To haste me hence, to find my fortunes folde," where fortune suddenly refers to his own well-being, and fold, the protective enclosure within which to preserve it. The lament over his outcast state becomes a threat to desert the queen as a matter of self-defense.

By 1593 Ralegh was referring to his home at Sherborne as "my fortun's folde" (Edwards, 2:80). Its equivalent in the late 1580s when he composed Poem 8 may well have consisted of the thousands of acres of land he had been granted in Munster in 1586. There too he obtained a castle at Youghal where he probably resided during his brief visits to Ireland. Indeed, several of Ralegh's biographers have suggested that "Like truthless dreames" belongs to the summer of 1589 when he first went to Ireland in person to examine his new holdings.[13] If so, the poem's allusions to "a countrey strange" and being "cleane from sight of land" entail literal applications.

The Fairy Queen.   Shortly after he returned from Ireland Ralegh presented Edmund Spenser and his *Faerie Queene* at court. Sir Walter commended his friend's great work with two very different poems. One ranks among his finest lyrics in its imaginative conception and execution; the second is a relatively awkward, less sophisticated effort that appears to have been something of an afterthought. Why Ralegh added this second and somewhat redundant commendatory poem to the first calls for some explanation.

He adapted Poem 9, "Me thought I saw the grave where Laura lay," to the medieval atmosphere of Spenser's work by entitling it "A Vision upon this Conceipt of the Faery Queene." The poem's effect as an old-fashioned dream vision is enhanced by its allegorical personifications of love, virtue, and oblivion. Ralegh uses these time worn trappings, however, to assert the Renaissance identity of his multifaceted poem. His form is the English or Shakespearean sonnet of three quatrains and a couplet. The shifting positions of the caesuras and the enjambment of lines 2–3 and 9–10 maintain the rhythmic flexibility that he had mastered by the mid-1580s. The theme of Spenser's superiority over the greatest poets of the past is developed from a characteristically Renaissance point of view, while Ralegh manages simultaneously to compliment Elizabeth as the ultimate beneficiary of Spenser's artistry.

In the first five lines Ralegh imagines Laura's tomb in the temple of the vestal virgins, an extraordinary combination of literary allusion and classical mythology that is Ralegh's invention, not Petrarch's. The sudden appearance of the Fairy Queen in the vision destroys this static scene. Love and virtue desert Laura to attend the Fairy Queen as Petrarch's ghost weeps; now Laura is attended by oblivion, and amid a chorus of anonymous ghostly groans

Homer's spirit is singled out as one who "curst th'accesse of that celestiall theife."

Here the "Faery Queene" is both Spenser's poem and Elizabeth, the queen it celebrates. This explains the focus upon Laura, the woman celebrated in the 360 lyrics of Petrarch's *Rime*. As a literary work, this collection is totally unlike Spenser's narrative; the comparison concerns only the idealized women immortalized by both poets. Ralegh contends that with the advent of Spenser's work, Petrarch's tribute to Laura and thus Laura herself will pass into oblivion, superseded by the superior tribute to Queen Elizabeth. Thus Ralegh, who had characterized Sidney as the "Petrarch of our time" (7.58), exalts Spenser above Europe's foremost vernacular poet. In the couplet he takes his praise a step further, for Homer, the greatest epic poet of classical antiquity, now reacts to the *Faerie Queene* as a work generically comparable to his *Iliad* and *Odyssey*. Ralegh portrays Elizabeth confiscating for herself the qualities of love and virtue formerly reserved to Laura, while Spenser exceeds both Homer and Petrarch, the finest poets among the ancients and the moderns. Ralegh's main vehicle for conveying so much meaning in so few words is the dual nature of his central figure, the Fairy Queen. His title specifies his focus on the "Conceipt of the Faery Queene," which is Spenser's central imaginative construct. She is the "celestiall theife" who steals away both personal and literary reputations. In this lyric Ralegh demonstrates his mastery by 1590 of sonnet form, which would be popularized in English by publication in the following year of Sidney's *Astrophil and Stella*. The poem demonstrates as well his ability to compress into this demanding form multiple levels of meaning, overt and suggested, such as would mark the highest development of the sonnet at the hands of such poets as Shakespeare, Michael Drayton, and Spenser himself.

In contrast with this polished sonnet, Ralegh's second commendatory poem for the *Faerie Queene*, "The prayse of meaner wits," is set forth in long-line poulter's-measure couplets, a form that was becoming old-fashioned even as Ralegh began his career at court.[14] By 1590 it was almost totally passé and a form that Ralegh never used before or afterward. The tone of the opening simile is sarcastic, for it affirms that inferior critics of the *Faerie Queene* are no more welcome than the cuckoo when the nightingale is singing. Ralegh then uses personifications to argue that only Elizabeth herself can properly criticize Spenser's work and that she is the living ideal upon which its virtues must be modeled. He concludes by noting that since only an angel could depict the queen's virtues accurately, she must "favour thy good will" rather than Spenser's actual achievement. Still, Ralegh himself values Spenser's verse above those of all other English authors.

The praise of the queen's perfections beyond the descriptions of all earlier writers (lines 9–10) echoes a central theme of the commendatory sonnet, but the main thrust of this curious lyric is the queen's role as final arbiter of Spenser's creativity. For a clue as to what prompted this poem we must turn to a lyric written by the earl of Essex in 1590 or 1591. It attacks in its first stanza "that cursed cuckowe's throate, / That so hath crost sweete Philomela's note," that is, the nightingale's song. It too praises the queen as virtue and beauty personified and attacks Ralegh through a number of allegorical symbols as well as with punning references to filthy or puddle "water" (Walter).[15] The similarities in language suggest some direct connection between the two poems but the exact circumstances are obscured by the earl's indecipherable symbolism. If he believed himself under attack in Ralegh's Poem 10, then he must have been among those "meaner wits" who presumed to praise the *Faerie Queene*. In fact, Essex's verse complaint seems to respond to injuries more serious than a mere literary squabble at court, although it may be that some such conflict was the basis of the quarrel and thus his motive for assimilating Ralegh's imagery and language. To some degree at any rate, Ralegh's second commendatory poem was involved in the feud between these two courtiers, and it elicited the earl's earliest known verses, a poem directed to the queen in defense of his position as her chief favorite.

Poem 11: "Now we have present made."   This poem also derives from an unspecified court occasion when Ralegh used these lines to celebrate the presentation of a gift to Elizabeth prior to 1592. He no doubt intended these verses to be performed before the queen in part-song, as indicated by the plural pronouns throughout and the musical setting for one of the three extant manuscript texts.[16] We know that Ralegh took part in the kinds of court entertainments often associated with such gift giving, for about 1587 he entertained the queen in a Shrovetide show along with Arthur Gorges and two other courtiers.[17] It was customary to present Elizabeth with gifts during or after such performances, and it was probably for some such occasion as this that Ralegh composed "Now we have present made."

Ralegh chose for this work the same *a b b a* rhyme scheme he had used in the elegy for Sidney. The basic rhythm, however, is iambic trimeter, although only twenty-two of the poem's thirty-two lines are regular examples of this meter. Moreover, about half of these strictly iambic lines are varied by final unstressed syllables resulting from the use of feminine rhyme. Ralegh also keeps these short lines from degenerating into a monotonous chant by adding substitute trochaic and anapestic feet. It is an innovative lyric form skillfully upheld by Ralegh's close attention to the sound of his verse.

Poem 11 repeats one of the themes developed in "The praise of meaner wits," that no earthly writer can justly portray the queen. Both poems insist that the task demands "a quill / Drawn from an angells winge" (lines 25–26, simply an "Angels quill" at 10.12). "Now we have present made" is the earliest extant poem by Ralegh to refer to Elizabeth as Cynthia, a motif he had devised no later than 1588 to judge from the crescent moon in the upper left-hand corner of his portrait painted in that year (see the frontispiece to this volume). In addition to Cynthia, she is equated with Phoebe and Diana, also names for the goddess of the moon; the association of these deities with chastity is clearly appropriate to the virgin queen. Flora, goddess of flowers and gardens, was already an established part of Elizabeth's iconography as queen of a bountiful land, but in the context of Ralegh's poem she is more particularly a goddess who possesses eternal youth. Elizabeth was not usually associated with Aurora, goddess of the dawn (line 3); Ralegh seems to have introduced this allusion to reinforce his theme of the queen's constant renewal, just as the dawn renews the day. The poem's first five stanzas develop insistently the idea of Elizabeth's perpetual beauty through a variety of rhetorical devices. Within the confines of these short-line stanzas Ralegh sets forth in stanzas 4 and 5 a compound simile comparing her changeless beauty to "elementall fier" and the undying passion "of vertues trew desire" (line 16.).

The poem's structure follows a logical progression from establishing Elizabeth as a goddess in the first twenty lines to the tornata of line 21 where she is left to personified servants, in contrast with Ralegh's previous treatment of the queen herself under such personifications as beauty and virtue. Again, "our prayses," the attempts of mere mortals, fail to do her justice; only supernatural powers can portray her correctly. Elizabeth has been rendered unobtainable, cut off even from accurate description by those around her. Her remoteness prepares for Ralegh's emphatic conclusion in the last two lines. The poet's enforced remove from the queen turns his love to woe, which can be described only by Sorrow, in contrast with a true description of Elizabeth by Cupid and the muses. The adoration, longing, and devotion implicit in this conclusion give it a force akin to the epigrammatic ending of a good sonnet. The turn is unexpected, and yet a natural consequence of the poem's emphasis throughout upon Elizabeth's divinely aloof isolation.

The *Revenge* Tract, 1591

By 1591 Ralegh had published under his own name commendatory verses for Gascoigne and Spenser. Late in that year, however, his first prose work, the *Revenge* tract, appeared anonymously. It was not attributed to him until Richard Hakluyt reprinted it in his *Principal Navigations* (1599–1600). The event Ralegh memorialized was the loss in late August of the queen's warship *Revenge* with its commander, Sir Richard Grenville, Ralegh's esteemed friend and kinsman. Sir Walter's purpose was to deflate Spanish and Catholic boasting over the victory while defending Grenville's behavior. Ralegh handled this latter task so well that Grenville became a folk hero. He was celebrated in Gervase Markham's narrative poem, the *Most Honorable Tragedie of Sir Richard Grinvile* (1595); Thomas Heywood described him as daring to combat "a whole Fleet of Spanish men a-warre," and William Browne yoked him with Drake as the two "Pillers great of Fame," while Tennyson commemorated the battle in "The Revenge, A Ballad of the Fleet."[18]

The *Revenge* tract is not confined to glorifying Grenville's last fight, however. From that event and its aftermath Ralegh extrapolates God's special protection of the Protestant English cause, then digresses to argue the futility of deserting to the enemy and the wisdom and virtue of rallying to defend Elizabeth. Ralegh's is the most detailed account of the incident and his discrepancies from the known facts are relatively minor. On the other hand, his interpretation of those facts is significantly affected by the patriotic fervor that guided his composition of this eminently successful propaganda piece.

Ralegh had ample cause to be profoundly moved by the loss of Grenville and his ship. Sir Richard had for years been a trusted participant in Ralegh's efforts to colonize Virginia as well as in his related privateering enterprises. Ralegh was himself responsible for spending £4,000 on behalf of the Crown toward preparing the ships for Howard's voyage, and he had invested in it nearly £5,000 of his own money.[19] Small wonder that during the Cadiz raid of 1596 when he confronted the first Spanish vessel to have grappled with Grenville's ship he wrote that he was "resolved to be revenged for the *Revenge*" (Edwards, 2:151). His subsequent references to Grenville are always laudatory, as in the "Invention of Ships" discourse where he mentions "the late renowned sir Richard Greenvil" (*Works*, 8:324).

Ralegh's attitude toward Sir Richard stands in sharp contrast with that of his cousin Arthur Gorges, who called Grenville's behavior rash, his decision to fight the Spaniards a gross error, and the ensuing defeat a "fond," that is, foolish incident.[20] Naval historians have generally sided with Gorges against Ralegh and popular sentiment. In late August 1591 the English squadron of six warships with their supporting supply vessels were in harbor at the Azores being cleaned and refitted after five months at sea. They were stationed among the islands to intercept the New World plate fleet, but they were themselves surprised by a Spanish armada of fifty-three sail. All of the queen's ships cleared the harbor in time, with the *Revenge* the last to depart. But instead of flying before the enemy, Grenville chose to engage them. He thus risked his men's lives and sacrificed one of Her Majesty's best ships in a contest that was by Ralegh's own admission "without hope or any likelihood of prevailing" (*Revenge*, 82). Ralegh's task was to put the best possible face on the disaster.

News of the battle reached England in early October. Ralegh's tract was ready for the press by late November. In the meantime he had gathered information with some diligence. He refers to interviews with surviving crew members from the *Revenge* and depositions by a Spanish captain (*Revenge*, 77, 81). Another eyewitness was Jacob Whiddon "who hovered all night to see the success" of the battle (78). Whiddon no doubt supplied Ralegh with a full account of the incident for he was a sea captain who had served Ralegh for years.[21] In addition to these sources, Ralegh also had access to reports taken from Spanish captives and turned over to the Privy Council. His summary of their account of Spanish losses after the taking of the *Revenge* forms an appendix to the tract that tallies exactly with the report sent to Lord Burghley on 16 November. A week later Burghley authorized the entry of Ralegh's pamphlet in the Stationers' Register.[22] Thus, the work was not only sanctioned by the government but prepared with the full cooperation of its chief minister.

Ralegh unified his treatise less through the story of the *Revenge* and its capture than by his relentless attacks upon Spanish deceit, ambition, and impotence. He begins by charging that the Spaniards and their sympathizers have lied about what really happened to the *Revenge*. He contrasts this minor and costly victory with English triumphs over Spain, notably the Armada of 1588, Drake's West Indian raid of 1585–86, and even the 1589 Portuguese expedition, which could be construed as a victory only in the sense that Spain mounted no effective opposition to the landing of English forces. Ralegh's opening strategy is to establish the overall scope of the contest, which he then uses to dilute this loss of a single royal ship.

Ralegh is equally skillful in his account of the battle itself. He begins his narrative at the point where Howard's ships are warned of the imminent approach of the Spanish fleet. His in-medias-res opening makes no mention of what the English ships were doing in the Azores, not that there was any secret about it. But his strategy is to portray the queen's forces as disadvantaged victims of Spanish aggression: "our ships being all pestered and rummaging, everything out of order, very light for want of ballast . . . the one half part of the men of every ship sick and utterly unserviceable"(*Revenge*, 75).

The spirited prose with which Ralegh describes the battle and Grenville's refusal to surrender the ship has been studied and quoted at length.[23] Equally prominent, however, is the corollary to his glorification of English bravery in the mocking, sarcastic rhetoric with which he satirizes the Spaniards. He notes that refugees from the Great Armada who were captured in Ireland were "all sent back again to their countries, to witness and recount the worthy achievements of their invincible and dreadful navy" (73). He recounts how the *St. Philip* closed with the *Revenge*, received a broadside, and "shifted her self with all diligence from her sides, utterly misliking her first entertainment" (77; this was the very ship that Ralegh later encountered in Cadiz harbor). After describing how English turncoats among the Spanish forces were so ragged that they stripped the worn-out clothing from prisoners taken with the *Revenge*, he concludes, "a notable testimony of their rich entertainment and great wages" (84). The style throughout pits sincere praise of the English resistance against sneering mockery of Spain and her Catholic sympathizers.

Ralegh excuses Howard and the other commanders in the voyage for not rescuing Grenville, and then proceeds to an account of the tremendous storm that raked the Spanish fleets a few days after their capture of the *Revenge*. This extraordinary natural disaster claimed many Spanish lives and ships with the sinking of the *Revenge* itself and two hundred of the enemy on board: "So it pleased them to honour the burial of that renowned ship . . . not suffering her to perish alone, for the great honour she achieved in her life time" (83). The unusually violent storm together with Spanish losses from previous storms in the Caribbean and from English privateers greatly reduced the number of ships that brought their treasure safely back to Spain. Ralegh interprets these cumulative losses as divine fulfillment of what Howard's expedition failed to accomplish: "Thus it hath pleased God to fight for us and to defend the justice of our cause against the ambitious and bloody pretences of the Spaniard, who seeking to devour all nations are themselves devoured. A manifest testimony how unjust and displeasing their attempts are in the sight of God" (83).

Ralegh's interpretation of the entire episode affirmed English heroism and God's intervention to counteract Spain's victory by dint of sheer numbers. The implications of all this were not left for the reader to decide but specifically driven home in the pamphlet's concluding pages. Ralegh was concerned with more than overall public morale, above all with the reactions of English Catholics, a substantial minority, who might be encouraged by this dramatic reversal to withdraw their allegiance from the queen and her government. To prevent them from defecting Ralegh seized upon another incident after the capture of the *Revenge*. He learned that Maurice Fitzjohn had attempted to lure the English prisoners into Spanish service. Fitzjohn was the son of the Irish traitor, John of Desmond and cousin to the earl of Desmond whose rebellion and execution made possible the Irish holdings granted to Ralegh, Spenser, and many other Englishmen.

Ralegh refutes in order the advantages that Fitzjohn offered the prisoners: better pay, promotion in rank, and practice of the true Catholic religion (84). The rebuttal comprises about one-fifth of the essay, a digression in which his irony and sarcasm reach their height. He cites the disasters in Fitzjohn's own family to illustrate the fatal consequences of rebelling against the queen, then adds, "If he had withal vaunted of this success of his own house, no doubt the argument would have moved much, and wrought great effect, which because he for that present forgot, I thought it good to remember in his behalf" (85). The digression continues with a condemnation of the Jesuits, who have ruined many great families by suborning them to renounce their obedience to the queen. As for true religion, Ralegh cites Bartholomew de las Casas's "The Spanish Cruelties"[24] on the slaughter of natives in Hispaniola, "besides many millions else in other places of the Indies, a poor and harmless people created of God, and might have been won to his knowledge" (86).

From these examples of Spanish hypocrisy and deceit Ralegh moves at once to his conclusion, urging his countrymen of all religions to maintain their due loyalty to Elizabeth. She becomes the center of attention toward the end of the treatise, a monarch honored both by earthly rulers and the heavenly ruler alike; she is one who "shall by the favour of God resist, repel, and confound all whatsoever attempts against her sacred person or kingdom" (87). He ends with a virtual pledge of allegiance, that "we her true and obedient vassals guided by the shining light of her virtues shall always love her, serve her, and obey her to the end of our lives" (87). The rousing cadences of this passage effectively gloss over a number of inconvenient facts: that Spain was protecting her ships from English aggression, that Howard's expedition failed of its purpose, and that the loss of the *Revenge* was far more damaging to English defenses than the cost in Spanish ships and men required to take her. Ralegh's tract is superb propaganda, its lofty patriotic appeal balanced by the satiric condemnation of England's enemies.

Chapter Three
Written in Disgrace

Most of Ralegh's poetry is occasional: his verse commendations for Gascoigne and Spenser, the elegy for Sidney, or poems such as "Fortune" and "Like truthless dreams" which were designed to counter the queen's predilection for Essex. In 1592 Ralegh faced a far graver setback to his career in Elizabeth's furious reaction to his secret marriage. Under the circumstances, his confinement in the Tower was predictable, but not so the five years of exile from court and sovereign that followed it. Ralegh was cut off from the center of bounty and power residing in the queen, to whom he owed everything. Granted, he did not lose all. He retained Sherborne and Durham House, his offices, and his income-producing patents. But he could not hope to better himself significantly until he regained Elizabeth's favor, and meanwhile a further offense might provoke her to punish him even more severely. For five years Ralegh devoted himself to the task of reinstating himself with the queen; nearly everything he wrote in prose and verse during this time was directed toward that one imperative goal.

By 1592 Ralegh's poetic skills had matured in harmony with the new styles that created the golden age of Elizabethan lyric and dramatic poetry. He had attempted the sonnet as well as short-line meters, modulating his rhythms with substitute feet and using enjambment to break the monotony of the mid-century end-stopped lockstep. Above all, he had freed his muse from the concern with sententiousness and sound for its own sake that had shackled creativity for so many poets of the 1560s and 1570s. If his verse still depended upon personification, alliteration, anaphora, and other trappings of the earlier style, those devices were now employed to promote structure and meaning rather than dominating his poems as ends in themselves. With an increasing emphasis upon thought and emotion came an increase in Ralegh's use of metaphor, simile, imagery, and the more complex tropes of an aesthetic devoted to meaning and impact above sound. Technically and aesthetically Ralegh had equipped himself for his most ambitious and powerful achievement in verse, the "Ocean to Scinthia" poems.

"Cynthia," Poems 12–15

Poems 12–15 survive in unique holograph copies at Hatfield House among the papers of the Cecil family, whose members contemporary with Ralegh included Lord Burghley, the Lord Treasurer, and his son, Sir Robert Cecil. Critical interpretation of these poems varies considerably in keeping with the supposed circumstances of their composition, for they have been assigned to almost every crisis in Ralegh's career from 1589 to 1618.[1] In addition much debate surrounds Ralegh's numbering of Poems 14 and 15: Are his numerals to be read as the eleventh and twelfth or the twenty-first and twenty-second books "of the Ocean to Scinthia"? Critics question as well the existence of some ten or twenty previous books: Are they lost, or do the numbers evoke a vast but bogus project in order to exaggerate Ralegh's devotion to Elizabeth? Finally, are the surviving poems final drafts or intermediate copies in the process of revision?

Beyond reasonable doubt Ralegh numbered Poems 14 and 15 the twenty-first and twenty-second books of the Cynthia series.[2] The only other testimony to the earlier books comes from Edmund Spenser, who alludes to Ralegh's "Cynthia" three times in the 1590 edition of the *Faerie Queene*.[3] Spenser praises Ralegh's "sweet verse," a "sweet" invention that glorifies the queen. Then in 1595 Spenser published his *Colin Clouts Come Home Againe*, a verse account of his journey to court during that winter now five years past. He signed his dedication of this volume to Ralegh on 27 December 1591, and it is clear that several passages in the poem were updated to fit the circumstances of 1595. Among them is the "song" with which Ralegh entertained him in Ireland prior to their journey. It is now described as "all a lamentable lay, / Of great unkindnesse, and of usage hard, / Of Cynthia . . . Which from her presence faultlesse him debard."[4] This discrepancy from Spenser's account of "Cynthia" in the *Faerie Queene* has puzzled scholars, causing Lefranc to dismiss Spenser as an unreliable source of information about Ralegh's poetry.[5] Katherine Koller is no doubt correct, however, in supposing that Spenser changed his account of the "Cynthia" project to fit the extant lament in order to build sympathy for his patron's bereavement in disgrace.[6] This conflation of the two circumstances, Ralegh, the favorite praising his sovereign, and Ralegh complaining in exile and despair, produced a further inconsistency in Spenser's poem as Ralegh mourns that Cynthia has "debard" him from her presence but then invites Spenser to "wend with him, his Cynthia to see" (line 186). Such contradictions attest to revision of Spenser's poem at this point, where originally he must have referred to "Cynthia" as the "sweet verse" of his other early references to it. Thus Ralegh had composed a work in honor of Elizabeth as Cynthia by 1590; at issue is its extent and circulation, if any.[7]

The remaining evidence for or against any earlier books in the Cynthia series is itself contradictory and uncertain. In several passages of Poem 14 Ralegh mentions the poetry he had previously written for Elizabeth. He echoes lines from Poems 8 and 11, but only once does he seem to refer to an unidentified verse that might belong to the lost, earlier portion of Cynthia. Lines 344 and 347 refer to Poem 11, yet the following lines leading up to the question, "Butt what hath it avaylde thee so to write" (line 355), cannot be aligned with any known verse by Ralegh, especially his description of the queen as

> Th'Idea remayninge of thos golden ages
> that bewtye bravinge heavens, and yearth imbaulminge
> which after worthless worlds but play onn stages,
> such didsst thow her longe since discribe, yet sythinge.
>   (lines 348–51)

If this apparently explicit allusion derives from a significant work in praise of Cynthia, we must wonder why Ralegh did not make more of it at the same time that he was reminding Elizabeth of relatively minor lyrics he had written for her. Perhaps he had not imparted any of this earlier "Cynthia" to the queen—Spenser says as much in the prefatory verses to book 3 of the *Faerie Queene*—in which case, why mention it at all?

The most likely sequence of events that fits the available evidence has Ralegh devising the Cynthia/moon conceit by 1588 and incorporating it into one or more poems in praise of the queen before 1590. Spenser read this work in 1589 and in return acquainted Ralegh with his ambitious glorification of Elizabeth in his great poem. Given Ralegh's enthusiasm for Spenser's work, it would be quite natural for him to plan an expansion of his own poetry into some fuller, "epic" tribute to the queen. However, had Ralegh composed so ambitious a work in Cynthia's praise, he would surely have sent it to her given the pressure of his ongoing rivalry with Essex and the disgrace of 1592. Lines 348–51 of Poem 14 may recall some lesser "Cynthia," but Elizabeth collected and preserved the more substantial literary works presented to her in manuscript. Had she received twenty books of the "Oceans love to Scinthia" or any approximation from Ralegh we should expect to find them among the Royal Manuscripts in the British Library along with similar "books" of verse by Gascoigne, George Puttenham, and Thomas Churchyard. Thus, while we may have lost one or two relatively modest poems, it is unlikely that Ralegh produced a monumental "Cynthia" prior to Poems 12–15. His designation of the later poetry as books 21 and 22 implies the existence of a much longer but quite imaginary work, the better to grace his protestations of eternal love for Elizabeth.

Judging from the quality of what has survived, it is regrettable that these alleged books never materialized. Poem 12 seems to be addressed to the recipient of the three following poems. Its form is predominately hexameter couplets bracketed by opening and closing lines in which internal rhyme produces the effect of trimeters, while line 4 is heptameter. The poem advises that these works should be kept secret, for readers will only interpret them as they are disposed for or against Ralegh, who needs neither the "dysdayne" of his enemies nor the "dyspaire" of his friends, seeing that his mind "exceeds" in both of these emotions. Already the ambiguity that marks all the "Cynthia" poems emerges in the admonition to "keipe thes amonge the rest, or say it was a dreame" (line 2). The antecedent of "thes" is presumably the cluster of poems that Ralegh transcribed in this manuscript, but do "the rest" refer to other poems, perhaps the earlier "Cynthia" verses, and what is the antecedent of "it" in the second half of the line? Less confusing are the pronouns in lines 5 and 7, which must refer not to the recipient nor to Cynthia but to the poet himself whose mind is overladen with disdain and despair.

Poem 13 is an English sonnet with substitute tetrameters in lines 1, 2, and 6. Ralegh laments his "boddy in the walls captived," where he is accompanied by personified sorrow and despair in contrast with his former access to "loves fire and bewtys light." The setting and theme serve as a prologue to Poem 14, "The 21th: and last booke of the Ocean to Scinthia." This is Ralegh's longest poem, some 522 lines of iambic pentameter crossrhyme, but with some dozen unrhymed lines, a concluding couplet, and four cancelled lines.[8] Despite its length, the poem is lyric rather than narrative; Ralegh complains as a rejected lover now deserted by the queen as Cynthia or Belphoebe. The poem dwells at length upon their past relationship and the immediate crisis. Ralegh's allusive style, however, yields few details that point to the exact context that governed the poem's purpose and meaning.

Poem 15 is entitled "The end of the bookes, of the Oceans love to Scinthia, and the beginninge of the 22 Boock, entreating of Sorrow." The form changes to iambic pentameter in three-line stanzas rhyming *a b a c d c e f e* that end abruptly in the midst of line 22. That Ralegh merely stopped transcribing here is indicated by Professor Lefranc's discovery of Poem 21. Lefranc classifies this text as an earlier state of Poems 22 and 23, the "Petition" to Queene Anne, with perhaps a dozen of its stanzas deriving from the original of Poem 15.[9] Poem 21 opens with the first two stanzas of Poem 15 verbatim; its third stanza begins with the "tender Staulkes" mentioned in the last line of Poem 15. The next twelve stanzas, lines 10–42, are linked to themes and images from the "Cynthia" series such as the "moss" and "unburied bones" similes of 15.19–21. If these stanzas bear witness to the original state of Poem 15, they show Ralegh extending the nature imagery from the ending of the "21st" book (Poem 14), into the twenty-second. He introduces as well a complaint about desertion by friends and kindred (21.25–36), which expands the overall scope of his lament beyond the loss of Elizabeth's favor. While it is impossible to know to what extent these lines from Poem 21 represent the "Cynthia" he composed in 1592–93, Lefranc's discovery certainly indicates that Ralegh finished more of his book than is preserved in the manuscript at Hatfield House.

The "Cynthia" poems are integrally associated with Ralegh's frame of mind during the imprisonment of 1592 and the ensuing disgrace. In Poem 13 he contrasts his physical imprisonment with his mind's captivation in "her auntient memory," a contrast that loses its complimentary force if both the imprisonments are figurative. This poem must therefore date from one of Ralegh's three confinements in the Tower of London, in the summer and fall of 1592, in late 1603 through 1616, and during August through October of 1618. The imprisonment theme is not developed in Poems 12, 14, or 15, yet 13 provides a thematic introduction to the following poems with its emphasis on his separation from Cynthia, his devotion to her, and his lack of any hope for reconciliation. The sonnet is clearly a prologue to the following two poems, all of which were transcribed by Ralegh serially in the Hatfield manuscript.

In Poem 14 Ralegh casts his relationship with the queen in the oxymoronic Petrarchan metaphor of a struggle with a fair warrior: "Twelve yeares intire I wasted in this warr / twelve yeares of my most happy younger dayes" (lines 120–21). If we assume that the struggle ended suddenly in July 1592 with Ralegh's imprisonment, then twelve years before coincides exactly with his earliest royal service as an army captain in July 1580. Granted, he might have recalled these dozen years of contention for Elizabeth's favor at a later date, but if the poem were a post-Elizabethan recollection we would expect some allusion to the nearly six full years of the "war's" resumption after June 1597 when Ralegh again became one of Elizabeth's prominent courtiers.

Similarly, the reference to being recalled from a voyage was timely in 1592 but not thereafter: "when I was gonn shee sent her memory / more stronge then weare ten thowsand shipps of warr / to call mee back. . ." (lines 63–65). The "Panama" voyage was Ralegh's personal undertaking; in late February 1592 Sir Thomas Heneage noted that he "hath his Comyssion signed to goe on his voiage," and a royal proclamation of 2 March described it as a "service of her majesty and her realm committed to Sir Walter Raleigh."[10] However, the queen recalled him from this voyage after it had sailed. His frustration comes out in the lines about having "to leve great honors thought / To leve my frinds, my fortune, my attempte / to leve the purpose I so longe had sought" (lines 65–67). This was, however, the last time that Elizabeth recalled him from the sea; indeed, the letters of marque issued to him in 1594 encouraged him to undertake voyages, as he did in 1595, 1596, and 1597.

Ralegh understandably downplays the event that led to his disgrace, his marriage, yet it emerges clearly enough in Poem 14 as the "error" that deprived him of Cynthia's favor. The queen was his "true fancy's mistris" in "Fortune," and his affection for her was "quite retired" in "Like truthless dreames" (Poem 8, line 3). In the twenty-first book his joys "died when first my fancy erred," where erring carries the sense of straying from its proper object, the queen. Ralegh consistently portrays his love for Elizabeth Throckmorton as his "error" that is equated with his "offence" at line 373 and termed a "frayle effect of mortall livinge" (line 445). In these vague references Ralegh demotes the love that led him to marry; it is nothing compared with his love for the queen, yet such a trifle has cost him all his sovereign's regard.[11] The Throckmorton marriage alone in Ralegh's relationship with the queen fits this allusion to a known, devastating crisis. Thus the 1592 dating connects this, Ralegh's most ambitious poetry, with an occasion compelling enough to have elicited it, in keeping with the functional, occasional nature of so much of his earlier verse.

The preservation of these poems at Hatfield House also makes sense in terms of the 1592 dating. By that year Cecil was acting as the queen's principal secretary and was probably her most intimate advisor. He was also Ralegh's friend, a poet, and a collector of verse.[12] He was the likeliest person of Ralegh's acquaintance not only to appreciate the "Cynthia" poems but to share them with the queen. Poems 12–15 are accordingly centered on the sheets and neatly copied in Ralegh's "fair" hand. The dozen or so minor corrections make the text a trifle rough for direct presentation to the queen yet acceptable for delivery to her through an intermediary such as Cecil. The sudden termination of Poem 15 marks a break in copying, not composition. Perhaps Ralegh was forced to interrupt his transcription, or he may have stopped at this point to dramatize his inability to proceed in such a task, having lost Elizabeth's favor.

For all of their ambiguity, disjointed syntax, and apparent disorganization, the Hatfield poems constitute an effective appeal for forgiveness comparable to the preceding complaints that Ralegh had addressed to Elizabeth in Poems 6 and 8. Above all, the complexities of Poem 14, the "twenty-first book" of the Cynthia series, are clarified in the light of these earlier complaints. He had good reason to follow up the strategies he had employed before, since we know that they were well received by the queen. To Poem 6 she had written a reassuring verse response, while whatever rift marred their relationship in 1589 found compensation in Ralegh's high favor from 1590 into the summer of 1592.[13] In Poem 14 Ralegh alludes to "Like truthless dreams" as a work that "my mishapp fortolde" (line 124), and he conveys the far greater magnitude of his present misfortune with a telling metaphor: "att middell day my soonn seemde under land / when any littell cloude did it obscure" (lines 130–31). Elizabeth, his sun, had seemed to leave him in utter darkness by retreating to the other side of the earth when her presence was actually only obscured by a cloud. Now, however, and throughout the "Cynthia" poems, the queen has abandoned him indeed to the darkness of a winter's night. His current difficulty is a catastrophic amplification of his former ones, and thus the essence of his poetic response is a creative enlargement upon the strategies he had previously used with success.

In Poem 8, as in Poem 6, the poet's despair was absolute. His joys were "past returne," leaving him only sorrow and the hope of a speedy death. In "Fortune" the queen and his joys were also lost to him forever. A similar hopelessness pervades the twenty-first book: "With youth, is deade the hope of loves returne" (line 287); "Thow lookest for light in vayne, and stormes arise / Shee sleaps thy death that erst thy danger syth-ed" (lines 489–90). Psychologically, Ralegh's strategy is identical in all three poems. His absolutism invites Elizabeth to assert her sovereign power by contradicting him. What he finds beyond repair she can renew and restore because she is a queen. He frequently reminds Elizabeth of her sunlike power, most explicitly perhaps in Poem 15, where he affirms that "shee cann renew, and cann create / green from the grounde, and floures, yeven out of stonn" (lines 16–17).

Elizabeth receives additional encouragement to exercise regal authority by restoring him to favor through a second strategy also found in Poem 6. There he had affirmed that fortune would never alter his devotion to her although she has succumbed to its power; similarly, he pledges eternal love in Poem 14 despite the dissolution of her love for him. The queen is thus challenged in both poems to demonstrate a strength of commitment equal to that of her steadfast servant.

To be convincing, Ralegh's expressions of abiding but hopeless love must be conveyed in an emotional style. The ambiguous references, disjointed syntax, and associative lurching from subject to subject create the effect of impulsive composition.[14] Yet this effect, upon closer scrutiny, turns out to be the result not of distraction but a calculated artistry designed to move the queen to relent. At line 73, for example, Ralegh launches a series of three epic similes to make the relatively minor point that motion may continue after the source of power has been removed, as in a dead body, the earth in winter, or a waterwheel after its current has been diverted. He uses a dozen lines to develop these analogues before applying them to the continuing labors of his "forsaken hart" and "withered minde" (line 85). The comparisons build to a powerful conclusion, but this is a deliberately crafted passage, not the spontaneous overflow of powerful emotions.

The poem's apparent formlessness is likewise deceptive. As we follow Ralegh's development of the main points which he communicates to Elizabeth, a pattern emerges that gives form to his apparently random oscillations between his present sufferings and memories of his past joys. Amid the "unrelieved grief"[15] that dominates the poem, Ralegh shifts his emphasis from the past to the present, and then to the future, giving Poem 14 a loose but appropriate structure.

The body of the poem is bracketed by a thematic introduction, lines 1–36, and a conclusion, lines 474–522, which together contain most of the pastoralism in the book. Above all, Ralegh conveys to Elizabeth his utter dejection, characteristic of the lover's lament, of course, but analyzed here in virtually epic detail. In the second section of the poem, lines 37–212, Ralegh dwells upon specific recollections of his past happiness in the queen's favor: the poetry he wrote for her, the interrupted voyage, and her immortal beauty. These nostalgic reminiscences conclude with his charge that love is transitory and that, for all her perfections, she retains "the affections of her kynde / yet free from evry yevill but crueltye" (lines 211–12).

A marked turn in the poem follows this guarded criticism of the queen: "But leve her prayse, speak thow of nought but wo." The charge of cruelty was scarcely praise, and more and worse criticism of Elizabeth will follow. In lines 213–461 he refers to his afflicted memories, yet the emphasis here is upon the present dilemma: the "tokens" he formerly received "ar now elcewhere disposde" (lines 263–64), and all his influence is gone, leaving his friends outcast and his enemies "deere beloved." This section of the poem began with an epic simile that compared the difficulty of retaining a woman's love to forcing a tempestuous stream from its accustomed channel: "onn houre deverts, onn instant overthrowes" all we have done, Ralegh complains. In contrast with her unstable affection for him, Ralegh introduces at line 300 his professions of unending love for her. These intertwined themes dominate this part of the work, and only after their estrangement has been portrayed in this light does Ralegh broach the subject of his "error" (line 338), the secret marriage that has caused him all this suffering. He acknowledges the causal relationship outright. The subtlety here concerns his vague language and diminution of the marriage to a single, momentary lapse that in no way reduced his passionate devotion to the queen. In the context of his abiding love for her, which is unaffected by her utter rejection of him, the Throckmorton match is reduced to an irrelevancy for which he is being unjustly punished.

In the concluding forty-eight lines of the poem Ralegh revives the pastoral atmosphere of its opening to characterize himself as a ruined shepherd who must now abandon his flocks: "Thus home I draw, as deaths longe night drawes onn" (line 509). His thoughts turn toward a future holding only sorrow and death for him, now that he is irrevocably deprived of her love: "her love hath end. my woe must ever last" (line 522).

If Elizabeth ever read this carefully designed complaint, she declined its invitation to restore her prostrate servant. Ralegh's criticism of her behavior is much stronger here than in Poem 6, for example, where she was portrayed as a more or less passive victim of fortune. In Poem 14 she is a fickle lover who deserts the poet without sufficient cause. The charge that "my love was falce" (line 465) is ambiguous, yet it seems to accuse the queen of infidelity. In the context of the amorous conventions in which he chose to write, moreover, Ralegh's criticism is doubly audacious, for his fall resulted from his desertion of the queen for Elizabeth Throckmorton. His reversal of the situation, charging the queen with lack of faith, is a bold rhetorical strategy akin to his portrayal of English forces as victims of Spanish aggression in the *Revenge* tract.

Although the twenty-first book has been termed the most significant blend of "pastoral, Petrarchan, medieval, and Platonic" traditions in praise of Elizabeth,[16] critics blame this variety of elements for contributing to the poem's apparent lack of unity. They note that the title is quite misleading, for Ralegh fails to develop the Cynthia-Ocean mythos or any other sustaining fiction. Elizabeth is identified with the sun rather than the moon, the predominant imagery concerns the earth, not the sea, while water in Poem 14 is generally a violent and threatening force rather than an attribute of the poet.[17] To say that Ralegh was highly eclectic need not imply, however, that the result was amorphous even within the larger organization of its parts into a past, present, and future pattern. Instead, Ralegh drew upon this array of styles and conventions to enhance his overall purpose of influencing the queen.

The poem's medieval-Petrarchan elements include the personifications of sorrow, love, joys, and the rest, a device typical of Spenser's allegory but prominent as well in Ralegh's style from the beginning. More important, Petrarchism fostered his pose as the distraught lover obsessed with a matchless but aloof woman in the courtly love tradition. His hyperbolic praise of the queen, with much of the language in which it is couched, belong to this tradition along with his equally hyperbolic lamentation of his own forlorn state. Again, Ralegh employed conventions familiar in his own verse long before 1592, and he drew specific allusions from his own poetry to remind Elizabeth of previous stages in their artificial courtly love relationship.

The Neoplatonic conventions of Renaissance love poetry offered Ralegh a solution to his dilemma of professing love for one woman after marrying another. He does term Elizabeth "Th'Idea remayninge of thos golden ages" (line 348), a platonic approach that he may have developed in earlier "Cynthia" poetry. Elizabeth, now in her late fifties, continued to expect tributes to her youth and beauty. Accordingly, the immortal beauty that Ralegh praises here as in Poem 11 goes beyond her spiritual qualities to her physical charms, as in his profession of love for "th'incarnat, snow driven white, and purest asure" (line 308), the perfect red and white of her complexion, traced with veins of blue.[18] Ralegh expresses a comprehensive love for the queen, yet he characterizes the quality of his love, the emotion itself, as a platonic essence. It is the "Idea" of line 12, his "essential love" (line 410), that has become an immortal, spiritual entity that animates his mind (lines 426–28; 438). In this way Ralegh uses Neoplatonism to magnify his commitment to Elizabeth without letting it exclude any of her attributes from his adoration.[19]

The passions of Poem 14 are further magnified by its unusual length and epic similes which, with the name Belphoebe, reveal Spenser's influence. Ralegh here uses extended similes for the first time, to impart an intensely emotional, elevated tone to his complaint. For at least one of his similes, the description of air imprisoned deep underground, he borrowed the cavern of Aeolus from an established epic, Virgil's *Aeneid* (1.52–59). For the pastoralism of Poem 14, however, Ralegh declined Spenser's English rusticity for Sidney's more elegant Italian style. The metaphor of the poet's heart as a sheepfold with false hope as his now broken sheephook (lines 497–508) was perhaps modeled on Sidney's "My sheepe are thoughts which I both guide and serve," where the sheephook is "wanne hope."[20]

These disparate styles, blended into an amorous lament designed to move the queen, gave Ralegh more emotional leverage than would have been possible with the Ocean-Cynthia metaphor. Comparing the lady to the sun, for example, was a Petrarchan commonplace. It was also a traditional royal symbol often applied to Elizabeth; it allowed Ralegh to stress the sovereign power that she is invited to exercise by redeeming him from the misery that he characterizes as fixed and immutable. The pastoral pose works, as it does throughout Renaissance love poetry, in tandem with courtly love elements to portray the lover's humility and the natural, in this case, ever-renewing, beauty of the beloved. Thus the conventions work together in furthering Ralegh's purpose, becoming in their cumulative effect something more than a skillful mingling of rhetorical commonplaces.

Ralegh deploys these conventions with a personal, emotion-laden voice to produce in the "Cynthia" series his finest poetic achievement. The sincere and convincing tone that marked individual passages in his elegy for Sidney, in "Like truthless dreams," "Fortune," and the conclusion of "Now we have present made," sounds repeatedly in the Cynthia poems. Ralegh achieves a colloquial tone in the description of his attempts to suppress his memories of the past: "Ah those I sought, but vaynly, to remove / And vaynly shall, by which I perrish livinge" (lines 171–72). Similar apostrophes, "Oh love it is but vayne, to say thow weare," "Oh, all in onn, oh heaven on yearth transparent" (lines 436, 43), convey personal feeling as do the emotional repetitions such as the anadiplosis in lines 491–92 followed by anaphora: "strive then no more, bow down thy weery eyes / Eyes, which to all thes woes thy hart have guided. / Shee is gonn, Shee is lost, shee is found, shee is ever faire." The impulsive effect gains too from the rambling sentences which, given Ralegh's sparse punctuation, often make it difficult to be sure just where a group of clauses reaches a full stop. In many passages this rhythmic, headlong impetus creates a Miltonic roll that is fed by enjambment.

We may wink at Ralegh's exaggerated flattery of the aging queen, and even at his protestations of undying love for her, yet considerations of context should not be allowed to diminish our appreciation of his achievement. The intimate, emotional tone of these poems sets them apart from that impersonal elegance so typical of Elizabethan love lyrics. Sidney's *Defence of Poetry* was first printed in 1595, and while Ralegh refers to it in *The History of the World* he may not have known of Sidney's theoretic aspirations for poetry at the time he wrote the "Cynthia" poems. Nevertheless, and particularly in Poem 14, Ralegh imparts to his verse that intensity of personal feeling or "energia" that Sidney praised as the mark of effective, moving poetry.

The "Succession" Tract

Ralegh's "Succession" tract, with its prefatory letter to the queen, forms a minor prose counterpart to the Cynthia poems. Both works are unfinished and survive in unique holograph copies at Hatfield House. As with the poems, Ralegh no doubt sent the prose tract to Sir Robert Cecil for delivery to the queen since Ralegh's fall had deprived him of direct communication with her. His letter mentions, moreover, another "paper contayninge the dangers, which might groe by the spanish faction in skotlande," which he had also sent to her. No copy of this work is known, and Ralegh admits that "how it pleased your Majestye to accept therof I know not" ("Succession," 42). His letter also echoes sentiments and phrasing from the Cynthia poems. He laments that his "errors ar eternal, and thos of other mortall," and that "your Majesty havinge left mee I am left all alone in the worlde." In closing, he reaffirms his obsession with "the memory of thos celestiall bewtes" emanating from the queen (43).

The four pages of argumentation that accompanied this letter serve, with the Cynthia poems, to flatter and placate Elizabeth. They defend her refusal to name a successor to the throne, a policy that was not even debatable so far as she was concerned. Had it been published, Ralegh's cogent defense of her position might have served as effective royal propaganda. Addressed to Elizabeth herself, however, it amounted to little more than an expression of loyalty.

The question of succession had haunted England from the moment Elizabeth came to the throne. During the first half of the reign her subjects had urged her to marry in order that she might produce an heir. After 1582 the controversy centered upon which of several possible claimants should rule when the queen died. Elizabeth fully understood, of course, that she would only weaken her own authority by diverting her subjects' attention to an acknowledged heir; thus the official policy of leaving the matter unresolved.

Ralegh's support of this policy displays his customary powers of organization and persuasive technique. He looks back upon Elizabeth's reign to demonstrate her sacrificial care for her people. The particular blessing he cites is her institution of the Protestant faith at a time when England stood weak and alone among hostile Catholic powers. For her subjects now to question her regard for their future welfare argued their lack of trust, or even insubordination. Ralegh then surveys the major candidates who might succeed Elizabeth. He points out not only their shortcomings but the difficulty of pleasing a majority of the people through the selection of any one of them; indeed, he suggests that widespread discontent or even civil war might result from a specific nomination. Ralegh then argues that a definite nomination could not guarantee a smooth transition of power anyway. He cites examples of legitimate heirs to the thrones of England and France who have found their regimes opposed or overthrown entirely.

In support of this last point Ralegh invokes the examples of Henry IV of France, the heirs of Edward IV, and Lady Jane Grey's challenge to Queen Mary. The listing of apt historical precedents typifies his argumentative style, as does the clear division of the essay into parts and his sarcastic treatment of his opponents, such as "thes great patriots" who insist that the queen settle the question at once. What else he meant to write on this occasion cannot be reconstructed; the tract, which seems to lack nothing but a conclusion, ends with the word "abortive."

Two minor aspects of what Ralegh did complete are worth noting for the light they shed on the development of his political thought. He suggests that naming James of Scotland heir to the throne might encourage him to precipitate the event by combining with Spain and with his brother-in-law, the king of Denmark, to invade England. Within a few days of composing the "Succession" tract Ralegh was warning his fellow members of Parliament that just such an invasion was likely because the king of Spain had corrupted both the king of Denmark and the nobility of Scotland.[21] This characterization of the king of Scotland was imprudent at best, although the larger point here is Ralegh's somewhat paranoid concern that several powers would unite to invade England. Similar fears crop up in his later writings. The driving force behind such a conspiracy as Ralegh perceived it was not Spain, much as Spain continued to be his particular bête noire for years to come. Rather, Catholicism was for Ralegh a permanent ideological force bent on England's destruction. Spain was an abiding but ultimately expendable instrument of this conspiracy. Increasingly, Ralegh viewed the Jesuits as a subversive political arm of the Catholic Church at work to destroy England from within as well as without. He had termed them "runagate Jesuits" in the *Revenge* pamphlet (85); in the "Succession" tract he blames them for attempting to assassinate the queen (43–44). He eventually combined the threat of international conspiracy with Jesuit leadership as it became increasingly difficult to maintain that Spain posed a genuine offensive threat to England.

The Guiana Tracts

If Elizabeth did in fact read the Cynthia poems or the "Succession" tract they failed to mollify her anger toward Ralegh. During the next two years he planned and set in motion a more substantial form of appeasement. In December 1594 the queen signed a commission that authorized him and his associates to plunder the king of Spain and his possessions, with the right to keep their gains less the Crown's ordinary customs.[22] On 6 February Ralegh set sail for the land he called Guiana, now part of northeastern Venezuela along the Orinoco River. He secured his line of retreat by dispersing the Spanish garrison on Trinidad and taking prisoner its commander, Don Antonio de Berrio. With one hundred men Ralegh then explored the river valley for several hundred miles inland, meeting and making friends with native chieftains and learning all he could about the topography and resources of the countryside. The gold-rich Indian civilization he expected to find never materialized, however, and he scrupulously forbade any looting of the natives he did encounter, nor did he take any major Spanish prizes during the voyage. As a result, he returned to England in September laden with dreams of empire rather than with treasure.

In the following year Ralegh published the *Discovery*, an enthusiastic account of the voyage that strongly encouraged English colonization in Guiana. He dedicated this book to Lord Charles Howard and Sir Robert Cecil, both of whom were leading privy councillors. A fuller understanding of Ralegh's intentions emerges, however, by comparing the *Discovery* with a shorter tract, "Of the Voyage for Guiana," composed by Ralegh or at his direction for the council or some of its members.[23] In this document Ralegh explained how the government could build upon his initial efforts not only to found an empire that would rival Spain's, but to begin the forceful subversion of Spanish holdings in the New World. He had long foreseen England's need to gain lasting strength through colonization. That was the ultimate goal of his effort to colonize Virginia. Now he adapted what he had learned in that venture to the circumstances in Guiana. The queen and her councillors, however, were eager for immediate gain; thus Ralegh's task as propagandist was to show that a lasting English presence in Guiana would yield greater returns than merely plundering the area. In the process he hoped as well "to appease so powerful a displeasure" as the queen still felt toward him (*Discovery*, 380).

The conflict between Ralegh's performance and official expectations resulted from a single important misapprehension. He believed that refugees from the Inca civilization had built in Guiana "the great city of Manoa" (397), termed by the Spaniards El Dorado, capital of a native empire far richer in gold than the one they had lost in Peru. This empire was Guiana proper, and Ralegh claimed only to have reached its borders. The existence of El Dorado was sworn to by a host of Spanish conquistadors including Berrio, who had spent a fortune trying to find it. In addition, such an empire was described by the Indians Ralegh met and talked with along the Orinoco.

As his treatise "Of the Voyage" makes clear, Ralegh had intended from the beginning to subdue Guiana and appropriate its wealth for English use. To accomplish this, however, he formulated a relatively humane plan for dealing with the native population, a plan that closely resembled his policy of fair

dealings with the Indians of Virginia. He insisted that the natives be converted to Christianity and taught the "liberall arts of civility" as well as warfare (146). But he argued that Christians have no right to conquer or kill
heathen peoples just because they are heathens (141–42). Ralegh envisioned
instead a partnership with the Indians that would lead to a blending of the
English and native populations. At first, he proposed, hostages from Guiana
would be brought to England, not only to ensure performance of the original
agreements between the two peoples but also to civilize these Indians and
marry them with English women (146). Ralegh's plan grew out of his respect
for the natives and their potential for becoming fellow citizens and allies in
the struggle against Spain. As a first step toward implementing this policy, he
left two of his men in Guiana and took back to England with him an Indian
named Cayworaco, son of the old King Topiawari.

Ralegh's idealistic proposals were too far ahead of his time to prevail with
the government, yet despite his misplaced faith in Manoa-El Dorado, the
plan was workable. In addition to its other natural resources the land does
contain gold, as gold rushes in the last century and during the 1980s have
demonstrated. Ralegh brought ore back to London and he repeatedly assured readers of the *Discovery* that gold, other precious metals, and gems
could be mined in the region. He established, moreover, a lasting rapport
with the Indians upon which a colony might have been developed along the
lines he suggested, for he returned to Guiana more than twenty years later to
find his name honored by the natives, who still wished to unite with England
in resisting Spanish domination.

Ralegh was ahead of his time in his understanding of propaganda methods as well as in plans for humane treatment of native populations. "Of the
Voyage" recommended that the Indians be given illustrated copies of Las
Casas's history of Spanish conquests and atrocities. He advised as well that
they be shown maps of England and northern Europe with emphasis upon
the French and Germans as allies of the great queen (144). Similarly, he had
encouraged or sponsored a half-dozen books and pamphlets in support of his
Virginia colony. The *Discovery* was his first important composition in support of English colonization.

The opening portion of his book, more than a third of the total narrative,
is devoted to the background of Guiana: its location, wealth, and the history
of Spanish efforts to find and conquer it. The account of Ralegh's journey up
the Orinoco River occupies about half the narrative, leaving the rest for a
summary conclusion that stresses the ease with which his countrymen might
obtain the wealth of Guiana versus the danger to England should Spain add
this prize to its already burgeoning empire.

The book became not only Ralegh's most popular work but the only one of his writings to exert an international influence. It saw four English editions in his lifetime, including the 1599 reprint in Hakluyt's *Principal Navigations*, four editions in German before the close of Elizabeth's reign, besides two in Latin and others in Dutch and French. True, other European powers were eyeing Guiana before Ralegh published his account of it; in the *Discovery* he claimed that the French were planning to settle in the area "this very year" (407). But the wide circulation of his book served to heighten the interest. A Dutch expedition reached Guiana in 1596; in the next few years Ralegh himself negotiated for a role in both Dutch and Swedish ventures to the same purpose.[24] He was determined to keep Spain from seizing Guiana whether or not his own country led the way. Yet by the time private Englishmen attempted settlement and trade in the region in 1604 and 1609, the provisions of King James's peace treaty with Spain had ensured their failure.[25]

The power of Ralegh's book derives from its lively, first-person narration, the tales of abundant gold, and his descriptions of the land as a second garden of Eden.[26] He uses a variety of rhetorical techniques to give his account the ring of authority, to make the places he describes as real as they are attractive. Much of what he says is documented by citations from Spanish authors and through translations of captured documents about Guiana that form an appendix to the discourse. He cites also the testimony of his prisoner, Berrio, who had mounted four exploratory expeditions into the mainland.

Ralegh creates empires brimming with treasure through the cumulative effect of his epic listings. In the dedicatory epistle, for example, he summarizes the territories that must be invaded if England tries to wrest away even a portion of Spain's empire: "there are besides within the land, which are indeed rich and populous, the towns and cities of Merida, Lagrita, S. Christophero, the great cities of Pampelone, S. Fe de Bogota, Tunia, and Mozo, where the emeralds are found, the towns and cities of Moriquito, Velis, la Villa de Leua, Palma, Unda, Angustura, the great city of Timana, Tocaima, S. Aguila, Pasto, Juago, the great city of Popayan itself, Los Remedios, and the rest" (*Discovery*, 382–83). Guiana too is composed of nations, kings, provinces, cities, and ports; he mentions the "Iwarawakeri" who live near the river Caroli not far from "other nations which also resist Inga and the Epuremei, called Cassepagotos, Eparegotos, and Arrawagotos" (443). He catalogs plants, animals, and rivers along with more tribes whose political orientations are exactly described, not to mention the products of the countryside itself: "great quantities of Brazil wood . . . abundance of cotton, of silk, of balsamum, and . . . of all sorts of gums, of Indian pepper, . . ." plus "pheasants, partridges, quails, rails, cranes, herons, and all other fowl; deer of all sorts, porkers, hares, lions, tigers, leopards" (462–63). Thus Ralegh imparts a sense of vivid reality to his account, behind which we glimpse only occasionally the expanse of tropical jungle dotted with stone-age villages and obscure Spanish outposts, the whole populated to a significant degree by cannibals, as Ralegh himself mentions more than once. Ralegh depicts a far grander place than that, "a country that hath yet her maidenhead, never sacked, turned, nor wrought; the face of the earth hath not been torn, nor the virtue and salt of the soil spent by manurance, the graves have not been opened for gold, the mines not broken with sledges, nor their images pulled down out of their temples" (464).

Some of the marvels recounted in the *Discovery* are even more incredible than the tales of plentiful gold. Ralegh saw oysters growing on trees (or stranded there, at least, at low tide), and he heard reports of a race of Amazon women, and of men whose heads grew beneath their shoulders. He attempted to convince his readers of the reality of these wonders by connecting them with similar accounts in old-world literature, in classical authors such as Pliny, and in the more modern *Cosmographie* of André Thevet and Mandeville's "Travels."[27] Ralegh appears even more gullible in stressing, both in the *Discovery* and "Of the Voyage," the report of an ancient prophecy found by the conquistadors of the Inca empire, stating that "from Inglatiera the Inga should be restored to Peru." Although he admits that "we are not greatly to rely upon prophesies" ("Of the Voyage," 139), his repeated references show that he believed that the Incas of Guiana, under English leadership, would be easily incited to undertake the reconquest of Peru.

The tone of sarcasm so characteristic of Ralegh's argumentative prose style largely disappears in the *Discovery*, while other traits of the author's personality color the narration. Of the boat ride upriver he writes, "there was never any prison in England that could be found more unsavoury and loathsome, especially to myself, who had for many years before been dieted and cared for in a sort far differing" (*Discovery*, 397). Ralegh's interest in pharmacology is evident in his discussion of the Indians' poisoned arrows and his desire to learn of the antidote for that poison. He pays tribute to Spenser and the *Faerie Queene* by naming a branch of the Orinoco the "river of the Red Cross, ourselves being the first Christians that ever came therein" (421). He laments the loss of Captain Whiddon and the death of a Negro servant who was killed by an alligator while swimming in the river (427). An engaging, personal tone pervades the book in keeping with its purported format as an account written especially for Cecil and Howard who are referred to from time to time in the narrative as "your lordship" and "your honour."

Ralegh and Essex

The earl of Essex prepared an elaborate entertainment to celebrate the queen's Accession Day on 17 November 1595. It culminated in a masque wherein Elizabeth was introduced to a blind Indian prince from "near the fountain of the Amazon." According to a prophecy, he was destined to expel from his homeland the "Castilians" who had encircled it but "not pierced near the heart."[28] The prince, who required an interpreter, may have been played by Cayworaco, the Indian who returned to England with Ralegh. At any rate, the earl's show borrowed from Ralegh's voyage and endorsed his contention that Guiana must not fall to Spain. Ralegh's disgrace signaled a rapprochement between the two men that began when Essex graciously consented to stand godfather to Ralegh's unfortunate son Damerei in 1592. Ralegh soon found his attention distracted from Guiana by the earl, who encouraged him to participate in the two major naval expeditions he commanded in 1596 and 1597.

The Cadiz Narrative, 1596. Ralegh described his role in the Cadiz raid of June–July 1596 in two similar but not identical letters, one written to his friend Henry, earl of Northumberland, and the other to Arthur Gorges.[29] The capture of Cadiz was preceded by a dangerous naval maneuver. Ralegh requested and obtained the precarious honor of leading this attack. It involved sailing under the town's fortifications and past the Spanish warships anchored beneath them. He ran this gauntlet without returning fire, saving his powder for the great Spanish galleons further down the channel, including the *St. Philip* and *St. Andrew*, both of which had grappled with the *Revenge*. Although the English flotilla was outnumbered at least three ships to one, it forced the channel and captured or burned the enemy fleet. The English then secured a landing zone on the peninsula where soldiers disembarked to fight their way back to Cadiz. Ralegh did not witness the city's fall, however, for he received a painful leg wound during the artillery duel with the *St. Philip*.[30] As a result he remained with the fleet while Cadiz was looted, and he ends his letter to Northumberland by complaining that the exploit has left him with a lame leg, "poverty and pain"(*Works*, 8:674).[31]

Ralegh's accounts of the battle, including his own heroism, are corroborated in all important respects by independent reports of the victory. He undoubtedly led the naval attack and was wounded during a firefight that lasted more than two hours. Both letters reveal the extent to which military discipline gave way to personal rivalries and emotions. While Ralegh conferred briefly with Essex aboard a ship to the rear of the action, Sir Francis Vere and Lord Thomas Howard edged their ships ahead of his. When Ralegh returned to his own vessel, he slipped past both his rivals' ships, then turned his own broadside in the channel to prevent their taking the lead again. And when Vere attempted to pull up to Ralegh by attaching a rope to his ship, Ralegh had it cut free—all in the midst of an enemy bombardment that damaged Ralegh's ship to the verge of sinking (671–72).

It is in the letter to Gorges, however, that Ralegh adds engaging personal touches not found in the more matter-of-fact letter to Northumberland. If, as Lefranc contends, these letters were written with an eye toward influencing opinion at court,[32] certainly the letter to Gorges was best calculated to do so. Arthur Gorges was, after all, a relative and confidant in regular attendance at court among the gentleman pensioners. To Northumberland, Ralegh remembered his "great duty to her majesty"(669), but he told Gorges of his French war cry, "Vive la Reigne de Angleterre," and his hope that his exploit "now seeme gracious in her eyes, to whom I haue giuen my lyffe"(344). This letter concludes with a further tribute to Elizabeth: Ralegh assigns the glory and thanks for their success to God, but then God "hath favored vs for her sake whome we serue," and to her belongs the honor and profit of the voyage (344). He nevertheless reserved some portion of the glory for himself, for after listing the English ships that followed his lead Ralegh exclaimed, "But Arthur your fleshe & blood, single in the head of all & against whome all the furious battery was bent"(343).

The "Opinion" and "Offensive" Tracts. Within months of the destruction of Spanish shipping at Cadiz, Philip II was preparing to launch a naval attack on England. By October the Privy Council had learned that a Spanish fleet seventy strong had been assembled to avenge the humiliating English victory. In early November the queen asked Essex to consult with seven named military advisors and to report to her their opinions just as her commanders had done during the Armada crisis. Had Ralegh not remained on amicable terms with Essex, the earl would not have insisted that he be added to the council of war along with his kinsman Sir George Carew, another veteran of the Cadiz raid. To the council that met on 3 November Essex submitted his "Articles," or rather questions about probable Spanish intentions and the best way to counter them ("Opinion," 675–76). Ralegh's "Opinion" responds to these questions. By 9 November Elizabeth had read his analysis, apparently without enthusiasm.[33]

Ralegh's brief treatise contends that Spain will not attempt an invasion before spring or summer and that the attack will be aimed at London rather than the western counties or the Isle of Wight. Ralegh suggests specific measures for repelling the invasion, yet his underlying thesis warns that England is vulnerable while awaiting a foreign attack from a purely defensive posture.

The "Offensive" tract is a more general and theoretical outline of military strategy that first argues the many disadvantages that beset a nation on the defensive. It must await the time and place of attack chosen by the aggressor and it stands to lose everything, whereas the invader can lose nothing more than his army. This part of the discourse ends with a long list of historical examples showing that invaders almost always succeed. Ralegh then turns to the advantages enjoyed by an invader. He specifies that an English attack on Spain would demoralize the enemy and prevent them from landing a strong force in England.

Lefranc suggests that the "Offensive" was written early in 1597. However, the parallels he cites between it and the "Opinion" may as easily be interpreted as evidence that the "Offensive" was an earlier "position paper" that Ralegh adapted in his "Opinion" to the specific recommendations he set forth in answer to Essex's questions. The list of successful invasions in the "Offensive," for instance, is repeated in order and almost verbatim in the "Opinion"(679), except for "Godmare de Fas," the "Reyster of Hess," the Earl of Nemours, and the Portuguese expedition of 1589 (208–9). Perhaps Ralegh amplified these examples as he drew on the "Opinion" to write the "Offensive," yet it seems more likely that he worked from this original but excluded a few of its details from the "Opinion."

Ralegh aspired to a seat on Elizabeth's Privy Council, an honor he never attained. Cecil affirmed at his trial, however, that privy councillors often consulted him on matters of state.[34] The war council of 3 November 1596 is one of the few recorded instances of a formal consultation that involved Ralegh, and from these two tracts we can reconstruct not only the substance of his advice but the orderly and well-researched way in which he presented it.

"The Lie."   The poem beginning "Goe soule the bodies guest" circulated in manuscript by 1595. None of its many texts was ascribed to Ralegh during his lifetime, yet a series of answering poems, two of them assuredly Elizabethan, attack Ralegh as its author.[35] Essex is connected with "The Lie" insofar as several of the verse responses to it can be traced to his circle, and it is just possible that he wrote two of these himself. Although Lefranc argues that the earl's partisans blamed "The Lie" on Ralegh between 1599 and 1603 in order to embarrass him, it seems doubtful that anyone would have taken so much trouble. By then, the Essex circle had more immediate charges to press against Ralegh, such as his role in the earl's disgrace and, after 1601, his execution. Moreover, the poem's iambic trimeter rhythm with five initial trochaic feet, feminine rhyme, and the pronounced enjambment of lines 9–10, 27–28, 45–46, and 73–74 closely resembles Ralegh's practice in "Now we have present made."

In Poem 16 the poet commands his soul to make accusations against contemporary institutions such as the court, church, and schools, against persons such as potentates and "men of high condition," and against such personified entities as love, beauty, wit, and faith. The couplet that closes each sixain orders the soul to "give the lie," that is, accuse of lying, any victim that denies these charges. So comprehensive a satire naturally invited contradictory replies, all the more so because of its unrelieved tone of bitter condemnation; Lefranc termed it a Puritan composition.[36] The poem is heavy-handed satire, a redundant chant devoid of the irony with which Ralegh injected wry humor into his argumentative prose style. Rudick notes that the poem fits Ralegh's disillusioned outlook between 1592 and 1595,[37] but in this case Ralegh's strong feelings inspired a very slight creative achievement notwithstanding the poem's contemporary popularity.

Early in 1597 Ralegh undertook preparations for another naval expedition against Spain. He was responsible for spending almost £19,000 to secure provisions for six thousand men.[38] He was regularly in the company of both Essex and Cecil, and by early March had managed at last to confer with the queen, although not in private. By April he was allowed to wait in the privy chamber, the room at court reserved for Elizabeth and her most favored retainers. On 2 June Cecil, with the approval of Essex, brought Ralegh before the queen, who restored him to his duties as captain of the Guard and allowed him to accompany her on her evening carriage ride.[39] The five years of disgrace were over, leaving Ralegh six years of more or less constant favor with his sovereign before the overwhelming disasters that befell him after the accession of King James.

Chapter Four
Transition to the New Regime

From a literary standpoint the last half-dozen years of Elizabeth's reign were among Ralegh's least productive. After his return to favor he busied himself with the parliamentary sessions of 1597 and 1601, and with campaigns for such offices as the vice-chamberlainship of the royal household and a seat on the Privy Council, neither of which he obtained. He was appointed governor of Jersey in 1600, and he continued his active service as captain of the Guard, lieutenant of Cornwall, and lord warden of the Stanneries.

To this period belong three works in prose, only one of which survives in final form. Shortly after returning from the "Islands" voyage, Ralegh composed his "Observations Concerning the Royal Navy and Sea-Service," a prose tract that he originally dedicated to the queen; it is treated below as revised by Ralegh for Prince Henry about 1608.[1] Sir Walter evidently jotted down his "Considerations concerning Reprysalles" in 1600 in defense of a privateering exploit performed on his behalf by his nephew, Sir John Gilbert.[2] Gilbert had seized "to Sir Wal: Raleighs use" a Dutch ship, the St. Mary, with a cargo of sugar belonging to Dutch and Venetian merchants. In retaliation Venice impounded "7 or 8 of the best English merchant ships." The Privy Council, however, deemed Venice a friendly power and moved for restitution of the prize.[3] Ralegh's "Considerations" form no fully developed treatise but merely outline the counterargument in which he links the St. Mary and its cargo with the Spanish war effort. By the end of the reign he had composed his lost "Discourse How War may be Made Against Spain and the Indies," which is known only from his allusion to it in the "Discourse Touching a War with Spain." The latter tract was addressed to King James and was no doubt put into final form between his accession in March 1603 and Ralegh's trial in November.

Late Elizabethan Poetry

"Nature," Poem 17. Only three poems can be connected with Ralegh between 1597 and 1603, and two of these attributions are quite tentative. The texts of Poem 17, which begins, "Nature that washt her hands in milk," are all of seventeenth-century origin, yet an earlier date of composition is suggested by its connection with the *Faerie Queene*. In book 3, canto 8, of Spenser's poem a witch creates a replica of the beautiful heroine Florimell. This "false Florimell" is a creature so marvelous "That euen Nature selfe enuide the same . . . The substance, whereof she the bodie made, / Was purest snow in massie mould congeald, / . . . In stead of eyes two burning lampes she set / In siluer sockets, shyning like the skyes" (stanzas 5–7). From this incident Ralegh took his cue, although in his more benign fiction it is Nature who forms the lady from "snow and silke" at the request of Cupid.

The first three stanzas of Poem 17 are light in tone, their sensuous diction enhanced by the lilting feminine rhyme:

> Her eyes he would should be of light,
> A Violett breath, and Lipps of Jelly,
> Her haire not blacke, nor over bright,
> And of the softest downe her Belly.
>   (lines 7–10)

The charming details of Nature forgetting to dry her hands, and of Love instructing her in the creation of the lady, are blunted at the end of the third stanza because the lady's "heart of stone" proves fatal to Cupid. The appearance of a personified Time in the fourth stanza, however, prepares for a resolution in the manner of the carpe diem seduction poem. Time does not wash nor dry his hands, and he "Turnes snow, and silke, and milke to dust" (line 24). At this point we expect Ralegh to address the mistress herself (as does Marvell in the third stanza of "To His Coy Mistress") to remind her that since Time will conquer even the beauty with which she has conquered Cupid, she must use well what little time she has left. Ralegh defeats this expectation instead by describing in the next stanza how Time "dimms, discoulers, and destroyes" the beauties listed in the opening stanzas. The poem concludes with an apostrophe to Time rather than to the lady, and the pessimism is further heightened by the assertion that Time steals not only "our youth, our Joyes and all we have," but, upon sealing our graves, "Shutts up the story of our dayes" (lines 32, 36). Thus Time consigns to oblivion even the memory of our existence.

In "Nature" Ralegh plays skillfully if morosely upon the conventions of the Renaissance love lyric before diverting his poem into the older memento mori tradition. The effect is as depressing as it is surprising. On the night before his beheading Ralegh is said to have inscribed the final stanza of this poem in his Bible (Poem 24), after adding a final couplet that relieved its pessimism.

Anatomies of Love. The poems tentatively assigned to Ralegh beginning "Conceipt begotten by the eyes" and "Passions are likened best to flouds and streames" (Poems ii and iii), deal with the nature of true and false love. "Conceipt" is subscribed "W. R." in the 1602 and subsequent editions of a printed anthology, the *Poetical Rhapsody*. These initials would point more conclusively to Ralegh were they preceded by S. or Sir, and the poem itself would more closely resemble Ralegh's style if its rhythms were less regular. Its eighteen tetrameter couplets are couched in an exaggerated iambic meter that lacks significant variation or enjambment. Even Ralegh's earliest canonical verses create more tensions within their forms than are found here. "Farewell falce Love" (Poem 4, ca. 1583) is an early and rather unimaginative anatomy of love, but it employs several substitute feet and run-on lines in its five stanzas. Similarly, "Fortune" (Poem 6, 1587) is a love lyric in couplets that boasts more rhythmic variations in its first four lines than "Conceipt" offers in its entirety. By the late 1580s Ralegh's ear was thoroughly attuned to the technical sophistication that made possible the great Elizabethan lyricism. Accordingly, Poem ii can be Ralegh's only if it is early work or a temporary lapse in his technical virtuosity.

Other aspects of this poem are more consistent with the attribution to Ralegh. The image of the seeds sown in the spring which "Die in the ground ere they be growne" (lines 7–8) and the symbolic abstractions such as Affection, Fortune, and Desire are typical of Ralegh's style if by no means uniquely his. Nor does their use generate that complexity of meaning common to Ralegh's later verse. Poem ii simply argues that infatuation, "Conceipt begotten by the eyes," is an unstable and transitory emotion. In his "Instructions" to young Walter, Ralegh made the same point in prose: "for desire dieth when it is attained and the affection perisheth when it is satisfied."[4] It is possible that he here recalled lines from "Conceipt," particularly 19–20 and 29–30:

> Desire himselfe runnes out of breath
> And getting, doth but gaine his death
>
> ....
>
> So fond Desire when it attaines,
> The life expires, the woe remaines.

The echoes between these two passages would bear more weight in the question of authorship were not the idea itself a commonplace, expressed with more vitriolic force, for example, in Shakespeare's Sonnet 129.

The similes in lines 7–12 and 25–30 develop the sense of instability leading up to the rather feeble turn in the last stanza: "some Poets faine would prove, / Affection to be perfit love." As in "Farewell falce Love," the poem assembles a long train of examples to belabor a point that only those few misguided poets of line 31 would contradict. The poem is competent, but if Ralegh's it does not rank among his finer efforts.

Poem iii, "Passions are likened best to flouds and streames," is better work more consistent with Ralegh's manner, yet rendered doubtful by the fact that it is attributed to him only in texts where these six lines are joined to a longer poem written by Sir Robert Ayton.[5] Unlike "Conceipt," Poem iii conveys a simple meaning with appropriate brevity: that deeply grounded feelings are not expressed in many words. Ralegh introduces the idea with a simile modeled upon one of the most popular poems of the age, "The lowest trees have tops," written by his fellow courtier, Sir Edward Dyer. Dyer concluded his verse with the couplet, "True hearts have ears and eyes, no tongues to speak; / They hear and see and sigh, and then they break," a somewhat more dramatic expression of the point in the sixain attributed to Ralegh. Dyer's lyric is made up of two sixain stanzas, the second of which begins, "Where waters smoothest run, deep are the fords." Poem iii seconds this comparison, bringing it to a crisp summation in the couplet, "They that are rich in wordes, in wordes discover, / That they are poore in that which makes a Lover." The meaning is not belabored and the verse is supple, with variations on the iambic meter in lines 1, 3, and 5, enjambment from lines 3 to 4, and feminine rhyme in the couplet.

Early Jacobean Prose

The loss of Durham House and most of his important offices within months of King James's accession must have discouraged Ralegh, but it did not prevent him from attempting to ingratiate himself with his new sovereign. He discussed foreign policy with James during a royal visit to Beddington Park, the home of Lady Ralegh's uncle, Sir Nicholas Carew. Sir Walter offered to invade the Spanish mainland personally on the king's behalf, but it seems unlikely that he presented him at this time with either his "War with Spain" tract or the lost "Discourse How War may be Made Against Spain and the Indies."[6] At his trial in November Ralegh defended himself from the charge that he worked for peace with Spain by referring to a tract he had written against it, which "I had intended to present unto the king." He went on to mention the Jesuits begging alms at church doors for King Philip, who retains "scarce one" of his twenty-five millions from the Indies. The appearance of these same details in "War with Spain"(399) shows that this must have been the treatise he was citing.[7] Thus, at the very time that he was accused of working to surrender his country to Spain, Ralegh was instead devising the strongest arguments he could muster to persuade James to continue the war effort.

    "War with Spain." Structurally, Ralegh's argument in the "War with Spain" parallels the one he used in the *Discovery*. There he had insisted that the anemic Spanish empire would be revitalized to the point of invincibility should it acquire the wealth of Guiana; therefore, England must seize the region for herself. In the "War with Spain" he contends that Spain will become irresistible if it annexes Dutch sea power to its own faltering navy. Ralegh fears that an Anglo-Spanish peace treaty will leave the Netherlands a prey to Catholic Europe. He notes that they are close neighbors to England and a remarkably industrious people whose navy is stronger than either England's or Spain's. Deprived of English support, Ralegh argues, the Dutch must either seek French aid or capitulate to Spain, for their own land forces cannot withstand the Catholic army in the southern Netherlands. With either France or Spain in control of the Dutch fleet, English shipping may easily be disrupted in the Channel and the Baltic; indeed, England could be successfully invaded under cover of invincible sea power.

    Ralegh urges the king to counter these gloomy projections by maintaining the Dutch alliance—their warships had, after all, participated in the Cadiz and "Islands" voyages among other joint ventures with the English during Elizabeth's reign. With their help a united Britain could prosecute the war against Spain more vigorously than ever. Again, Ralegh underscores Spanish vulnerability by stressing not only Philip's bankruptcy but the crumbling disarray of his empire: "in Peru many of the chiefest and best towns are recovered from him by the natives"(309).

    Ralegh's orderly treatise confronts James with numerous dangers to his regime if he appeases Spain, balanced by the manifold advantages of ongoing hostilities. The Netherlands become the strategic and deciding factor in either policy. Ralegh's tone is humble and duly flattering; he assures the king that "your majesty can better judge by a word, than another can by a volume" (302). He vows that his advice "proceedeth from an humble and faithful heart, which your majesty cannot beat from the love of your royal person and good estate"(315–16). Unfortunately, Ralegh's belligerency flew in the face of two complementary strains in his sovereign's character, the desire for peace and dread of violence. Nor did Ralegh take into account the enormous costs of continuing the war, or the Dutch resolve to maintain their political and religious independence with or without foreign assistance. Within the year James had committed his new kingdom to peace with Spain and Ralegh found himself convicted of high treason on the absurd charge of plotting the Spanish conquest of England.

First Years of Imprisonment

Advice to His Son. Professor Latham's discovery of a unique prologue or epilogue to Ralegh's "Instructions to His Son" strongly suggests that he composed this work while awaiting death at Winchester between 17 November and his reprieve on 9 December following.[8] In the manuscript Ralegh assures his son that he is ready "to departe this world," in which "I have had my parte . . . and nowe must give place to fresh gamesters. Farewell" (208). Instead, Ralegh spent the next thirteen years a prisoner in the Tower of London, during which time his eldest son Walter, for whom the "Instructions" were no doubt written, studied at Oxford, traveled on the Continent under the supervision of Ben Jonson (1613), and fled to the Netherlands in 1615 to avoid punishment for dueling. The tract saw very little manuscript circulation, but its publication in 1632 was a great success, calling for seven editions in the next four years.

The practice of handing down advice to one's son was well established by the time Ralegh, in anticipation of his imminent death, penned this treatise for young Wat. As Latham notes, he may have known King James's *Basilicon Doron*, although most of James's advice to the prince and heir apparent was irrelevant to Ralegh's purposes. It is less probable that Ralegh was guided by the advice that his friend, Henry, earl of Northumberland, drew up for his son, since that work was composed in the Tower in 1609 and was thus more likely to have been influenced by Ralegh's discourse than vice versa.[9] Two earlier father-to-son tracts, however, could have influenced Ralegh's work; these are Lord Burghley's "Precepts," written for Robert Cecil during the 1580s, and Sir Henry Sidney's advice to Philip, written in 1566 and published in 1591. Burghley's tract was not printed until 1617, but it circulated widely in manuscript. Ralegh may have acquired a copy through his close association with Cecil, its recipient. Furthermore, he admitted at his trial that when Cecil gave him access to Burghley's study after his death in 1598, he came away with several manuscripts, the "Precepts," perhaps, among them.[10]

Ralegh and Sir Henry Sidney addressed sons who were not yet in their teens, yet their exhortations overlap on only a few rather obvious points: love God, avoid loose speech, and refrain from drunkenness. By contrast, Lord Burghley's "Precepts," composed when Robert was at least twenty,[11] coincide with Ralegh's "Instructions" on a number of issues both general and specific. Both tracts are divided into ten parts, with the "Precepts" far less well developed than the topics covered in Ralegh's ten "chapters." Both deal with the selection of a wife and servants, the dangers of loose jesting, and of pledging oneself in surety for another. Where Burghley warns that jesting that conveys the truth will offend those who become its objects, Ralegh notes that "as there is nothing more shameful and dishonest than to do wrong, so truth itself cutteth his throat that carrieth her publicly in every place" (25). Burghley urges Robert to abstain from lawsuits, but to pursue them vigorously once entered as a warning to others, whereas Ralegh applies this same strategy to "public disputations" that lead to quarreling: "If thou be once engaged, carry thyself bravely that they may fear thee after" (24). Latham observes that a number of Ralegh's recommendations to his son Wat contradict his own experience.[12] The influence of the "Precepts" may explain some of these discrepancies, especially those concerned with choosing a well-to-do wife and not trusting "any friend . . . with any matter that may endanger thine estate" (19), principles that Ralegh had, to this stage of his career, violated with impunity.

Ralegh lends authority to his advice through frequent quotations, most of them from the Bible but drawing as well on Pliny, Hesiod, and Euripides among others. He was no doubt working rapidly and drawing on a commonplace book for the illustrative citations. He avoids a dry, pedantic tone, however, by his personal and direct address to his son: "and believe thy father in this and print it in thy thought"; "I myself have lost thereby more than I am worth" (28–29). He enlivens his style with simple comparisons such as the unacknowledged borrowing from Greene's *Mourning Garment*, the simile that "as a wolf resembles a dog, so doth a flatterer a friend," and that drunkenness "destroyeth the body as ivy doth the old tree or as the worm that engendereth in the kernel of the nut"(24,30).

Ralegh develops his points logically enough within each section of the treatise, yet the overall principle of organization is problematic. He begins with advice on the choice of friends, then moves to the choice of a wife in chapter 2; to avoiding flatterers in chapter 3; to speech and deportment in public, the management of his estate, and of his servants in chapter 6. The sequence does not necessarily follow the chronological occurrence of these decisions in life, the order of their increasing or decreasing importance, or their order in the "Precepts." To this extent the "Instructions" differ from Ralegh's normal practice of establishing clear patterns of organization in his prose writings.

Ralegh was certainly capable of showmanship when the circumstances required it: witness his bravado in the capture of Fayal, the overwrought emotionalism of his "Cynthia" poems, and his abortive attempt at suicide with a table knife shortly after his arrest in 1603.[13] But for all the theatricality of his own career, he does not recommend acting or deceptive display to his son. In contrast, Burghley urged Robert to cultivate the friendship of a great man by giving him many small gifts, and to behave with humble familiarity before social inferiors since that is an easy way to make a favorable impression on common folk. But Ralegh, who was accused of being a "Machiavellian" schemer, makes no mention of such politic artifice; he urges Wat instead to protect himself from the deceptive behavior of dishonest servants, false friends, and flatterers, while guiding his own life with reason in the pursuit of the truth.

"Three thinges there be," Poem iv.   "Three thinges there be," if Ralegh's, complements his "Instructions" by replacing its concrete advice with a very general warning that turns out to be, in effect, no warning at all. The first of this lyric's three crossrhyme quatrains poses the riddle, what three things mar each other when they meet? The puzzle is solved in the second quatrain in the general terms of line 5, followed by clarification in the next three lines: the wooden gallows, its rope, and the poem's addressee ("my pretty knave") mar one another when they meet together at a hanging. The final stanza then restates the first one in light of this answer.

Even on its most literal level Poem iv does not really threaten the child with hanging, as Latham suggests,[14] for its implicit warning is undercut first by the riddling format, the "deere boy" of line 9, and the failure to address any of the circumstances that might cause "the wood, the weed, the wagge" to "assemble" for their fatal meeting. The "Instructions" provide concrete advice for evading such difficulties; these verses entertain more than they warn by presenting a grim theme in a whimsical but personal manner. It is difficult to imagine that any son, least of all the irrepressible Wat Ralegh, would tremble with anxiety at the affectionate teasing conveyed in these stanzas.

"What is our life," Poem 18.   A far more serious lyric, and one to which Ralegh has a strong claim, is the eight couplets of "What is our life," which Rudick assigns to the early years of Ralegh's imprisonment.[15] The poem became one of the most popular of the seventeenth century, with two prints and at least forty manuscript copies by mid-century. Its appeal derives from its concise development of the already hackneyed conceit that the "world's a stage," a recurrent motif in Ralegh's verse and prose. He described

Sir Philip Sidney's passing from "this worldly stage"(Poem 7.36), and he often refers to life as a tragedy and to this "stage-play world" in the "Cynthia" poems and *The History of the World*.[16] Ralegh's outlook in Poem 18 is grim but entirely orthodox, a far cry from even his contemporary reputation in some quarters as an atheist and the patron of Thomas Harriot and other intellectuals who espoused subversive ideas. "Our mirth" occupies only the brief interludes in the serious business of our roles in "time's short tragedy" (line 4). Heaven looks on, beholding those who "act amiss," a focus not balanced by any reference to salvation or eternal reward. Moreover, "The graves that hide us from the parching sun / Are but drawn curtains till the play be done"; this final couplet expands the frame of reference to provide an unsettling but undefined conclusion. As Rudick notes, we are forced to consider that our lives transcend the conceit. Life extends beyond the "play of passion" on this earth, for the grave is only another interlude before the finale of the Last Judgment.[17] The sudden extension of the metaphor into the afterlife is accomplished in the last five words of the poem, thus lifting it above the commonplace comparison even though the extension is dictated by Christian belief in God's judgment. The sombre tone and apprehensive conclusion are likewise of a piece with the brooding pessimism that stressed divine justice rather than mercy and salvation throughout *The History of the World*.

Ralegh and Prince Henry

The prince was scarcely nine, a few months younger than Wat Ralegh, when he came to England as heir apparent to James's newly acquired throne. By his early teens Henry was clearly on the way to becoming a reverse mirror image of his father in temperament as well as political and philosophical makeup. He sympathized with the more zealous Prostestants in contrast with James's toleration of Catholicism. He countered his father's pacifism with a keen interest in military affairs both in respect to his personal skill at arms and in matters of national policy. And despite the king's lethargy in pursuit of empire, his son expressed interest in Ralegh's Guiana project and became a shareholder in the Virginia company. He attracted to himself a large following among those who longed for an assertive foreign policy and the imperial expansion of English Protestantism.

The extent to which Ralegh helped shape any of these tendencies in the prince is unclear—neither is it clear just when Ralegh began to influence him at all. Ralegh's biographers assume that Queen Anne introduced her son to Sir Walter early in his term of imprisonment, although no evidence of such direct contact with the royal family has surfaced. Sir Arthur Gorges may have

facilitated some sort of contact between Henry and Sir Walter, for he dedicated his account of the "Islands" voyage to the prince in 1607 and gained an
appointment in his household in 1610. The earliest documented connection
between the two seems to be the revised "Observations . . . on the Royal
Navy," which, with the letter to Henry on naval affairs that apparently preceded it, probably dates from the latter part of 1608. By the winter of
1608–9 Ralegh had begun work on *The History of the World*, at Henry's bid-
ding.[18] The foundation for so vast an undertaking presumably did not rest
upon a brief or superficial acquaintance. Thus Ralegh and the prince had no
doubt found some efficient means of communication by 1608, the year in
which Henry turned fourteen. Thereafter, Ralegh claimed that Henry had
read portions of his *History of the World*, while most of the prose works written by or attributed to Ralegh from 1608 through 1612 are connected with
the prince: the fragmentary tracts on the "Art of Warre by Sea" and the "Seat
of Government," the two marriage tracts (which are addressed to Henry but
not certainly Ralegh's), and the "Jesuit" dialogue.

   The Naval Tracts.

"Observations"

The "Observations," originally composed for Queen Elizabeth, drew immediately on Ralegh's experience in the expedition of 1597. He incorpo-
rated as well what he had learned at Cadiz, in setting forth his own voyages of
exploration, and from equipping royal fleets in 1591 and 1592. He deals
first with the problems of ill-qualified naval officers, poorly designed ships,
and the disadvantages of stationing the royal fleet at Rochester, thereby leaving the entire south and west coasts vulnerable to surprise attacks. He then
treats a host of lesser, more specific problems: English warships tend to be so
overladen with cannon as to be unseaworthy, their caulking materials quickly
deteriorate, and in contrast with merchantmen, the food and drink aboard
warships is so poor that sailors dread royal service. Ralegh also questions the
integrity of the officers who press mariners into service, the location of galleys
far below deck, and the lack of armor and weapons that could be easily supplied on every ship with the income that would be generated by selling off the
surplus ordnance (348).

   Ralegh offered solutions to each of the problems he raised, but by the time
he revised the treatise for Henry, the state of the English navy had in fact
worsened. James's deteriorating fleet became the subject of a royal investigation, which nevertheless produced no substantive reforms. Ralegh thought it
necessary to expand the section on ill-qualified officers, and in deference to
the peace with Spain he spoke of England's enemies in general rather than of

Spain alone as in his original. His reference to the West Country being "so often dismayed with alarms as they have of late years been" (342) seems, however, to harken back to the fears of Spanish invasion during the late 1590s. The revised conclusion defends the necessity of maintaining a powerful navy, for the current peace, Ralegh argues, has "proceeded out of the former trial of our forces in times of war and enmity" (349). Were England's strength to decline further, "those proud mastering spirits, finding us at such advantage, would be more ready and willing to shake us by the ears as enemies, than to take us by the hands as friends."[19]

"Of the Art of Warre by Sea"

In *The History of the World* Ralegh claimed to have undertaken a treatise "Of the Art of Warre by Sea" for Prince Henry: "but God hath spared me the labour of finishing it by his loss" (5:1; *Works*, 6:83). The surviving fragments consist of notes and outlines for the tract, although it is possible that the "Discourse of the Invention of Ships" was a part of it that Ralegh expanded toward the end of his life and detached from the original treatise. Otherwise, all that remains of the "Art of Warre" are three sets of notes. Two of these in Ralegh's handwriting in the Cotton manuscript provide similar outlines of the tract, the second of which is divided into chapters. The third set of notes, in Jones MS B60, is made up of narrative excerpts that can be assigned to their corresponding locations in the outlines. This manuscript, however, seems to present a different pattern of organization for the treatise in that a paragraph labeled as its first chapter deals with the subject of ports, a topic that appears toward the middle of the first outline in the Cotton manuscript. The comparison in this same passage between war on land and on sea (600) suggests that Ralegh envisioned his treatise as something of a naval counterpart to Machiavelli's *Art of War*, a work he cited on three other occasions.[20]

Ralegh apparently envisioned a work in fifteen chapters beginning with a history of naval combat. The sections that follow on the "building & vitling of shipps," their "burden . . . fittest for the warr," and ordnance suitable for warships (599) were probably to have been supplied by or adapted from the "Observations." The rest of the discourse would have consisted primarily of advice on how the English fleet might best be employed to counter the naval power of Spain, Portugal, Turkey, and the Netherlands. Ralegh intended once more to inform the prince as well as to encourage him in the aggressive use of English seapower: "ther is nothing *that* so much discouers the judgment of a Prince as his enterprises" (598). These fragments are also of interest for what they reveal about Ralegh's comprehensive maritime strategy, for the finished tract was to incorporate many of his favorite themes, some of which found thorough development elsewhere. These include his concern over the silting in of English ports, the exportation of cannon manufactured in England (mentioned in the "Marriage" tract and more fully treated in the "Jesuit" dialogue), the ease with which Spain's colonies might be wrested from her, and the importance of "forcible trades" (598), that is, trading in areas where hostile competitors or states forced merchantmen to arm themselves. Ralegh also planned to explain this latter point in his unfinished "Seat of Government" treatise (540). Another idea developed in the "Jesuit" and "Invention" tracts and, here attributed to Themistocles, affirms "That hee that commaunds the sea, commaunds the trade, and hee that is lord of the Trade of the world is lord of the wealth of the worlde."[21] The truth of this maxim would be demonstrated in the course of the next few centuries by the growth of the British Empire.

"On the Seat of Government."   Lefranc dates the composition of this fragment to 1604–16, although the two references to Exodus and Deuteronomy in just two and one-half pages of text suggest that Ralegh composed it about the time he was dealing with the same Old Testament material for book 2 of *The History of the World*, about 1609–10. These few leaves are not addressed to Prince Henry, yet they seem to form an appropriate royal counterpart to the "Instructions" Ralegh penned for his own son. "The Seat of Government" tells how to hold and exercise royal power through a due regard for civil justice and martial discipline. It opens with a comparison of earthly kings to the cedars of Lebanon, the former rooting their power "in the hardy hearts of their faithful subjects" (538). As in the "Instructions," Ralegh invests this treatise with clarifying comparisons, such as "the unjust magistrate that fancieth to himself a solid and untransparable [opaque] body of gold," and a continuation of the tree imagery in his description of the laboring class as "the fruit trees of the land" (539). He had advised Wat to "let reason be thy schoolmistress" (20), and the "Seat of Government" places a similar emphasis on reason as the faculty that teaches kings to win the hearts of their people, and to recognize that reason and love are the bonds that maintain royal authority over the governed.[22]

After dividing his treatise into two parts, civil justice and martial discipline, Ralegh begins to explain how justice should be administered with respect to three classes of citizens, laborers, merchants, and the gentry—and here the discourse ends. Had Ralegh completed it, he might well have qualified or contradicted the advice directed to Henry in the king's *Basilicon Doron*, at least with regard to the administration of civil justice. Apparently,

Henry's death caused Ralegh to abandon this project as well as the "Art of Warre by Sea."

The Marriage Tracts. Although the "Discourse Touching a Match . . . Between the Lady Elizabeth and the Prince of Piedmont" may have been composed a year or more before the "Discourse Touching a Marriage between Prince Henry . . . and a Daughter of Savoy," both works deal with the same extended series of marriage negotiations.[23] Those involving Henry's sister, the Princess Elizabeth, ended as far as Savoy was concerned with the signing of her marriage articles with Frederick, Prince Palatine of the Rhine, in May 1612. Henry, however, was still considering an alliance with Savoy at the time of his death in November. These tracts were credited to Ralegh and printed for the first time in 1750. In support of this late attribution only one copy of the "Marriage" discourse is assigned to Ralegh among the numerous earlier manuscript copies of both tracts. His authorship of either work is accordingly open to doubt.

The "Match" purports to be written for an unnamed recipient addressed as "sir," at "the commandment of my lorde the prince"(223, 228). In orderly fashion it presents the three motives for political marriages of the sort proposed by the duke of Savoy: the uniting or enlarging of kingdoms, ending wars, and joining forces against another power. Most of the essay demonstrates that none of these reasons applies to the relationship between England and Savoy. The author suggests instead that this proposal smacks of a Spanish plot, for Spain dominates the utterly dependent Savoyans. After citing the personal disadvantages of such a match to Elizabeth herself, including the possibility of harm from Jesuits or other popish plots against her, the treatise concludes with the suggestion that she consider a marriage with the Prince Palatine.

Fully half of the "Match" is devoted to a rather medieval listing of historical examples in support of two points. First comes a summary of Henry VIII's campaigns in France to show that even with support far surpassing anything that Savoy could muster, English forces were unable to secure a lasting foothold in France. Second, a long list of duplicitous Spanish marriages and offers of marriage is enumerated to suggest that Philip will use this marriage to gain political leverage in England. As we have seen in the *Discovery*, Ralegh characteristically uses multiple examples in his argumentative prose to establish his authority on the subject and to add weight and conviction to his points. Here, however, the arguments are inefficiently belabored; no need to summarize Henry's campaigns one by one to establish by analogy that Savoy would make a feeble ally in any renewed English attempt on France.

With regard to examples of Spanish duplicity in marital negotiations, the author promises to "remember unto you some few, and leave the rest to your own reading" (228), yet the subsequent listing consumes five of the tract's fourteen pages. If this is Ralegh's work, he drew many of these examples from his previous research. Several of those pertaining to King Ferdinand had appeared in the "War with Spain" where he also claimed to have fully described "the like practice" of Charles V in his lost "Discourse How War may be made against Spain and the Indies" (308). Perhaps Ralegh was overly eager to put all he had found on this subject to good use. Still, its bulk overwhelms the "Match," and to little avail at that for want of a specific application to the Savoyan-English proposals. We are told that the Catholics might be tempted to harm Prince Henry and Prince Charles in order to claim the throne through Elizabeth, but so awkward a scenario must have appeared too unlikely to pursue. If Ralegh is responsible for the "Match," it is his clumsiest display of persuasive technique.

Other aspects of the discourse are more characteristic of Ralegh's manner. An account of the Emperor Charles V's evasions of his marital obligations concludes, "By this you may see to what great advantage these princes used the sacrament of marriage" (231), and there is another flash of Raleghean sarcasm in the observation that the duke of Savoy "hath no port, (his ditch of Villa Franca excepted)" (236). The tract's overall condemnation of Catholicism takes on a particular ad hominem edge in descriptions of the prospective bridegroom as a "poor popish prince" and a "prince jesuited" (234, 236). Finally, the "Match" shares a substantial portion of its text with the "Marriage" tract, along with several minor points that were among Ralegh's favorite themes. These overlapping elements, however, do not necessarily connect him with either work, nor do they absolutely confirm a common authorship.

The "Marriage" discourse amplifies most of the arguments so laboriously set forth in the "Match," but the result is a far more skillfully fashioned essay. Its eight-point outline methodically investigates the advantages to Savoy of the proposed match with Prince Henry. Treachery in international marriage alliances is illustrated in five concise examples, the first of which, Spain's luring of Henry VIII into the Biscayan campaign, was cited in the "War with Spain" (308) as well as in the "Match." A similar list of bogus alliances in *The History of the World* (4:6; *Works*, 5:511), includes the "Austrians," the Emperor Charles V, Francis I, and the dukes of Milan. The entire passage that establishes Savoy's dependence on Spain borrows almost word for word from the catalog of the duke's offspring in the "Match" (225, 241–42), and this point is expanded to show that Savoy could not take up arms against France, the Pope, or the Holy Roman Empire on England's behalf. The proposed marriage would thus saddle England with an impotent ally, or worse, provide

an entrée for Catholic intrigues aimed at the conquest of Britain. The tract develops what is only a vague threat in the "Match" by noting that the Spanish Infanta, whose claim to the English throne was championed in Robert Parsons's massive *Conference about the next Succession to the Crowne of Ingland*, now resides in the Netherlands in command of the best army in Europe, an army that "may be passed over into England in one night."[24]

The "Marriage" tract concludes, as does the "Match," by considering the personal disadvantages of the proposal and then offering an alternative plan. Henry is advised in this strong finale to refrain from marriage until he has "somewhat repaired his estate" (250), that is, freed himself from the crushing debt that James continued to settle upon the Crown. The prince is then urged to marry one of the daughters of Henry IV of France. Would Ralegh have proposed such a Catholic alliance? The main advantage according to the treatise would transcend the resulting Anglo-French alliance, for "By holding France, we hold the Low Countries, which will make us invincible; for they dare not abandon us both" (252). Dutch control of the balance of power in Europe was a cornerstone of Ralegh's European political philosophy, a thesis he argued in the "War with Spain" and in the "Jesuit" dialogue. He sought French aid in his final assault on Guiana, and he tried to escape to France when the collapse of that venture threatened his life in 1618. For Ralegh, a Catholic marriage was perhaps not too high a price to pay for an Anglo-French-Dutch alliance that would ensure England's safety from Catholic aggression. On the other hand, should those forces attack in the wake of a Savoyan match, he asks, "from whom may we hope for help? . . . our friends inhabit beyond the mountains; our enemies hard at hand. We leave those that are strongest and nearest us," the French, "for those that are weakest and furthest off" ("Marriage," 252).

This lively conclusion has the ring of Ralegh's most spirited prose, while several other passages in the discourse argue strongly for his composition of it. The author recalls, for example, the days "in my time" when "one of her majesty's ships" could defeat forty of the Dutch, but now they are armed with English ordnance and can "take us one to one, and not give us a good-morrow" (248). A similar reminiscence occurs in the "War with Spain" (304–5), and Ralegh stresses the point again in the "Jesuit" dialogue (sig. E6v). The insistence that England might readily seize the West Indies is another of his pet projects that also crops up in the "Marriage" tract. Finally, the author observes that if the duke should offer Geneva to England, James "might well answer him, as Alexander did Darius, that the gift of those things that are not in our possession is not thankworthy" (243). Ralegh cites this same remark in book 4 of his *History of the World*, which, according to Lefranc, he had completed by early September 1612.[25]

In style, content, and manner of exposition this work bears all the marks of Ralegh's authorship. The degree to which its structure and themes overlap with the "Match" suggests that he wrote that discourse also, yet the case remains circumstantial. Both works grew out of the entourage associated with Henry that included many of Ralegh's friends and sympathizers, among them Gorges, to whom one manuscript of the "Marriage" tract was originally attributed.[26] Gorges and others in this coterie no doubt enjoyed ready access to Ralegh's output; his "War with Spain" survives in sixteen manuscripts, the "Marriage" treatise in more than two dozen copies, and the "Match" in eleven. He could have lifted ideas and whole passages from this latter work in composing the "Marriage" tract, or similar borrowings within Henry's circle could explain the echoes of Ralegh's authentic works in both the marriage tracts.

As the last years of Elizabeth's reign marked the lowest ebb in Ralegh's output as a writer, the middle years of his imprisonment, from about 1608–12, are his most prolific. His foremost task during this period was the five massive books of *The History of the World*, but in addition he composed at least four and perhaps a half-dozen shorter pieces for the prince and his circle. To some extent then, all of his prose beginning with the "Instructions" was immediately addressed to adolescent readers. There is nothing juvenile or condescending, however, in these works. His advice to his son Wat was meant to guide his adult understanding just as his advice to Henry—on improving the navy, governing his subjects, and parrying the Catholic threat to England—all was aimed at fashioning Britain's next king to Ralegh's aggressive, Protestant specifications. The energies he had formerly invested in courtiership and voyages were now channeled primarily into writing. The works of this period comprise, moreover, the formulations of his mature thinking, for he was now in his fifties and able to draw on a lifetime of diverse experiences, wide reading, and careful reflection. If the tone of these works is often sober to the point of pessimism, they were composed nevertheless by a man who believed that he still had much to contribute to the future welfare of his country.

Chapter Five
Confronting the King

Between 1611 and 1615 Ralegh finished the five books of his *History of the World*, plus the "Jesuit" and *Prerogative of Parliaments* dialogues. In these three works, far more than in his earlier writings for Prince Henry, Ralegh vents his increasing frustration with the Jacobean regime. The criticism is so blatantly set forth in the "Jesuit" dialogue as to preclude any significant circulation of that work even in manuscript. In 1614 James forbade the sale of the newly printed *History of the World* because of its unacceptable treatment of kings, and, in fact, Ralegh's attacks on the king in this massive work are more frequent and diversified than James and his councillors may have realized. The *Prerogative* purports to be dutifully committed to the best interests of the king, to whom it is dedicated. It is, nevertheless, a carefully researched attack on James's failure to adapt his philosophy of governance to the English tradition of cooperation between Crown and Parliament. This tract saw wide manuscript circulation and was surreptitiously printed within a few years of the king's death.

"A Dialogue between a Jesuit and Recusant"

Ralegh composed this tract during the first half of 1611,[1] probably for the eyes of Henry and a narrow readership within his circle. Certainly the one reference to Henry in the dialogue was meant to flatter him: "England hath a young Prince, that thinks his life an imprisonment till he exercise his Courage in some notable enterprize" (sig. E2v). The dialogue did not reach print until 1700, and survives in only one manuscript, in comparison with eleven manuscripts for the "Match" and more than twenty for the "Marriage" tract. The dialogue, a compendium of Ralegh's favorite precepts, achieves multiple purposes. It condemns the malice, hypocrisy, and political ambition of Catholic Europe, as epitomized in its Jesuit leadership. The publication in 1610 of the *Apologia pro Henrico Garneto* gave Ralegh further motive for attacking this religious order. Its Jesuit author, writing under the pseudonym Andreas Eudaemon-Joannis, twice called him a Puritan, a fact that Ralegh angrily denounced in *The History of the World* (5:5; *Works*, 7:659). The Jesuits, Ralegh contends, promote an international conspiracy to conquer all of Protestant Europe. James's pacifism and his toleration of Catholicism render him little more than a dupe of this conspiracy. The treatise ends with an astonishing rehearsal of the king's failures, especially his alienation from his subjects amid the growing poverty of the central government. Many of these ideas and even their argumentative structures appear in Ralegh's works before and after 1611, but the dialogue form marks a new departure in his polemical writings. Here he explores the satiric potentialities of speaking through fictitious personae.

Of Ralegh's responsibility for the work there can be little doubt. The correspondences with his other writings are detailed and widely scattered within the canon. The reference to the breaking of the Spanish banks at Seville (sig. E4v), for instance, also crops up in "War with Spain" (303) and was mentioned by Ralegh at his trial. The claim that the older Spanish settlers in the West Indies hate newcomers as the Irish hate the English (sig. E5) is echoed by the charge in the "Marriage" tract that the king of Spain is more hated by the natives "than the English are by the Irish" (246). The Recusant's adage that whoever commands the seas commands trade, and through it wealth and the world (sig. E6v) is repeated in the "Warre by Sea" fragment (600) and the "Invention of Ships" tract (330). The example of Stevena Borough shelling and sailing successfully past Elsinore Castle (sig. E5v) is cited in book 5 of The History of the World (Works 6:108–9, with Stevena corrected to William). Both works note as well that papists murdered Henry IV of France after he had converted to Catholicism (History, Book 2:19; Works, 4:559–60; "Jesuit," sig. C6v).[2]

This dialogue is entirely in Ralegh's vein with regard to the development of its arguments as well as in purpose and content. His concern with research and supporting evidence emerges as the Jesuit describes the creation of a Catholic empire in the Baltic by surveying the histories of Prussia, Poland, and Lithuania from the thirteenth century to the present. Similarly, he delves into Islamic history to show how internal feuding allowed King Ferdinand to drive the Saracens from Spain. This background material, limited to a few pages of the larger discourse, is typical of Ralegh's argumentative methods. It may substantiate as well his claim that he had already "hewn out" some of the later books of his History (Book 5:6; Works, 7:901).

Fictional dialogues of the type that Ralegh attempted here for the first time had become a well-established medium of Renaissance propaganda under the Tudors. He probably knew the "Euphues and Atheos" dialogue appended to John Lyly's popular prose narrative Euphues (1579), and he certainly knew the three-way conversation of "Leicester's Commonwealth," a

Catholic attack on England's Protestant government as well as upon the earl of Leicester.[3] The "Jesuit" dialogue may also owe something to such explicitly religious works in the same vein as *A Dialogue betweene a Vertuous Gentleman and a Popish Priest* (1581), George Gifford's *Dialogue betweene a Papist and a Protestant* (1582), and *A Conference Betwixt a Mother, A Devout Recusant, and her Sonne, a Zealous Protestant* (1600). Moreover, within a year of composing the "Jesuit" tract Ralegh was studying the king's *Daemonologie*, a dialogue about witches and witchcraft that Ralegh cites in the preface and in book 1 of the *History*. He thus had a number of models for his dialogue, yet he achieves in it an ironic tone and dramatic tension seldom found in these representative examples of the genre.

This tension was all the more difficult to manage because of Ralegh's choice of speakers, a Jesuit and his "host," an English recusant. Lyly exploited the inherent tensions between an atheist and his sombre Christian speaker, Euphues, just as the Protestant–Catholic dialogues held obvious potential for conflict. Ralegh nevertheless generated conflict within the opening paragraphs of his work.

The dialogue begins with the Englishman welcoming his spiritual advisor back to England and acknowledging receipt of his "last learned Letter" dispatched from Rome (sig. C4). The Jesuit then bewilders his host by presenting him with a papal pardon for his sins. The Recusant wonders how he can receive a general pardon that requires no penance merely because he relieves "saints," that is Jesuits, who are sanctified before they suffer or die. Ralegh enlivens his dialogue through his characterization of the Recusant, who raises doubts and questions that the Jesuit finds increasingly bothersome. When the Recusant contends that the Jesuits aim not only at free public worship but absolute Catholic dominion over England, the Jesuit tells him to air all his doubts by speaking as if he were a heretic. The mechanism for heightening confrontation is to some degree artificial, but not wholly improbable given the Jesuit's arrogant, authoritative manner. His host undertakes the role of heretic with such enthusiasm, moreover, as to blur the distinction between the pose and his actual beliefs. As the dialogue unfolds, we increasingly sense an ironic dimension in much of what the Recusant has to say.

The first part of the dialogue after this introduction consists of the charges leveled by the Recusant-as-heretic. Through this persona, Ralegh counters Catholic appeals for the right to worship openly by reciting the acts of political terrorism he blames on the Jesuits. They are charged with assassinating the last two kings of France and William of Orange, and of plotting the murder of Queen Elizabeth. The Recusant turns next to the Jesuit's prediction that Catholic nations will force England to grant further concessions to its recusant minority. One by one Ralegh lists his favorite themes concerning the great international rivalry: Spain's weakness and inability to launch an invasion, her failure to harm England, and the English victories over Spain in 1588, at Lisbon, and at Cadiz. The Recusant notes that a thousand English soldiers could seize a few strategic bases in the West Indies and deprive Spain of her New World treasure. Some of these ideas crop up in Ralegh's prose as early as the *Revenge* pamphlet, and all of them recur in his later writings. New to the "Jesuit" dialogue, however, is the contention that English Catholics are treated tolerably well and will not rise up against their king (sig. E1v).

Ralegh not only vents his contempt for the Jesuits more forcibly here than in his other writings; he also combines ironic attacks with dramatic self-revelations that give the dialogue its best satiric moments. In his pose as heretic the Recusant makes a devastating comparison of Jesuits to the Apostles: "They humbled themselves, ye exalt your selves," they preached the Gospel, you lock up the Bible, "they raised the dead, ye kill the living" (sig. C5v). The Jesuit characterizes himself as an unscrupulous subversive agent when he abruptly refuses to tell the Recusant whether or not the mission to England involves anything more than saving souls. He insists furthermore that Catholics need not obey all the rules of Scripture, whereas they must obey the commands of his order (sig. D1v). Speaking in his own character, the Recusant does not openly defy his coreligionist with regard to these issues. Ralegh leaves ambiguous the degree to which the Recusant has become disillusioned with the Jesuit, although he hints at a considerable breach in one passage. When the Recusant asks whether or not the Jesuit could disobey a direct order from his superior to kill the king, he is told that "It is a sawcy question, mine Host, and I am not bound to resolve you therein." To this the Recusant responds, "I desire it not, holy Father, for I am resolved already" (sig. D6).

The Jesuit dominates the second part of the dialogue as he explains that the peace treaty between Spain and England (1604) and the truce between Spain and the Netherlands (1609) "hath a deep and dark bottom" (sig. E4v). He conjures up the new threat to Protestant Europe that will result from Polish-Lithuanian expansion into Russia under King Sigismund III. Ralegh develops here a timely if somewhat paranoid analysis of international events, for Polish forces had in fact occupied Moscow in 1610 and were not effectively repelled until 1612. Sigismund was furthermore a devout Catholic who planned to conquer Sweden and create a Polish empire in northern Europe. The Jesuit argues that this empire could one day cut off vital naval supplies from the Baltic, then overcome Sweden, Denmark, the Netherlands, and England through sheer force of numbers.

The dialogue concludes with a blunt, critical discussion of James's inept rule that marks Ralegh's most skillful use of his characters for satiric purposes. The Jesuit charges that James could not resist an all-out Catholic invasion because he "wants all that should make a king fearful to his enemies"; above all, he is poor and unloved by his subjects (sig. F2). Ralegh contrives his dialogue so that his principal satiric victim, the Jesuit, attacks his secondary victim, the king. The Recusant is left to manage a lame defense of the king that actually extends the satiric criticism. He makes no attempt to deny the Jesuit's charges, alleging only that James can easily regain his subjects' love. And what if he has given away more to his Scottish favorites in eight years than Queen Elizabeth gave in forty? The Crown rather than the commonwealth is the poorer for it (sigs. F2–2v). As for the unpopular "impositions" (the customs on imports that the king could not get Parliament to countenance in 1610), the Recusant yields the point: these unpopular taxes violate English law and tradition, but then many laws are routinely broken. On the subject of imported luxuries the Recusant makes his only telling point in this part of the dialogue by claiming that formerly "the Noblemen and Gentlemen lived in their Counties and kept Hospitality, they fed the poor, and were beloved and followed; but now forsooth my Lady must live in *London*, and consume more in covering of her tail than would serve to feed a hundred honest men" (sigs. F2v–3). It is an outburst worthy of Jonathan Swift, yet in context it does nothing to counter the Jesuit's charge that James has levied unpopular and illegal taxes.

Beyond this daring attack on the king and his policies, the dialogue includes other ad hominem attacks that would scarcely have been tolerated had the work come to official notice. When the Recusant asks where a Catholic fleet in the Baltic would find sufficient armament, the Jesuit replies that England has armed all of Europe. Indeed, the late Lord Treasurer "Buckhurst would have armed Hell itself for Money."[4] Both the Lord Treasurer and his son, the second Lord Buckhurst, had profited from the export of ordnance. Although father and son were dead by 1610, this personal assault on peers of the realm amounted to libel, as Ralegh no doubt understood. In the same context he attacked a living trader in ordnance, "that honest Milliners Son of Abchurch Lane, called Ferne." When the Recusant protests that Ferne is now a knight, the Jesuit quips that he deserves the promotion for his good service to the king of Spain. These slanders, along with the unflattering treatment of the king, make the "Jesuit" dialogue an effective and daring satire.[5]

The dialogue ends with a final reminder of the latent irony in the Recusant's dealings with the Jesuit, for he bids him farewell with the promise to "tell you more plainly my mind at our next meeting" (sig. F3v). Ralegh has deployed his arguments in a telling fictional context, and with a more balanced give and take between his speakers than occurs in the contemporary dialogues he might have used for models. The gentleman of the 1581 *Dialogue*, for example, dominates his "popish" parson, who readily submits to the case against him. Atheos and the Recusant Mother of the 1600 *Conference* are also easily converted. Only Gifford's papist is defiant to the end, yet his objections are lost amid the Protestant's long-winded orations. Nor does James succeed much better at bringing lively discussion into his *Daemonologie*. There, Philomathes expresses some doubt about the existence of witches, but he readily assents to everything claimed for them in Epistemon's lengthy explanations. In contrast, Ralegh allows both his speakers to participate on nearly equal terms; their often double-edged exchanges drive home his multiple satiric points in lively fashion.

The History of the World

Ralegh's *History of the World* was registered for publication on 15 April 1611. The million-odd words of his magnum opus took more than three years to print, during which time he continued work on the final books and the preface. The *History* was published, anonymously, late in 1614, and was almost immediately suppressed by the government.[6] Ralegh's title is in several respects a misnomer, for the *History* reaches only into the second century B.C. and deals almost exclusively with Mediterranean civilizations. Ralegh could hardly be expected to treat Far Eastern history, but it is strange that he does not even acknowledge the problem of New World history, especially in book 1 where he deals with the "plantation" of the earth after Noah's flood. Ralegh does refer to the New World in anecdotal or illustrative fashion, but his main subject is Hebraic and classical history. He draws primarily on well-established sources, the Bible preeminent among them, to produce not a history of the world in the broadest sense but primarily a history of the memorable acts of important people. With few exceptions it is a story of the exercise of political and military power. Cultural history—the arts, technology, law, and the rest—is relegated to digressions. These are often lengthy, yet they lack the development and continuity that would make the *History* truly comprehensive. As F. Smith Fussner observes, Ralegh was not trying to develop a new and original history—not in this first volume, at least.[7] How he might have handled the late Tudor period, to which he was a participating eyewitness, is quite another matter. He declined that undertaking, however, with the warning that he who follows truth too closely at the heels takes the risk that "it may strike out his teeth" (preface, *Works*, 2.1xiii). Instead, he combined and reevaluated what was known (or believed) concerning the origins of the world and its major events to the eve of the Christian era.

Ralegh disposed his *History* into five books, with a preface, and extensive chronological tables at the end. Books 1 and 2 focus on Old Testament history from creation to the Babylonian captivity. Books 3 and 4 treat the Persian Empire, the Peloponnesian War, the conquests of Alexander the Great, and the division of his empire by his captains after his death. Book 5 is centered on Roman history, with a detailed account of Hannibal's role in the second Punic War, Rome's triumph over Carthage, and the absorption of Macedonia into the empire.

In many respects the first two books of Old Testament history are alike in texture and emphasis, while the last three, treating Greco-Roman or "classical" history, form a different kind of unity.[8] The first two books deal at length with thematic issues, particularly with respect to chronology and geography. Ralegh deduces from conflicting authorities the exact year of the creation, the date of Noah's flood, and of Abraham's birth. He spends an entire chapter determining the location of the Garden of Eden. He insists that the Queen of Saba or Sheba was an Arab, after demonstrating the geographical impossibility of her residence in Ethiopia. He includes condensed histories, from biblical times to his own, of all the major cities that figure in the Old Testament. This thematic approach is not so much abandoned as merely abbreviated in books 3–5, which are more concerned with uninterrupted narration. Ralegh continues to analyze and interpret what he relates, but he maintains a greater sense of continuity even as he moves from one city-state or empire to the next.

The *History* was a vast intellectual undertaking that became virtually encyclopedic because, as Ralegh admits in the preface, he freely embellished his text with digressions. A number of these digressions amount to "position papers" as well developed as his "Offensive" or "War with Spain." He discusses witchcraft and necromancy in book 1, the nature and function of law in book 2, the superiority of English armies to those of Rome or of Alexander the Great, plus a history of duels in book 5, and the evidence for the existence of Amazons in book 4. Ralegh admits to treating this last topic at some length solely because his own account of these warrior women in the *Discovery* had been held up to ridicule (*Works*, 5:352).

Many of these digressions, such as those on law and dueling, were based on a substantial amount of research, testifying to Ralegh's personal interest in them. But was he also responsible for the massive and complicated bulk of the entire work? Ben Jonson charged that "the best wits of England were Employed for making of his historie. Ben himself had written a piece to him of *the* punick warre which he altered and set in his booke."[9] The charge cannot be wholly discounted, for Jonson was tutoring Wat Ralegh in 1612–13, and he wrote commendatory verses that were printed with the *History.* "Mr. John Talbote" no doubt assisted in the task, for Ralegh eulogized him as "an excellent generall skoller" who had spent eleven years with him in the Tower ("Journal," 190–91). Ralegh's chaplain, the learned divine Robert Burhill, also helped him with the task, for Burhill's widow claimed that her husband had read much Greek and Hebrew for the project, especially with regard to its chronology.[10] Burhill's association with Ralegh during these years is likewise indicated by his authorship of *De Potestate Regia* (1613), a detailed refutation of another tract published by the Jesuit who had accused Ralegh of Puritanism in 1610. Ralegh admitted in the preface that he knew no Hebrew and had received help from "learned friends"; thus, in book 2, chapter 7, he attributes a note on Hebrew grammar to "a skilful Hebrician," presumably Burhill (*Works,* 3:226).

Whatever Jonson among others may have contributed to the *History,* he grants that Ralegh "altered" it before incorporating it into the book. Modern critics agree that it was Ralegh who polished the consistent style and tone of the final product.[11] The author's first-person interjections frequently remind the reader of his individual presence throughout the work. Speaking of the castle where St. George was born, for instance, Ralegh demurs that "I leave everyman to his own belief" with regard to his encounter with the dragon (2:7; *Works,* 3:235). He affirms that predestination exists but that it applies only to salvation, then drops the subject with the abrupt disclaimer, "as for the manifold questions hereof arising, I leave them to the divines" (1:1; *Works,* 2:37). The *History*'s narrative style, of which more will be said later, points as well to a work crafted in all important respects by a single hand.

How Ralegh worked cannot be known in any detail, although it is clear from the repetition of ideas, anecdotes, and even phrasing from his other writings in prose and verse that he drew upon a permanent store of information, whether books, manuscripts, or his own memory.[12] Aubrey reported that he always carried a "Trunke of Bookes" with him when he went to sea, and shortly before his death he asked Bess to send him "some paper bookes of myne" (that is, manuscripts) "in the bottome of the sedar chist." After the reprieve of 1603 Cecil had searched a "little Trunk" that belonged to Ralegh where he found a number of manuscripts, including "a little collection of comonplaces." Such a self-compiled reference work would have been quite useful to Ralegh as he applied himself to the *History*'s diverse subject matter.[13] British Library Additional MS 57555 is, moreover, a document primarily in Ralegh's handwriting that he undoubtedly used in preparing the *History.* Most of this manuscript is given to headings under the letters of the alphabet for various geographical features of the Mediterranean world, particularly the Holy Land, interspersed with carefully drawn maps. Several of these maps influenced or served as models for those that were printed in the *History*. His alphabetical entries include biblical and scholarly notes on the places enumerated, while the ample blank space under almost every letter suggests that Ralegh never filled out this table as he had originally intended. The alphabetical listing is followed by a catalog of the library Ralegh had assembled in the Tower to the extent of some five hundred volumes.[14] The manuscript thus reveals both his methodical approach to his task and the fact that he could readily consult a library adequate to so large a project, for scores of the titles listed in it can be aligned with passages drawn from them in the *History*.

Ralegh's lengthy consideration of problems of geography and chronology, especially in books 1 and 2, have brought down much unfavorable criticism of the work. Certainly, so many pages devoted to such matters reduce the book's interest for the modern reader, but only because these issues have been resolved by accurate maps and historical timetables. More than a century after Ralegh published the *History* Sir Isaac Newton pondered and wrote about the same problems of chronology in the ancient world.[15] The questions remained viable, just as they were of fundamental importance to Ralegh's integrity as a historian. His oft-cited goal for the work was to establish the truth, to which end the when and where of world events constituted the basic parameters for every narrative. Ralegh found that by comparing sources and synchronizing events he could correct a number of received errors. Dido and Aeneas, for example, could never have been lovers, for they lived centuries apart, nor was Deucalion's flood identical with Noah's (2:8; 1:7; *Works*, 3:282, 2:195). Ralegh justified his attention to geography by explaining that "all story, without the knowledge of the places wherein the actions were performed, as it wanteth a great part of the pleasure, so it no way enricheth the knowledge and understanding of the reader; neither doth any thing serve to retain what we read in our memories, so well as these pictures and descriptions do" (2:3; *Works*, 3:61).

Ralegh's commitment to truth was bounded by one unquestioned authority, the Bible. Moses, he affirms, wrote the Pentateuch "not after any man's opinion, he wrote the truth" (1:4; *Works*, 2:121). Ralegh presumes nevertheless to correct mistranslations of Scripture. He notes the error that gave horns to Moses, and he contradicts the Vulgate and Geneva Bibles where they affirm that Shem was Noah's eldest son rather than his youngest. He also denies, the text to the contrary, that the spirit raised before Saul by the Witch of Endor was Samuel's on grounds that souls of the blessed cannot be conjured

(1:8; *Works*, 2:404). Unable to fit the Book of Judith into his chronology, Ralegh declares it uncanonical, although in so doing he was quite in accord with the compilers of the King James version.

Ralegh treated his other sources with the same commitment to reason that he had recommended to his son in the "Instructions" and to Prince Henry in the "Seat of Government": "to me . . . where the scriptures are silent, the voice of reason hath the best hearing" (1:9; *Works*, 2:358). He could therefore write that "I reverence the judgments of the [Church] fathers, but I know they were mistaken in particulars" (2:15; *Works*, 3:19). He often ridicules the fabrications of Friar Annius of Viterbo, yet he accepts his testimony over that of the learned Protestant scholar, Joseph Scaliger, where the Catholic's account is "more probable, and more agreeable to approved histories."[16] Ralegh's critical appraisal of his sources often makes him concede that the truth about some subjects simply cannot be known. His frustration in the pursuit emerges with particular candor in his account of the Roman campaign against the Carthagenians in Spain. Ralegh suspects that the Roman accounts of the war's later stages are biased, yet no Carthagenian sources had survived. His pragmatic efforts to cope with this difficulty conclude with the apology, "I am weary of rehearsing so many particularities, whereof I can believe so few. But since we find no better certainties, we must content ourselves with these" (5:3; *Works*, 6:317). Strathmann bases his analysis of Ralegh's skepticism in large part upon its application in the *History*, while Fussner praises Ralegh's critical evaluation of his sources, his "discrimination in judging probabilities," among his most admirable traits as a seventeenth-century historian.[17]

In contrast with his methodology, Ralegh's philosophy of history has come in for rather less praise from modern critics. Ralegh argued that the truthful record of the past gives "life in our understanding" by showing us instance after instance in which God's plan unfolds to reward virtue and punish sin (preface, *Works*, 2:v). Presumably, such an enlivened understanding would cause readers of the *History* to lead virtuous lives, yet this benefit is undercut in several ways. First, God's will directs and orders every event toward the fulfillment of His ultimate but unknowable plan. God works through second causes, which may be anything from the influence of the stars to the temporary lapse of a ruler's sanity, but the result is the same: "There is not therefore the smallest accident which may seem unto men as falling out by chance, and of no consequence, but that the same is caused by God to effect somewhat else by" (2:5; *Works*, 3:176–77). Ralegh asserts with a fatalism that echoes the lines of "What is our life?", God "is the author of all our tragedies"; He has "appointed us all the parts we are to play" (preface, *Works*, 2:xlii).

Accordingly, what practical benefit can accrue from the reading or writing of history? The insistence on an absolute divine providence, as Racin explains, obviates the value of history, for whatever we may learn from the past cannot be applied to changing the future in a manner contrary to God's will. We are doomed to carry out that will, nor can this be a uniformly blessed task for fallen man. In the postlapsarian world man is doomed to commit sins for which he will inevitably be punished. Racin concludes that Ralegh was unique among late Renaissance historians in denying that we can profit from knowing historical truth, at least to the extent that such knowledge could improve our lot beyond the confines of God's overarching plan.[18]

In addition, Fussner points out a secondary problem of particular relevance to the didactic thrust of Ralegh's work. His providential bias makes it impossible for him to differentiate between the causal and the accidental in history in cases where virtuous men are punished while the wicked flourish.[19] Ralegh, however, like Milton, acknowledged the existence of evil as a part of God's plan. The devil is constantly at work in the *History* as a second cause, yet no more able to thwart God's final intentions than is the Satan of *Paradise Lost*. Ralegh explicitly states his belief that God permits evil for His own purposes, for example, in His judgment of Olympias, mother of Alexander the Great, whose death God "appointed," just as He had "permitted her to live, and fulfil the rest of her wickedness" (4:3; *Works*, 5:439). Thus the logical problem noted by Fussner applies only to instances where evildoers receive no final punishment and the virtuous no ultimate reward.

The *History* was grounded upon Ralegh's broadest religious and philosophical convictions. At the same time he used the digressions to explore a wide range of tangential subjects. Many of these were probably included especially for the prince's benefit, although the same could be said of the work's overall didacticism. The asides on military strategy, however, were in Ralegh's view especially pertinent for Henry, and he comments on a variety of such topics from naval strategy to the difficulty of resisting an invading army, to the dangers of making a retreat in full view of the enemy (5:2; *Works*, 5:308, 6:210–11). Ralegh likewise airs his own political theories in a number of passages. Those treating of kingship would have been particularly relevant to Henry, of course. They include rather long digressions on the nature of kingship in book 2, chapter 16, and the comparison of tyranny with virtuous kingship in book 5, chapter 2. A number of other themes would have been familiar to Henry from other works that Ralegh had already addressed to him, such as the subordination of priests to secular rulers (2:346), or the importance to kings of gaining their subjects' love (a repeated motif, e.g., *Works*, 4:576, 5:508, 6:76–77). As the *History* unfolds, the digressions of a substantive and illustrative nature give way, as Lefranc observes, to personal recollections, perhaps because Ralegh's chief patron and reader died as the last two books were being brought to completion.[20]

A great deal of what Ralegh had to say about kingship was both instructive for Henry and at the same time implicitly or openly critical of his father's rule. As a result, it seems unlikely that either the king or any of his councillors with their wits about them read the *History* from cover to cover. Had they done so, they would never have sold the confiscated copies of the book, as they did after Ralegh's release from the Tower in 1616, whatever profit accrued to the royal coffers. Lefranc demonstrates that Ralegh's analyses of the events he narrates create, in their cumulative effect, a thorough condemnation of the king and his policies. James had banned publication of the work because he allegedly objected to Ralegh's treatment of Henry VIII. In a letter of early 1615 the king mentioned "Sir Walter Raleigh's description of the kings that he hates, whomof he speaketh nothing but evil."[21] Yet James might have surmised this much about the book merely from its preface. Had he read on he would have found Ralegh baiting him with a mixture of irony, flattery, and effrontery that made of the *History* an instrument of all-out reproach.[22]

Ralegh conducted his assault on the Jacobean regime through a variety of satiric techniques coupled with disclaimers and even praise of the king that worked to deny so much as a semblance of disparagement. Indeed, James would have found many passages in the work wholly to his liking. In the digression on dueling, for example, Ralegh commends his sovereign for outlawing "the *deadly feud*" (5:3; *Works*, 6:465), nor is there discernible irony in his flattering contrast of James with Joash, who sacked the Temple in Jerusalem, whereas "the most virtuous king of our age" has declined to ravage the church (2:22; *Works*, 4:645). Ralegh fully agreed with James as well in declaring that kings were appointed by God and not by law, and that they obeyed the law not by compulsion but only by choice and with a due "regard of the common good" (2:4; *Works*, 3:145; and see 1:9). Both precepts appear likewise in the king's *True Lawe of Free Monarchies*.

In the larger context, however, passages such as these form a thin, discontinuous smokescreen. At the end of the preface, for example, Ralegh denies that he alludes allegorically to the present in his treatment of the past. Yet his interpretive practice throughout the work renders this disclaimer nothing less than advance notice to the reader to be alert for parallels with contemporary events. Ralegh shows his own awareness of the pattern as he points out Old Testament archetypes, such as Moses' transformation of bitter water into sweet, which he interprets as "a plain type and figure of our Saviour" (2:3;

Works, 3:90). He also jumps repeatedly from past events to their modern counterparts.[23] Accordingly, where he fails to mention recent applications, contemporary readers could readily supply them in dozens of passages to the detriment of James and his government. Thus in his discussion of fortune in book 1 Ralegh asks why "so many worthy and wise men depend upon so many unworthy and empty-headed fools?" The blame, he submits, cannot be pinned on fortune but rather on the weakness of those in power, where "princes, or those that govern, endure no other discourse than their own flatteries" (1:2; *Works*, 2:40). He describes Artaxerxes as a ruler filled "with the persuasion, which princes not endued with an especial grace do readily entertain, that his own will was the supreme law of his subject, and the rule by which all things were to be measured, and adjudged to be good or evil" (3:12; *Works*, 5:263–64). The correspondences in these passages with James's notorious self-indulgence in drink, hunting, and dallying with his minions, could hardly have escaped contemporary readers.

Ralegh's portraits of the weak King Ninias and the insolent Rehoboam are often cited as mirrors in which James was to see his own image. Ralegh seems to defend by analogy James's pacifism in his assessment of King David's military career: "so greatly doth the Lord and King of all detest homicide," that kings who hope to become great through their wars always offend God (2:17; *Works*, 4:506). Yet the distinction between David's military aggrandizement and a good ruler's just responsibility to defend his people emerges in Ralegh's sarcastic treatment of Ptolomy's response to Antiochus' invasion of Egypt. Ralegh scorns Ptolomy for ruling through two of his advisors, "himself being loath to have his pleasures interrupted with business of so small importance as the safety of his kingdom." And when Antiochus' forces are repelled, Ralegh adds that the king quickly agreed to peace, "it being much against the nature of Ptolomy to vex himself thus with the tedious business of war."[24]

Perhaps the most representative instance of Ralegh's elusive yet daring attacks on James concerns his account of the death of the Macedonian tyrant, Perseus. His miserable end in a Roman jail leads Ralegh to surmise that, had he foreseen his fate, "He would rather have been very gentle, and would have considered that the greatest oppressors, and the most undertrodden wretches, are all subject unto one high Power, governing all alike with absolute command" (5:6; *Works*, 7:896). As if to drive home the reflection on James, Ralegh laments at some length in the same passage the tendency of some kings to be swayed by flatterers, minions, and harlots, often to the detriment of their entire lineage. But then Ralegh masks his hostile intent with an ironic quotation from James's own writings, that God will punish "'such kings as think this world ordained for them, without controlment to turn it up side down at their pleasure.'"[25] God's punishment of a tyrant leads Ralegh to lament the way other kings are brought to similar disgrace and ruin, and then to cap the satiric digression with assenting words written by the object of his attack.

In two instances Ralegh dwells upon historical episodes that satirize James through allegories of the injustice inflicted on Ralegh himself. Lefranc suggests that Ralegh treated at length the downfall of Philotas, a trusted official under Alexander the Great, because of its similarities to his own unfair trial and excessive punishment.[26] More to the point is a digression within the digression on duels, which concerns "guileful killing by the pen," that is, by willful miscarriages of justice. Ralegh cites two French examples "(that I may not speak of any English judge)." The second case involves an admiral of France prosecuted by the chancellor. Although nothing could be proved against him, the admiral lost "his estate, offices, and liberty," though not his life. To this point both cases take aim at Sir Edward Coke, Ralegh's vicious prosecutor in the trial of 1603. Ralegh takes vicarious revenge by noting that both the French judges were punished for their misprision. The unflattering contrast with James concerns the behavior of the French king, who had instigated the admiral's trial in the first place. This monarch not only punishes his chancellor's injustice, he restores the admiral to his estates and offices (5:3; *Works*, 6:466–68).

In addition to these attacks by analogy, James is somewhat more directly satirized in several passages. Ralegh's generalizations about kingship often apply to James in exact and derogatory fashion. A case in point is Ralegh's account of personal promotions and honors that kings distribute merely for "silver or favour." Of course, James's habit of rewarding and ennobling unworthy favorites ranked among his least defensible abuses of power, and Ralegh heightened the condemnation by adding that these are honors "which kings, with the change of their fancies, wish they knew well how to wipe off again" (1:8; *Works*, 2:351).

Ralegh's most audacious frontal attack on his sovereign occurs in the digression on kingship in book 2, chapter 16. The text is 1 Samuel 8–20, the very passage that James had quoted in full in the *True Lawe* to support his claim that kings rule by divine right. Ralegh's approach to the subject focuses on Samuel's threat that a king will seize his people's fields, vineyards, and other properties to give away to his favorites. Some readers, Ralegh notes, see in this a description of "the power of a king governed by his own affections, and not a king that feareth God." Others, however, "construe this text . . . as teaching us what subjects ought with patience to bear at their sovereign's hand" (*Works*, 4:472). James had developed the latter interpretation by arguing from this same verse that God conferred absolute authority on kings, whose subjects were bound to endure any degree of tyranny from them rather than rebel.[27] Ralegh counters this self-serving thesis by citing the foundation of divine law in Deuteronomy 23, where God demands that kings obey His mandates. Accordingly, no unjust appropriation of the subject's goods "shall be lawful for the king" (*Works*, 4:473). Then, after his thorough refutation of James's interpretation of the passage, Ralegh concludes with unassuming deference, "Such in effect is their disputation, who think this place to contain the description of a tyrant"; a tyrant, that is, being a king who takes his subjects' property for his own use (as James took Sherborne to bestow on Sir Robert Carr, some readers might recall). Ralegh then returns to the alternate view, that the passage denotes what subjects should willingly suffer at their sovereign's hand. These arguments, he concedes, "as they are many and forcible, so are they well known to all; being excellently handled in that princely discourse of the true Law of free Monarchies, which treatise I may not presume to abridge, much less here to insert." Thus Ralegh declines to repeat James's arguments, presuming only to refute his central thesis, with lengthy, direct rebuttal, mock praise, and a transparently false humility.

If Lefranc's interpretation of the *History*'s overall thrust as a condemnation of the king is correct, it goes far toward explaining the work's pessimism and its lack of any emphasis upon forgiveness of sin or redemption. These qualities are noted by most critics of the *History*; however, how Ralegh planned to deal with mankind's salvation after the Christian era is not known. Much of the pessimism he expressed about human affairs may simply derive from orthodox Christian belief in fallen man's hopeless spiritual condition in the pre-Christian world. Meanwhile, Ralegh's attention to God's justice and punishment of sin performs a requisite function in the satiric attack on James, an attack, Lefranc suggests, that in itself offered a new ray of hope. The faltering Jacobean regime had effectively smothered the spirit of patriotic optimism engendered by the "Tudor myth." In that interpretation of English history the Wars of the Roses were resolved with the advent of the House of Tudor, which itself culminated in Elizabeth's reign. Against the disappointing anticlimax of James's rule, Ralegh opposed the relentless assertions of his providential history, which promised that the king's tyranny would meet with divine retribution.[28]

Ralegh's sporadic and varied attacks on the king will not lure many modern readers to pore over all five books of the *History*. Fortunately, the work yields other dividends in many chapters and sections, most of which are included in Patrides's abridgment. In the first two chapters, for instance,

Ralegh sets forth his understanding of the creation and the nature of the cos-
mos. The result is in large measure restated in Tillyard's *Elizabethan World
Picture* and C. S. Lewis's *The Discarded Image*. Ralegh discusses the nature
of God, and of man's body, soul, and psychological makeup, noting the effects of sin upon all three. He describes man's relation to the world in a
microcosm/macrocosm analogy, likening the body's four humors to the four
elements that compose all earthly things. He compares the seven ages of man
to the qualities of the seven planets, and he adapts his interpretation of history to the medieval concept of the seven ages of the world, from the age of
gold through silver, brass, and so forth in a declining order that conforms to
the declining vitality of the earth and all it holds.[29] Thus the encyclopedic
scope that Ralegh imposed on the *History* results in a "world picture" far
transcending the chronological and historical limits of the first five books.

The work is also valuable for its retelling in Ralegh's fine prose of a great
many good stories, both historical and legendary. In book 3, chapter 10, he
summarizes Xenophon's *Anabasis* and includes full but engaging accounts
of the Peloponnesian War, the campaigns of Alexander the Great, and
Hannibal's invasion of Italy. Ralegh distrusted the classical myths as historical sources, yet he recounts most of them for whatever vestigial or allegorical
truth they may contain. Book 2, chapter 13, is devoted almost entirely to
Greek mythology: the stories of Pluto and Proserpina, Tantalus, Medusa,
Daedalus and Icarus, Oedipus, Theseus, and others, followed in chapter 14
by an account of the Trojan War. He warns the reader that these tales no
doubt distort the truth and that many of them can be understood only allegorically. Prometheus' punishment for bringing down fire to mankind,
Ralegh explains, must be read as a type of the discomforts that plague a restless, inquisitive mind (2:16; *Works*, 3:188). He concludes that there must
have been many men named Hercules, although their various exploits were
all attributed to the son of Alcmena. Some of the adventures of these multiple Herculeses must be genuine, he concludes, and "others perhaps must be
allegorically understood" (2:16; *Works*, 4:492). Other myths he rejects outright: "for myself I think it but a loud lie" he insists against Plutarch's claim
that the giant Antaeus was sixty cubits tall (2:13; *Works*, 4:407–8). Ralegh
derides, doubts, and interprets, but he incorporates nearly all of ancient
Greek mythology into the *History*.

Ralegh's treatment of the classical myths is but one aspect of his personal
response to a much larger Renaissance intellectual task, the reconciliation of
ancient culture with Christian belief. His lack of reverence for the classical
heritage is sharply at odds with the respect accorded to it by such contemporaries as Ben Jonson and John Milton. Ralegh singles out a few wise heathens

such as Plato, Pythagoras, and the mythical Orpheus, who rejected the pantheistic legends in favor of monotheistic beliefs (1:6; *Works*, 2:179–84). He is otherwise surprisingly contemptuous of Greek and Roman culture. With Milton he holds that the pagan oracles were controlled by the devil, and that they ceased when Christ entered the world.[30] But he is far less charitable than Milton with regard to the ancient world's understanding of the gods. Milton sided with the view that they were fallen angels and thus superior if satanic beings whom even the brightest of mankind might easily have mistaken for gods before the advent of true, revealed religion. For Ralegh, however, the pagan gods were merely giants or men of extraordinary ability. They were deified through mere human ignorance and the distorting fictions of poets. He accuses the Greeks of being wholesale "corrupters of all truth," "a nation of all others under the sun most deluded by Satan" (1:7; 1:9; *Works*, 2:189, 313). The Romans fare no better. He repeatedly derides their foolish, divided policies and the internal rivalries that left Rome unable to cope effectively with Hannibal. Thereafter, in the ultimate triumph of the empire over the entire Mediterranean world Ralegh brands the victors "ravens and spoilers of all estates" (2:9; *Works*, 3:292). Ralegh was little in awe of the classical past that gave the Renaissance its name and its cultural identity.

A final and pervasive virtue of the *History* is its style. Most of Ralegh's working sources for the project were in Latin, and during most of his life Ciceronian Latin was deemed the most elegant style for imitation in the vernacular. Accordingly, some of the *History*'s chief stylistic effects show the influence of classical Latin prose. The periodic sentence is a salient characteristic of both Cicero's style and Ralegh's. Typically, the subject is qualified at the beginning of the sentence by adverbial and adjectival elements that are often couched in absolute, participial constructions directly modeled on Latin practice: "being again pressed with want of water, they . . ."; "Elijah . . . misliking that Ochozias sought help" (2:4; 2:9; *Works*, 3:91, 4:299). The main predicate is thus delayed until the end of the sentence, as in this example from book 4, chapter 6: "For Demetrius, at his return from the idle pursuit of young Antiochus, finding all quite lost, was glad to save himself, with four thousand horse and five thousand foot, by a speedy retreat unto Ephesus, whence he made great haste towards Athens, as to the place that for his sake would suffer any extremity" (*Works*, 4:509).

Clearly, an unrelieved procession of such long and involved sentences would encumber rather than enliven Ralegh's narrative. Fortunately, his ear was as sensitive to prose as to poetic rhythms. He varies the lengths and cadences of his sentences to produce the ever-changing texture of his prose, thus creating the "successful modulation of an infinitely varied tone."[31] Moreover,

Ralegh heightens the sense of immediacy in his largely past-tense narration by shifting to present tense from time to time, another borrowing from classical Latin prose.

His style is likewise filled with passages of that particular vitality, wit, and power that had long characterized his writing. His interpretations of events are often delivered in first-person asides and laced with bitter, derisive, or epigrammatic sarcasm. He dismisses King Ahaziah as one who "was much busied in doing little, and that with ill success" (2:20; *Works*, 4:594). Of the doubtful authenticity of a work attributed to one Aristaeus, Ralegh scoffs that "a new edition of it is come forth, *purged from faults*, (as the papists term those books, wherein they have changed what they please)" (5:5; *Works*, 7:641n). The tone is occasionally enhanced by figurative language, as in the description of Alexander the Great's general, Antigonus, who "valued the loss of his men, money, and ships, no otherwise then as the paring of his nails" (4:5; *Works*, 5:464). Simile and metaphor are used sparingly, but with apt imagination for the most part. Ralegh explains that the Roman consul Fabius cautiously approached Hannibal with his inexperienced army "first to look on the lion afar off, that in the end they might sit on his tail" (5:3; *Works*, 6:252). In a few instances Ralegh expands his figurative language to reinforce a point as in the observation that "great alterations" in human affairs are "storm-like, sudden and violent; and that it is then overlate to repair the decayed and broken banks, when great rivers are once swollen, fast-running, and enraged."[32]

A minor aspect of the *History*'s style, its incorporation of scores of verse excerpts, takes on a particular interest in light of Ralegh's lifelong devotion to poetry. In addition, he reveals more about his attitudes toward the art of poetry in this work than in all of his other writings combined. Ralegh included here only three passages of English verse by other poets, two of them by Arthur Golding and one from Samuel Daniel's play, *Philotas*.[33] Ralegh himself translated from Latin sixty-three verses for the *History* besides a sixain stanza, Poem 19, which Rudick classifies as original because it does not correspond with any verse in the source to which Ralegh attributes it. None of these excerpts is noteworthy as poetry except perhaps in the variety of forms they employ. In a half-dozen instances he translated the long-line Latin originals into fourteener couplets, and there are several hexameters, for the extra syllables per line help compensate for the conciseness of the Latin. Twenty of the translations use heroic couplets, but not on a line-by-line basis. The twelve lines of Poem 38, for example, translate only eight and one-half lines from Virgil. Elsewhere Ralegh uses rhyme royal, ballad stanza, triplets, crossrhyme, and a variety of long and short meters. He largely disregards elegance of expression or imaginative rendering of the originals; the translations are literal, workmanlike, and seemingly governed by the same principle he followed in providing English translations for the prose sources he quoted in the original languages.

From Ralegh's direct comments about poetry and poets in the *History* one might conclude that he despised both. He repeatedly mentions "fables and poetical fictions" (2:24; *Works*, 4:701). The Greeks, he notes, did not believe that Sicily was a highly desirable country because its praises were "delivered only by poets" (5:1; *Works*, 6:31). Ralegh's interest in chronology, moreover, did not extend to matters poetical, for he dismisses efforts to establish the age of Homer with the remark, "For myself, I am not much troubled when this poet lived" (2:16; *Works*, 4:497). To reconcile this denigrating attitude with his own career as a practicing poet we must keep in mind that Ralegh was speaking as a historian. He was obliged to evaluate a number of early sources that were either written in verse or tinged by what would now be called creative writing, or both. Small wonder that he invoked that ancient charge against poetry, that it deals in fictions and is thus deceptive. His longest translated verse in the *History* is the eighteen-line epigram that asserts that Dido never met Aeneas; therefore, "Readers, beleeve Historians," for "Poets are liers, and for verses sake / Will make the Gods of Humane crimes partake" (Poem 6). In the *Defence of Poetry* Sir Philip Sidney refuted this charge while submitting that history failed to inspire right living because it recorded many examples of vice rewarded and virtue punished. But Ralegh insisted that the pattern of God's justice could be traced throughout human history, and he resented the blending of real and mythical events that, he deduced, must characterize so many ancient narratives.[34]

But if poetry in the sense of creative writing was a liability from the historian's point of view, it was nevertheless functional and even pleasurable in its own right. Ralegh admits that many worthy deeds have been forgotten for want of a "sacred Poet" to memorialize them. He resents Virgil's fabrications about Dido and Aeneas, yet praises him as "the prince of Latin poets" (3:1; *Works*, 5:39). Ralegh grants that "both profit and delight" may be found in poetry, "yet small profit to those which are delighted overmuch" (2:14; *Works*, 4:448). This passage defines the central problem. Poetry delights the reader with pleasing fictions couched in apt and ornamental language. Its emotional impact is therefore undeniable, although the unwary will suffer, for, in Ralegh's view, anyone must suffer who allows emotion to overwhelm reason. This rationale for the peculiar efficacy of poetry helps to explain his own use of verse, especially in the "Cynthia" poems he wrote to placate the queen after revelation of the

Throckmorton marriage. He played on her emotions in verse that was filled with remorseful complaints, hyperbolic praise, and offhanded diminution of his offense. The medium was poetry in part because the facts of the case left so little room for a reasoned defense.

The *History*'s rich, personal style and its running battle with the first Stuart king account for much of its seventeenth-century popularity, as witnessed by eight editions and two significant abridgments by the century's end. Furthermore, the problems of chronology and geography that Ralegh addressed remained pertinent, while Puritans and other dissenters, in England and America, relished Ralegh's providential interpretation of history, his support for limited monarchy, and his condemnation of tyrants. Lord Protector Cromwell could recommend the *History* to his son for its military and political advice as well as its morally pleasing view of world events. On the other hand, antiroyalist enthusiasm for the work often distorted its author's political views. Ralegh abhorred mob rule as much as he did tyranny. He advocated instead the cooperation between Crown and Parliament that would be hammered out through centuries of English constitutional development.

The Prerogative of Parliaments

The *Prerogative* speaks directly to the problem of maintaining this traditional balance of power. Ralegh's treatise is occasional work that must be understood in its historical context, a series of events in the aftermath of the Parliament of 1614. James's second Parliament met for only three months and passed no bills, least of all the financial relief in the form of a subsidy that the Crown so desperately needed. Instead, the House of Commons questioned the king's prerogative by opposing his impositions, the taxes on imports imposed by royal mandate rather than passed by law in Parliament. Ralegh had already touched on this issue in the "Jesuit" dialogue, where the Recusant defends the tax. The Commons not only refused to legitimize the impositions, they complained of many other abuses stemming from James's irresponsible rule. The chorus of unrest culminated on 7 June with a speech by John Hoskyns, a member whom Ralegh had known for many years as a fellow Middle Templar. Hoskyns attacked the king's prodigal gifts to his Scottish favorites, a notorious grievance that Ralegh had likewise mentioned in his earlier dialogue. But Hoskyns went as far as to propose that the Scots be treated to a new "Sicilian Vespers," alluding to the Sicilian massacre of French forces of occupation in 1282. For his impudence Hoskyns was confined to the Tower of London for a year, along with Dr. Lionel Sharpe and Sir Charles Cornwallis, who were condemned as instigators of Hoskyns's speech.[35]

James dissolved Parliament in June and placed his hopes for financial relief on the dowry he would obtain if Prince Charles married a Spanish princess. Meanwhile, members of the House of Lords showed their loyalty to the Crown by subscribing to a free gift or benevolence. The bishops were to offer James their best piece of plate or its cash value. Efforts to collect the benevolence throughout the kingdom, however, met with scant enthusiasm. A Wiltshire gentleman, Oliver St. John, wrote to dissuade the town of Marlborough from any such contribution. For this he was tried in Star Chamber, the name given to the king's Privy Council when it sat as a judicial body. St. John was jailed for some six weeks, then released in mid-June of 1615.[36]

Ralegh must have composed the *Prerogative* shortly afterward, during the summer of 1615. He addressed a political environment in which opposition to the Crown in speech or writing was routinely suppressed, whether committed by members of Parliament or ordinary citizens. The king had no intention of summoning Parliament again despite the fact that he was often unable to pay even the tradesmen who supplied the royal court. Yet he fueled his subjects' anger with his unabated spending on court entertainments and lavish rewards to favorites. Ralegh had long understood that a harmonious relationship between Crown and Parliament depended on popular support for the sovereign of the kind that Queen Elizabeth had enjoyed. James would ease the bankruptcy of the central government only by healing this rift between himself and his people.

In his "Fortune" and "Cynthia" poems Ralegh had complained that Elizabeth was responsible for his sufferings as an outcast favorite. In dedicating the *Prerogative* to James, however, he made the equally fictitious claim that his suffering and imprisonment resulted from "the borrowed authority of my sovereign misinformed" (153). Indeed, Ralegh blames all the shortcomings of the king's reign upon greedy favorites and self-serving councillors. But, as Lefranc observes, a tinge of sarcasm marks this dedication to the king with regard both to those councillors, now "rotten," who led the king to imprison Ralegh, and the very idea of parliamentary as opposed to royal prerogative.[37] In the dialogue Ralegh takes it upon himself to become the good advisor James lacks. He instructs his sovereign in the constitutional history of England from Norman times to the present, showing how Crown and Parliament have learned to work together for the common good. Ralegh's alleged purpose is to convince James that this traditional harmony, though fraught with tensions and compromises, is the best way to resolve the immediate crisis. But as with the "War with Spain" tract, so again in the *Preroga-*

tive, Ralegh pitted himself squarely against one of James's most staunchly
ingrained principles, in this case his belief in absolute rule. The question is,
did he knowingly oppose the king and thus create a hidden purpose beneath
the work's overtly benign and didactic surface?

The dialogue format allowed Ralegh both to distance himself from the
message he set forth as well as to enliven the mass of historical evidence he
presented to the king. The *Prerogative* opens with a Privy Councillor and Justice of the Peace discussing the St. John case. Their agreement that the Crown
needs additional income ushers in the main topic, whether or not the king
should convene another parliament. The Privy Councillor opposes the idea
on grounds that Parliament diminishes the authority and honor of the
Crown. Ralegh's spokesman is the Justice of the Peace, who presents all the
arguments for calling another parliament. The Councillor begins the debate
by rehearsing the loss of Crown prerogative to Parliament and through
Magna Carta. The Justice then takes the initiative, demonstrating "that the
kings of England have never received loss by parliament, or prejudice"(163).
The remainder of the dialogue follows a chronological survey of the parliaments of each reign beginning with those of Henry III. Even Ralegh's concise
accounts of the relations between Crown and Parliament make rather dry
reading, yet the accounts are functional, for time after time they set before
James the subsidies that Parliament granted to his predecessors. Edward I,
Henry IV, and Henry V, for example, each received three subsidies in their
first twelve years on the throne, whereas James had concluded his twelfth
year without a penny from his parliaments.

Although the Justice's alleged purpose is merely to demonstrate that Parliament has not diminished the royal prerogative, the Councillor's questions
and objections cause him to digress from his historical survey. In these digressions, the nature of James's incompetence is held up to searching scrutiny
through carefully selected analogous circumstances, the same device Ralegh
had used in the *History*.

Thus when the Councillor objects that Parliament affronted Edward III by
insisting that he discharge some of his favorite servants, the Justice responds
that "It grieved the subjects to feed these cormorants" who devoured what
Parliament had granted to the king (183). The Councillor condemns Parliament for forcing Richard II to dismiss his Lord Chancellor, but the Justice
parries: Richard retained all the money Parliament had granted him, yet he
was bound "to believe the general council of the kingdom" because he fancied
"a man all the world hated, (the king's passion overcoming his judgment"
(188). The parallels are too striking to be overlooked, the criticism scarcely
veiled by the dialogue's diaphanous fiction. Ralegh's condemnation of

James is further magnified in light of the thesis so often illustrated in the *History* that anyone who submits to passion inevitably sins.[38]

The assault on the king intensifies as Ralegh's Justice defends the appointment of a commission to regulate the gifts that Richard II conferred on his subjects. The Councillor argues that "it is some dishonour to a king to have his judgment called in question," to which the Justice replies, "That is true, my lord; but in this, or whensoever the like shall be granted in the future, the king's judgment is not examined, but their knavery that abused the king. Nay, by your favour, the contrary is true, that when a king will suffer himself to be eaten up by a company of petty fellows, by himself raised, therein both his judgment and courage is disputed" (190). The application to James is a perfect fit. Here is a vitriolic assessment of the king's prodigal, inept manner of rule. His indulgence of minions, the "petty fellows," had caused in Ralegh's opinion much of the Crown's insolvency while alienating the people's affections from their sovereign.

From this condemnation by analogy Ralegh guides the digression toward a more overt rehearsal of the king's failures. The Justice, arguing from precedent, advises James to put aside some of his income so that the ordinary expenses of the central government are met first. Not surprisingly, Ralegh's Justice uses the royal navy to illustrate this point, since "those poor men, as well carpenters as ship-keepers must be paid" (193). But this practice would necessarily reduce the king's bounty to favorites and deprive them of their priority claims upon exchequer receipts. Here the Councillor interrupts to defend his immediate self-interest, unconsciously revealing his own affiliation with those selfish parasites who drain the treasury: "what will become of our new-year's-gifts, our presents and gratuities" from the king? (194). When told that poor men should have their wages before rich favorites absorb ever more, the Councillor abandons all pretense of statesmanship or rule of law: "what care we what petty fellows say? or what care we for your papers? Have we not the king's ears? who dares contest with us? Though we cannot be revenged on such as you are for telling the truth, yet upon some other pretence, we will clap you up, and you shall sue to us ere you get out" (194–95). This outburst steers the digression toward an unflattering comparison of James with Queen Elizabeth, who, the Justice recalls, termed herself " 'the queen of the small, as well as of the great' " (195).

With the parliamentary history complete, Ralegh's Justice argues that James should convene Parliament, and by heeding this "general council of the kingdom" above the selfish clamor of his favorites on the Privy Council, he will regain the love of his people (212–13). James was in no frame of mind to take this step, yet he would not have found the entire *Prerogative* offensive. His councillors and favorites become scapegoats for all the problems that have marred his reign. The Justice concedes, moreover, that Parliament has no more authority than does the Privy Council, both of which are limited to advising the king (213), a point James had underscored in the *True Lawe*. Yet the dialogue violates an even more cherished tenet of his political philosophy by presuming to judge the king, a privilege that James had reserved to God alone. Worse yet, the ultimate verdict is failure, however much blame is shunted off on royal councillors. It was a commonplace of Renaissance courtesy books, such as Castiglione's *Courtier,* that wise rulers surrounded themselves with honest, experienced advisors, whereas James, in Ralegh's view, had been flattered and deceived by his chosen favorites from the beginning of his reign. In this weakness he resembles Richard II, who was deposed in part because of his devotion to unworthy favorites. James is then contrasted with Elizabeth, whose success Ralegh attributes to her concern for her meanest subjects above the claims of her greatest lords. In the final analysis the chief target of the *Prerogative* is the king himself, whose susceptibility to shallow, selfish advisors has dissolved his people's love and emptied his coffers.

It is difficult to imagine that Ralegh addressed this dialogue to James with the expectation that he might read it, grasp its truth, and reform his style of kingship. Ralegh's sincere belief in the solution he proposed is beyond question; the recurrence of these same ideas in his other writings testifies to that. Perhaps he was unaware of his new sovereign's commitment to peace when he addressed the "War with Spain" to him in 1603, but by 1615 he was well acquainted with James's commitment to absolute rule, and he knew what irresponsible extremes of self-indulgence this belief had fostered in the king. From the beginning then, Ralegh devised the *Prerogative* as a powerful condemnation of James, muted in a fictional dialogue that purports to absolve him of blame while offering sound advice wholly dedicated to his best interests.

By 1615 Ralegh had good reason to attack the king, and he was in a unique position to do so. James had spared his life, but had confined him to the Tower for a dozen years by now; the condemned prisoner lacked even a legal identity. Ralegh had suffered further from the king's devotion to his minions when James seized Sherborne as a present for Robert Carr. Prince Henry had forestalled the transfer, but with his death Ralegh lost the estate as well as his best hope for pardon and release from imprisonment. He probably felt that he had little left to lose.

Ralegh fashioned the dialogue to allow his spokesman to dominate its speeches, including the digressions that set forth the most damaging reflections on the king. In other respects this speaker is closely identified with

Ralegh, who had served as Justice of the Peace in Dorsetshire. Moreover, the Justice recalls, somewhat gratuitously, that he had moved in the House of Commons during one of Elizabeth's parliaments to levy a subsidy only on the wealthier citizens, a point Ralegh himself had argued in the House on 9 November 1601.[39] Ralegh's identification with the Justice also helps to account for the tone of the dialogue's concluding exchanges. Unlike the *Revenge* pamphlet, or the "Succession" tract that Ralegh had dedicated to Elizabeth, this work ends without a word of praise for its dedicatee, his accomplishments, or the hope that God's blessing will follow his affairs. The Justice defies the Councillor's threats to his personal safety, and when asked, "What is it then you hope for or seek?," he responds, "Neither riches, nor honour, or thanks; but only seek to satisfy his majesty, . . . that I have lived and will die an honest man" (221). The Justice has the last word, and in light of all that has preceded it, his defiant tone scarcely concludes the piece on a note that James would have found very satisfying.

In these three major prose works Ralegh leveled a variety of charges against James, and he presented them in ever bolder fashion. The "Jesuit" dialogue is a coterie piece in which the king becomes an important but secondary victim of the conversation. Ralegh derides his poverty and lack of rapport with his subjects that have combined to leave England vulnerable to an international Catholic conspiracy. The attack on James in the *History* is pervasive, yet disguised by Ralegh's disavowal in the Preface that he glances at any modern parallels and by the sheer bulk of the work in which those incriminating but oblique parallels are submerged. Ralegh's overall strategy here was to turn James's own philosophy of kingship against him by agreeing that God will judge and punish tyrants, then demonstrating that the qualities of tyrants in the historical record coincide with James's own record. The *Prerogative* accuses James of listening to greedy favorites instead of the wiser counsel represented by Parliament assembled. As a result, he has been unable to adapt his regime to the kingdom he obtained in 1603. This criticism was the most blatant of all, given its dedication to James and its survival in some thirty manuscript copies. Thus publication of these three works follows an ascending scale of audacity, albeit the most stinging condemnation of James comes in the *History*, which assures him that God will punish his tyranny.

Chapter Six

The Last Years

Tower Remnants

In Commendation of Gorges's Lucan, Poem 20. It was perhaps not mere coincidence that Sir Arthur Gorges chose to translate Lucan's *Pharsalia*, and to publish it in the same year that Ralegh's *History* came from the press. The *Pharsalia*, an account of the Roman republic's struggle to prevent one-man rule, was written by a Latin poet who fell victim to a later emperor. Ralegh's commendatory poem is unusual in its neglect of the work itself. Gorges is the center of praise in these verses while the translation provides merely a convenient excuse for that praise. The sonnet draws a parallel between the Roman poet who suffered under Nero and Gorges, whose refusal "to clime / By flattery, or seeking worthless men," has left him "bruis'd." Gorges gained neither office nor reward from King James, although his "scarres" amounted, so far as is known, to nothing worse than this lack of promotion. Ralegh praises his cousin's steadfastness now, and formerly "in just, and in religious warres," referring to the "Islands" voyage where Gorges fought shoulder to shoulder with Ralegh at the taking of Fayal.

Ralegh establishes Sir Arthur's strength of character (and consequent official neglect) in the first two quatrains. In the third he urges him to maintain his lofty resolution in order to gain "a lasting state / . . . free from infamy." The couplet returns to the comparison between Gorges and Lucan, who resemble each other in courage as in poetic accomplishment. Ralegh's ending is rather pedestrian in conception as in its epigrammatic force, which is drained by the broken rhythm and syntax of line 13, "Such is thy *Lucan*, whom so to translate."

The poem honoring Gorges was the last verse Ralegh is known to have composed before his release from the Tower. Between 1615 and his death in 1618 Ralegh was primarily occupied with three types of writing. He worked on the "Invention of Ships" and "Cause of War," both of which may date entirely from these years or mark continuations of discourses he had begun for Prince Henry. Second, he composed a variety of works relating to the Guiana undertaking, including proposals for the attempt, documents directly related to the voyage itself, and in its aftermath the "Apology." Poems 21, 22, 23, and possibly 24 entreat Queen Anne's intervention to save his life, and may date from the autumn of 1618. Third is the small group of documents connected with Ralegh's execution, including his reworking of the last stanza of Poem 17 into Poem 25, his speech from the scaffold, and another speech that he may have written but did not deliver on that occasion.

"A Discourse of the Invention of Ships." Beyond doubt this short discourse belongs to one or more longer works that either have been lost or were never completed. Its diverse contents fall into two parts. The first deals historically with the independent invention of ships by various cultures around the world, recent advances in naval technology, and brief naval histories of Venice and Genoa (317–26). Aside from the consideration of naval ordnance (324), none of this material fits Ralegh's outline of the "Art of War by Sea" in the Cotton Manuscript. He seems instead to be writing a general history of shipping without a particular military focus.

The account of Genoa's declining sea power leads him to reflect that "all the states and kingdoms of the world have changed form and policy" (326), which serves as an abrupt transition to a paragraph on the decline of the Holy Roman Empire. The rest of the tract traces the recent economic and political expansion of Spain, France, England, and, in more detail, the Netherlands. Naval matters are reintroduced to show that despite Dutch sea power, England could still muster a fleet to conquer theirs (329). This revision of his earlier thinking argues a relatively late date of composition, for Ralegh had contended in the "War with Spain" and later tracts that the Dutch navy equaled or surpassed England's.[1] He then rehearses three of his favorite themes: the damaging effects of exporting cannon of English manufacture, the importance of "trade by force" to the development of a strong navy, and the necessity of close ties between England and the Netherlands. Next, the treatment of England's critical influence upon Dutch commerce turns the discourse to the subject of impositions, with which it concludes.

Four references in the second part of the tract, as Lefranc observes, indicate that this section belongs to a larger work.[2] Ralegh states that he has already "proved" that the Church of Rome diminished the power of the Holy Roman Empire (326), although no such argument appears in the extant text. He promises to say more about the Hanse towns "hereafter" (327), then drops the subject, and he notes upon his first mention of the "Newcastle trade" that he has "digressed" from this subject. In the final paragraph he refers to the "conclusion of this chapter." The question is, for what kind of work would either part of this discourse make up a chapter? The history of ships makes an ungainly preface to a discourse about the political and commercial status of Europe, while those topics are but intermittently related to naval matters.

The treatment of customs duties (impositions) toward the end of the "Invention" enhances the miscellaneous nature of the tract, but it does help to define Ralegh's political thinking. In the "Jesuit" dialogue the Recusant had defended the king's impositions on grounds that England needed fewer imported luxuries. Ralegh had likewise blamed the decline of Roman power on luxuries from the east (*History*, book 5:3, 5:5; *Works*, 6:362, 763), yet the Recusant is not consistently his spokesman, so that his attitude toward these taxes cannot be certainly known from this witness alone. The "Invention" reveals his sincere support for the impositions, again because the "trumperies" they tax weaken the nation (333). On the other hand, Parliament opposed the impositions as unlawful seizures of the subject's goods; they were forcible acquisitions by the Crown of the very kind that characterized a tyrant, as Ralegh had argued in the *History*. Thus he approved of the impositions themselves, but not the way they had been levied without recourse to Parliament.

The casual, disorganized nature of the "Invention" is reinforced by its personal tone. The first-person address throughout makes it read more like a letter than a formal discourse. The prose is dotted with such expressions as "for my own opinion," and "sure I am," in addition to which Ralegh interjects several reminiscences. He laments the sinking of the *Mary Rose*, with the loss of Lord Carew's cousin and Sir Richard Grenville's father aboard (324), and he recalls his own leave-taking with the Prince of Orange in 1582 (the only record of this interview, 331). The aura of familiarity here goes well beyond that of the *History* or even the "Marriage" tract, and much beyond the relatively formal tone of the "Match." Ralegh's intended audience, whether the prince, friends, or relatives, was throughout a readership with whom he felt at ease.

The relationship of the "Invention" to Ralegh's other works could be more easily reconstructed if we knew when he composed it. The first section belongs to 1605 at the earliest, for Ralegh terms Sir George Carew, Lord Carew (324), an honor he attained in that year. The reference to *Trades Increase* in the second part shows that Ralegh was writing in 1615 or later.[3] The "Invention" survives in six manuscripts and the 1650 printed text; a critical edition of the text might reveal whether Ralegh or someone else spliced together these disparate materials. Meanwhile, the received text leaves its purpose something of a mystery.

"A Discourse of the Original and Fundamental Cause of . . . War." The "Cause of War" is better unified than the "Invention, although it too covers a broad range of topics and shows unmistakable signs of incompletion or textual corruption. Lefranc argues that it is in fact two separate discourses, the first about war, the second on the growth of the temporal power of the papacy, whether fused by Ralegh or someone else it is impossible to say. Lefranc also believes this to have been the last work that Ralegh composed in the Tower,[4] although it may have been drafted in whole or part in 1612. Ralegh notes that he has "briefly shewed in another work" that wars of "forcible transplantations" cause the most extreme miseries (255), an allusion to book 2, chapter 28, of the *History* (*Works*, 4:804). Ralegh need not be referring here to the *History* in its entirety for he had finished book 2, by Lefranc's calculation, in 1611.[5] In the "Cause of War" Ralegh also deals extensively with the Punic Wars, a subject that was fresh in his mind as he wrote book 5 of the *History* in 1613–14. Two other datable allusions point tentatively to composition closer to 1612 than 1616. He mentions the colony "lately" established in the Somer Islands (255), a reference to the settlement of Bermuda under auspices of the Virginia Company in 1612. He also alludes to the wars in the Netherlands during "these last forty years" (277), which again points to 1612 since the Dutch revolt against Spanish occupation began in April 1572. Thus the discourse was begun no earlier than 1612, nor is there compelling evidence to extend its completion more than a year or two beyond that date.

As with the "Invention," the various textual states of the "Cause of War" obscure its purpose. The discussion of the papacy, which occupies about a third of the tract, occurs at different places in several of the manuscript copies, and as a totally separate appendage to the printed text of 1702.[6] The dislocation of this material largely accounts for the uncharacteristic disorganization of the received text.

Ralegh's initial plan for the "Cause of War" was simple and direct. After defining war as a necessary activity of fallen mankind, he discusses its three varieties, the necessary or natural war, voluntary or arbitrary war, and unnatural, civil war. War is necessary, for example, to acquire more territory for an overpopulated land faced with disease or starvation. Voluntary wars are instigated by princes for various reasons: to control the population, especially its unruly elements or "swelling humours" (258), to gain revenge, or, most often, from mere ambition. Civil war, Ralegh contends, normally results from the ambition and treachery of a few powerful men who manage to persuade others to join them in rebellions whose ultimate motives these followers do not understand (283–84).

This simple three-point outline is disrupted by the long section on papal intervention in political affairs that is used to illustrate wars caused by ambition. Then, after the discussion of civil war, Ralegh returns to voluntary war as represented by Rome's conflict with Carthage, but with extended and irrelevant attention to Hannibal's career and the sabotage of his Italian campaign by Hanno and the Carthagenian senate. Ralegh treated these same events in the *History* in the long second and third chapters of book 5. The discourse then takes up the Roman civil wars and the Wars of the Roses before concluding. It would be strange if this backtracking to voluntary and civil war represented Ralegh's final intentions for the tract, given his customary regard for clear organization.

In the absence of a critical edition it is nevertheless possible to evaluate in isolation what Ralegh intended for certain parts of the discourse. The papal material constitutes his most thorough attack on the Church of Rome. With it he combines a number of his favorite political and philosophical beliefs. He attributes papal acquisition of temporal power to the same drive to dominate others that he had described in the *History* as natural to all men (5:2; *Works*, 6:146). The pursuit of this ambition by religious institutions, however, Ralegh traces back to the founders of Islam (269). Thus the popes are guilty of a heathen practice that, Ralegh had often argued before, was entirely foreign to Christian belief and tradition.[7] With his typical concern for supporting evidence he then summarizes the growth in papal influence over temporal affairs, from the Church's domination of the Holy Roman Empire to its intervention in European wars, among them the revolt of the Netherlands and England's Wars of the Roses. Ralegh's attack on Rome can stand as an essay by itself, but it is not out of place as an illustration of voluntary war caused by worldly ambition. He asserts throughout that the papacy has expanded its influence by playing a critical role in the majority of recent European conflicts. At issue is the disproportionate length of this example to the remainder of the treatise.

The analysis of unnatural or civil war which follows this section of the tract opens with a consideration of rebellion that attacks the Jacobean regime implicitly yet quite as forcefully as in equally oblique passages from the *History* or the "Jesuit" and *Prerogative* dialogues. Ralegh had already taken aim at the king through an unflattering comparison to Queen Elizabeth, for after citing her strong measures to defend her merchants from Spanish aggression, he noted that her strength "made her glorious in all nations . . . yet served it not for a precedent for others of less virtue to follow" (262). Ralegh's disarming introduction to the section on civil war insists that such wars are always harmful (279), and that to stir up "factions, rumours, and discourses, which alienate the minds of people, and impeach and weaken the government, is a degree of treason, and consequently a breach of the sixth Commandment"

(280). In the next paragraph, however, he affirms that where the administrators of a society's laws are "visibly and incurably defective in preserving the whole," they "may be removed." He warns that this is the utmost limit of the subjects' power, then defines even more vividly, and with transparent application to James's crisis of government, the conditions that justify such a revolt. With all due caution, and always remembering the dangers of rebellion, the populace is licensed under certain circumstances to overthrow the government: "where the person or persons possessing the supreme power are incurably defective, and this plainly appears to the majority of the people, they have a right to change the same, I think naturally they must" (281).

The attack on the king intensifies as Ralegh examines those qualities that typify a corrupt kingdom. He begins by comparing a prince and his subjects to a father and his family, the same analogy that James had used throughout the *True Law*. If the servants of the king's household (his appointed officers, in other words) "be overrun with the deadly sin of pride and luxury, sloth and rapine, it is a fair sign of its utter ruin." Where the government's ministers are corrupt and self-serving, and their offices obtained by "money, or favour purely," rather than by desert, the stage is set for civil war. The similarity to James's manner of rule required no further comment. But Ralegh then undercuts the relevance of this entire argument to the larger discourse by admitting that civil war rarely results from such poor government (283). And why? Because where the majority concurs that such incompetence must be rooted out, the government is unable to "gain a party strong enough to make a civil war" (283). This sudden shift in direction caps his insulting, derisive attack on James's policies and their likely consequences. After devoting some five pages to this bogus cause of civil war, for the sole purpose of its gratuitous satire, Ralegh summarizes the actual cause of civil war in a single paragraph.

Equally digressive is the long account of Hannibal's career during the second Punic War (285–92). Earlier in the tract Ralegh had cited this war as an instance of voluntary conflict caused by fear or the desire to prevent future domination (263–64). The later, extended rehearsal of these matters drives home the thesis, also developed in the *History*, that Hannibal was betrayed by jealous politicians at home, especially Hanno who "under the disguise of being a patriot, ruined his country" (292). And as in the *History*, Ralegh pits Hanno's false, self-serving statesmanship against the true patriotism of the Roman Consul, Atilius Regulus (290–91; 5:1; *Works*, 6:92). Here, and in the examples of Varro and Penula, Ralegh may have glanced at similarly shallow men in James's government, but the hit, if it is one, is far from palpable. This section of the essay strays from the subject of arbitrary war without commenting in an effective satiric fashion upon contemporary affairs.

The "Invention" and "Cause of War" are far better developed than the "Art of Warre by Sea" fragments, yet they too impart a sense of unfinished ambiguity. Their overlap with both topics and specific examples from the *History* argues that they were not written for Prince Henry, who apparently had full access to that work until the time of his death. On the other hand, separate treatises on the history of ships, causes of war, and the belligerency of the Church of Rome were lessons that Ralegh left out of the *History*, yet might well have addressed to the prince. The repeated attacks on James and his councillors, and the reiterative account of the second Punic War point to composition after the *History* had been suppressed late in 1614. These fragments may belong to a projected larger work that Ralegh designed to salvage part of what he had put into the suppressed *History*, and to disseminate ideas and findings he had not covered there.

One clue to the connection between these tracts is Ralegh's claim in the "Invention" that he had already dealt with papal hegemony over the Empire (326). This is recounted, as we have seen, in the "Cause of War" (271–74). Furthermore, most manuscript copies of these works circulated together, and after Henry's death in 1612, an obvious recipient for them was at hand in the person of Prince Charles. The eight manuscripts of the "Marriage" tract which entitle it a work about Charles's choice of a bride suggest that Ralegh may have addressed a copy of it to the prince. Perhaps he began the "Invention" and "Cause of War" in hopes of securing a new royal patron, only to abandon them as it became clear that Charles did not share his brother's sympathy for the aging prisoner in the Tower.

The Guiana Documents, 1607–18

Plans and Proposals.   During his imprisonment Ralegh maintained his ties with Guiana and continued to believe that it was a land rich in gold that must be made subject to England as soon as possible. Queen Anne's brother, King Christian of Denmark, asked James to release Ralegh for service as his admiral, no doubt with a view toward establishing a Danish presence in Guiana.[8] Meanwhile, Ralegh had proposed to Cecil in 1607 that he be allowed to organize another Guiana venture, and at Cecil's urging he revived this plan in 1611. He wrote Queen Anne about the project, enclosing a copy of his letter to Cecil and begging her to intervene with James. He wrote the king directly to outline the benefits of the project while claiming to "have spent my sorrowfull tymes of ymprisonmente in the studdye of your Majesties servyce, and saffetye."[9] In 1615 he sent Secretary Winwood copies of his letters to Cecil and the king coupled with renewed assurances that he wished to undertake the voyage for "no other end nor desire then to pay his Ma*je*stie some part of the Debt I owe him.""[S]eeing," he continued, that "the same death which strikes us downe in the worthiest accons, doth not spare to strangle us in taking our vn*pro*fitable ease I should thinke myselfe exceeding happy to encounter him in the way of his Ma*je*sties service."[10] Undated letters survive to the Privy Council and to John Ramsay, Viscount Haddington, to whom he offered supreme command of the expedition. In 1607 Ralegh had estimated the cost of the voyage at £5,000. An unaddressed rationale for the project from about 1614 includes a detailed estimate of the cost at something over £9,500. Harlow puts the final cost of the undertaking at some £30,000.[11]

A complete analysis of Ralegh's persuasive strategies in these documents is impossible here, although the main points can be summarized. He offered the king a ready source of gold, to the "dispight of yo*ur* Malitious enemyes Abroade; and of yo*ur* gruntinge sub*jec*ts att home." The treasure, he warns, "cannot lye hidden longe."[12] Ralegh promised not to offend "any *Chri*stian prince" in the course of the enterprise, yet noted in his detailed estimate of expenses that he had claimed Guiana for England years before and that the native population had accepted English sovereignty.[13] As for his own allegiance, Ralegh repeatedly urged that the officers set over him on the voyage be instructed to "cast me into the Sea" should he attempt to escape or deviate in any way from the mission.[14] The major change in his argumentative strategy is his omission of any reference to El Dorado, the Indian empire of gold that had dominated his enthusiasm for Guiana in the *Discovery*. Subsequent exploration had disproved the legends, but Ralegh still believed in the mines and in the gold ore he had seen with his own eyes.

James was finally led to approve the venture by the combined pressures of his remediless poverty, Winwood's influence as secretary, and the bribery-induced support of the new royal favorite, George Villiers. On 19 March 1616 Ralegh was released from the Tower. His preparations for the Guiana enterprise took more than a year; indeed, letters patent authorizing it were not signed until 26 August. Their terms provided for a twenty percent return of all profits to the king, but gave Ralegh absolute command of the expedition including the right to draw up "such Orders, Ordinances, Constitutions, direccions, & instruccions" as he saw fit.[15] The "Orders to be observed by the Commanders of the Fleet," issued on 3 May 1617, were undoubtedly approved by Ralegh, but were adapted from earlier naval orders which may or may not be his. Their emphasis on the conduct of battles at sea and procedures for an armed landing suggest that these instructions were originally drawn up for an all-out military operation such as the "Islands" voyage of

1597.[16] The closing paragraphs of the "Orders," however, are specifically adapted to the Guiana enterprise and reflect Ralegh's own experiences there. He commands the men not to harm or steal from the Indians but to "use them with all courtesy" (688). He warns them not to eat anything that the natives avoid and, recalling the fate of his unfortunate servant during the first voyage to Guiana, he warns them not to swim in the alligator-infested rivers.

The "Journal," 19 August 1617–13 February 1618. Ralegh's autograph journal of the second Guiana voyage covers six crucial months of the year-long undertaking. It is filled with nautical data regarding distances sailed, wind directions, tides, and the like, yet it includes several good narratives as well. Above all, it chronicles the misfortunes that beset the enterprise from the very beginning.

His fleet of fourteen ships left Plymouth on 12 June, but the "Journal" entries begin some two months later after a seven-week layover in Ireland due to bad weather. At Lanzarota in the Canary Islands the English party was denied water or the right to trade for supplies. Ralegh told the Spanish governor "that did I not know that it would offend the King my soveraine, I would pull his Moriscos out of ther towne by the eares" (181). He was better received at Gomera where he exchanged gifts with the English-born governess of the island. By this time, however, disease had broken out in the ships and henceforth the dead are named on almost a daily basis. The governor wrote to Gondomar, the Spanish ambassador in London, to commend Ralegh's fair dealings with his people, but his testimony was undercut by the desertion of Captain John Bayley, who returned to England to accuse Ralegh of turning pirate.[17]

The fleet proceeded to the Cape Verde Islands off the west coast of Africa, then turned on 4 October for the crossing to South America. A mid-Atlantic calm lengthened to over a month what should have been a two-week voyage. Water rations were halved on 24 October. All of Ralegh's servants succumbed to disease except for his pages, and on the last of the month he too caught the fever. For the next twenty days, he wrote, "I never receaved any sustenance but now and then a stewed prune but dranck every houre day and night, and sweat so strongly as I changed my shirts thrise every day and thrise every night" (197).

They reached the South American coast 11 November and were off the mouth of the Orinoco by the fourteenth when Ralegh wrote Bess. He had renewed contact with the natives from his first landings along the coast, finding "my old sarvant Leonard" who had lived several years in England, and another Indian who had spent two years with him in the Tower (197–98). "To tell you that I might be here King of the Indians," he confided to his wife, "were a vanitie; but my name hath still lived among them."[18] The rest of the letter recounts the miseries suffered and good men lost.

Ralegh was too weak to lead the expedition upriver, but dispatched it on 10 December under command of his trusted friend Captain Lawrence Keymis. For two months Ralegh's larger ships hovered off the coast to guard the escape route and prevent an anticipated Spanish incursion, since James had forced Ralegh to supply Gondomar with a detailed itinerary of the voyage months before he sailed.[19] By early February Indians had brought rumors to the coast that the English company upriver had taken the Spanish town of Santo Tomé with the loss of two of their captains. Presumably Ralegh stopped making entries in the journal when he received Keymis's letter with the news that Ralegh's son Wat had been killed in the assault on the town.

The "Apology." The exploring party returned to the ships after more than two months on the Orinoco, without finding the mine or bringing back any ore. Keymis committed suicide after Ralegh refused to accept his excuses for the mission's failure. Ralegh's subsequent efforts to take further action then ran afoul of his demoralized and unruly comrades. His plans to attack the Spanish plate fleet or to refit the entire expedition in Newfoundland for another attempt on Guiana were thwarted as captains deserted for home or for privateering expeditions. By late March Ralegh had only four ships left, and three of these deserted on the return voyage, leaving the *Destiny* to enter Plymouth Harbor alone on 21 June 1618.[20] There his kinsman, Sir Lewis Stukely, Vice-Admiral of Devonshire, took him into custody for the journey to London.

From sea Ralegh had addressed letters to Winwood, Lord Carew, and to Bess, defending his actions and explaining why the mission failed. Now he needed time to prepare a more elaborate defense given the growing evidence of official condemnation. A royal proclamation of 9 June denounced the voyage and blamed Ralegh and his men for breaking the peace with Spain contrary to their orders. James and his court were traveling on summer progress toward Salisbury; when Ralegh arrived in the town with Stukely he made use of a drug that left him "so broken out all over that yt is verely thought to be a kind of leprosie."[21] The ruse gave him a few precious days' delay in which to pen the "Apology" and to await some opportunity for contacting the king.

Ralegh designed the "Apology" as a wholesale defense of his conduct of the mission and its rationale. It refutes in the order of events various charges made against him including a written list of accusations drawn up by some of his captains and sent to Lord Admiral Howard.[22] The wording and organization of several passages show that he consulted the "Journal" as he wrote; in his assertion, for example, that he kept his men from sacking Lanzarota, in the description of their arrival at Gomera, and of the problems with shallow waters off the coast of Guiana (484–86, 488; "Journal," 181, 183, 202).

Ralegh's defensive strategy involved placing his disastrous enterprise in the context of other unsuccessful expeditions, from an imperial invasion of Africa to the defeat of Drake and Hawkins in the West Indies, to Sir John Norris's failure to take Lisbon in 1589 (an exploit Ralegh had counted among England's triumphs over Spain in the *Revenge* tract, 74). Ralegh is uncharitable in blaming his failure on his volunteers whom he describes, "some forty gentlemen excepted," as "the very scum of the world, drunkards, blasphemers and such others as their fathers, brothers, and friends thought it an exceeding good gain to be discharged of" (480). He had needed these men and was in no position to be very selective about who joined the expedition. They had suffered greatly in search of the gold mine he had promised, and many of them lost their lives in the attempt. A more valid excuse is Ralegh's complaint that he was unable to lead in person the critical Orinoco leg of the journey. This may well have doomed the entire mission to failure, and it is a handicap that sets Ralegh apart from the other commanders in his historical survey of even greater failures.

Ralegh returns to Drake later in the essay to show that "as good success admits no examination of errors, so the contrary allows of no excuse, howe reasonable or just soever" (486). Both Drake and Cavendish, he argues, owed their initial success to luck; when "chance had left them to the trial of their own virtues," both perished (487). This allows him to attribute his own failure to the unlucky combination of bad weather, disease, and unworthy followers. Thus, for his own persuasive needs Ralegh deals only with what he considered to be "second causes." Yet he explained at length in the *History* that what appears to be mere chance is instead God's hand at work through second causes toward His ultimate purpose. Ralegh adhered to this overall philosophy in urging Bess to "obey the Will and Providence of God" in accepting the loss of their son.[23] In the "Apology," however, he could hardly submit that his Guiana project failed because it ran counter to the will of God, so Ralegh prudently chose to interpret his failure in the more favorable light of its susceptibility to bad luck.

Ralegh saved his most telling and crucial arguments for the last third of the "Apology." He responded to the charge that he knew nothing about a mine and had never expected to find one in Guiana by asking why, if the voyage were merely to escape the Tower, "did I not keep my liberty when I had it?" (498). Why, he asks, did I sell all I owned, risking my life and my son's on an empty hope? "What madness could have made me undertake this journey, but the assurance of the mine; thereby to have done his majesty service, to have bettered my country by the trade, and to have restored my wife and children their states they had lost" (498).

With regard to invading Spanish territory, Ralegh confronts James with his own insistence that Ralegh provide the Spanish ambassador with a complete itinerary of the voyage in advance. Moreover, the king had, upon condition, approved of the plan to work a gold mine in Guiana. It follows that "either the country is the king's or not the king's" (501). If not, then robbing Spain of its gold there would have been quite as illegal as attacking and burning the town. But if England had a right to the mine, then Santo Tomé was a foreign outpost encroaching on English territory. To clinch the case Ralegh cites the recent slaughter of thirty-six unarmed English traders by their Spanish hosts in the West Indies.[24] Accordingly, there was no peace to be broken between England and Spain in the New World, and therefore so much the less blame can be attached to the Englishmen who captured Santo Tomé after the Spaniards ambushed them in the first place.

Ralegh no doubt hoped to provide James and his council with the "Apology" when they came to Salisbury but there is no evidence that he succeeded. However, the treatise began circulating almost at once in manuscript. Chamberlain noted on 20 August that Ralegh "hath made a long apologie for himself," and the twenty-eight extant copies of the work testify to its widespread popularity.[25]

Verses for Queen Anne, Poems 21, 22, 23, 24. From his house in London Ralegh tried to escape to France on the night of 9 August; he was apprehended and sent once more to the Tower. It was soon rumored that he would be executed by recourse to the conviction of 1603.[26] Ralegh had some two and a half months in which to stave off further punishment, but it was not until 24 September that he addressed a letter to the king, a succinct rehearsal of the arguments in his favor that he had developed more fully in the "Apology." He emphasized, however, that he had returned to England despite the warnings of his companions in order to fulfill his pledge to the king and in full confidence of "your Majesties goodnes."[27]

At about the same time Ralegh may also have written an appeal in verse to Queen Anne, although Professor Lefranc assigns all three states of this poem to the weeks between Ralegh's conviction on 17 November and his reprieve on 9 December 1603.[28] However, the collection of papers in which the unique copy of Poem 21 occurs includes unusual documents connected with Ralegh that date from 1603 through 1618; thus the single leaf of verse among them could belong to any of those years. It is alternatively possible that Ralegh began a draft of the appeal in 1603 but completed it for submis-

sion to the queen only when prompted by the crisis of 1618. In any event
Lefranc's discovery of the unique manuscript of Poem 21, transcribed below,
brings to light another intermediary draft of the "Petition" that sheds new
light upon the "Cynthia" series as well as on Ralegh's creative practices.[29]

1.   My daye's delight, my Spring tyme Joyes Foredon,
        Which in the dawne and rising Sunn of youth
        Had theare creation and weare First begunn,

2.   Doe in the Evninge and the winter sadd
        Present my minde, which takes my tyme's accompt   [5
        The greves remayninge of the Joy it had.

3.   My tender Staulkes nowe clad with rugged ryndes,
        Whose former Fruite was of such mixture made
        As with the Harmefull blast and Easterne winde,

4.   In creapt the eating worme, and in the hart   [10
        And kirnell taketh liffe and Nurrishment,
        Till it had all devowrd the better part,

5.   Which when my wants presented to my tast,
        Then hopefull of the good myne owne hands planted,
        Of all my toyle, I found False Fruite at last,   [15

6.   Love all eaten owt, but in owtward showe,
        My Elder Fortune Cutt by newe mishapp,
        The False internall, then I only knewe;

7.   For as no Fortune stands, so no man's love
        Stayes by the wretched and disconsolate,   [20
        All old affections From newe Sorrowes move,

8.   Mosse by unburied bones, Ivy by walles,
        Whome liffe and People have abandond,
        Till th'one be rotten, stayes, till th'other Falls.

9.   Butt Frindshipps, Kindred, and love's memorie   [25
        Dye, coole, Extinguishe, hering or beholdinge
        The voice of woe, or Face of misorye,

10.   For Frends in all are like those winter showers
        Which come uncalde, but then Forbeare to Fall

When Harmefull heate hath burnt both
Leaves and Flowers; [30

11. Then what we sometyme weare, theie knowe no more,
Whenas those Stormes of Powerfull destanie
Have once defaste the Forme we had before.

12. For if theare did in Cynders but remayne
The smalest heate of Love's long lasting Fyers [35
I could not call forr right, and call in vayne;

13. Or had truth Power, the Guiltlesse could not fall,
Mallice wynn glory, or revenge tryumphe.
But truth alone cannott incownter all—

14. All love, and all desert of Former tymes, [40
Mallice hath covered from my Sufferaigne's Ies,
And lardgly layd abroade Suspected Crymes,

15. Burying the Former with theare memorye,
Teaching offence to Speake before it goe,
Disguising private hate with Publique dewty. [45

16. Cold walles, to you I sighe, but you are sencelesse,
Yett sencefull all alike, as are those frends,
Frends only of my Sometyme happinesse.

17. To whome then shall I crye, to whome shall wrong
Cast downe her teares, or hold upp Folded hands? [50
To her to whome compassion doth belonge,

18. To her whoe ys the First and maye alone
Be caled Empresse of the *Brittayns*;
Whoe should have mercie If a *Queene* have none?

19. Whoe can resist Strong hate, Fearce Injurye? [55
Or whoe releve th'oppressed State of truth?
Whoe is companion elce, to powerfull Majestie?

20. Butt you greate, Goodliest, Gracefull Princesse,
Whoe hath browght glorie, and posteritie
Unto a widdowe land and People hopelesse, [60

21.   Parfayt our comforts by protecting those
        Whome hate, and no selfguile hath runied;
        All in the Feild are yours, whatever growes,

22.   Aswell the humble bryar under shade
        As are the talest Cedars which obscure them;   [65
        Love, Nature, right, have you theare princesse made;

23.   Save then your owne, whose liffe in your defence
        I scornde to keepe, and could have Joyed to loose;
        For love, distruction is no recompence.

24.   If I have sold my dewty, sold my Fayth   [70
        To Strangers, which was only dewe to one,
        Nothing I should esteme so deere as death;

25.   Butt if both God and tyme shall make you knowe
        That I, your humble vassall, am opprest,
        Then cast your Iyes on undeserved woe,   [75

26.   That I and myne maye never morne the misse
        Of her we had, butt prayse our living *Queene*,
        Whoe brings us equall, If not greater blisse.

Lefranc's reading of the textual evidence in light of the competing historical contexts is quite plausible, but it cannot wholly override the contemporary evidence of William Drummond's title to the unique draft of Poem 23, "S. W. Raghlies Petition to the Queene 1618." Lefranc suggests that Drummond acquired a copy of the poem from Ben Jonson, who visited him in January 1619, but that the Scottish poet was misinformed or misunderstood his guest as to the date and purpose of the work. Jonson, however, had been the Ralegh family's confidant since at least 1611 and was well-qualified to supply his host with a correct account of the circumstances behind the poem's composition.

A final point of external evidence concerns Queen Anne's failure, so far as is known, to intervene on Ralegh's behalf in 1603. Ralegh still might have appealed to her for mercy then, perhaps with the encouragement of Sir George Carew, who had recently become an officer in her household.[30] After 1603, however, Anne became convinced of Ralegh's innocence. In her effort to save him in 1618 she is said to have written "very earnestly to the King," and she wrote as well to Villiers, now earl of Buckingham, asking him to move James "that sir Valter Raleigh's life may not be called in question."[31]

The strongest evidence for the earlier dating of the poem is, in the final analysis, the content of the three texts, to which Poem 21 adds nothing of substance to the testimony of Poems 22 and 23. Ralegh's denial, for example, that he had "sold my duetye, sold my faithe, / To strangers" (23.28–29, 21.70–71), could refer to Cobham's charge in 1603 that Ralegh was seeking a Spanish pension. On the other hand, he was likewise accused in 1618 of possessing a commission from the king of France whom he planned to serve, and this charge was connected with his alleged offer of £10,000 to Stukely to escape with him to France.[32] Whether or not the French offered to pay Ralegh to defect, he was sharply questioned about an interview with the French ambassador before his attempted escape.[33] The ambassador was placed in custody by order of the Privy Council on 9 September, and Anglo-French diplomatic relations were suspended for some eight months after Ralegh's execution.

More telling as evidence for the 1603 dating is the treatment of Queen Anne's accession as a recent event that "hath browght glorie and posteritie / Unto a widdowe land and People hopeless" (21.59–60). Ralegh even proposes that if Anne can save him, "I and myne may never morne the misse / Of her we had, butt prayse our living *Queene*" (21.77–78). Still, "glorie and posteritie" were Anne's foremost achievements in 1618 as in 1603, while Elizabeth's death and the events of her reign were understandably current in Ralegh's mind to the end of his life. He repeatedly invoked her memory in his Jacobean writings, and on the night of his arrest he identified a ring he was wearing as a gift from Elizabeth. Similarly, he took pains at his own execution to deny that he had rejoiced at the earl of Essex's beheading, now some seventeen years past. The Raleghs found good cause to remember and mourn Elizabeth's reign throughout the reign of her successor.

Poem 23 omits the stanza found in both of the earlier drafts of the poem that describes England as a "widdowe land and People hopelesse." This suggests an alternate explanation of the circumstances that connect all three texts. The earlier versions, Poems 21 and 22, may represent Ralegh's adaptations of Poem 15 to the crisis of 1603. He failed to complete the petition during those few weeks when he was also occupied with writing a number of letters as well as the "Instructions to his Son." Instead of sending a verse appeal to the queen at that time he saved his revision along with copies of his other poems. Working from these papers in 1618, he adapted his work in Poems 21 and 22 to the new crisis and, shortly afterward, adapted Poem 25 from the concluding stanza of "Nature that washt her hands."

The similarities between the imprisonments of 1603 and 1618 minimize the importance of knowing which occasion elicited the three poems in question. Lefranc's discovery is of much greater interest for revealing how Ralegh worked from Poem 15, a complaint designed to appease Elizabeth, through Poems 21 and 22, to Poem 23, an appeal to Queen Anne to save his life. The dominant trends in this creative process reduced the "Petition" from a "book" of the Ocean to Cynthia to a concise but still compelling plea for rescue. Ralegh eliminated the pastoral metaphors and imagery that were probably left over from the original state of Poem 15, and he replaced the complaint of his desertion by friends and kindred with the lament for his vulnerability to fortune, malice, and envy. Ten of the final version's twelve stanzas survive relatively intact from Poem 21, with only one new stanza introduced in Poem 22 plus a second stanza unique to Poem 23. The survival of stanzas 23–26 in both Poems 21 and 23 indicates that Poem 22 originally included these lines and is incomplete in the unique manuscript copy, BL Additional MS. 27407. Poem 24, which is also termed Ralegh's address to Queen Anne in the face of disaster, may have belonged to this same petition; if so, the pastoralism of its "broken pipes" hung on the willow tree was likewise dropped in favor of a more straightforward approach.

Ralegh begins Poem 23, which can stand as a final version of the petition, with stanza 9 of Poem 22 (Poem 21, stanza 13), by changing "Or" to "O": "O had Truth Power the guiltlesse could not fall." Stanzas 1–6 pose the problem by portraying Ralegh as the victim of abstract personifications, abandoned by friends and mercy and afflicted by fortune and malice. He transforms the personification in Poem 22 of "wronge" casting down her tears into an immediate, first-person question, "Then unto whom shall I unfold my wrong / Cast downe my teares or hold up foulded hands?" (22.19–20). This rhetorical question marks the turn in the poem's rhetorical structure; the answer of course is the queen, who is still termed "empresse of the Brittaines." She is here praised not for her bounty to the nation at large as in Poems 21 and 22, but for her ability to preserve Ralegh and his family.

The four concluding stanzas of direct appeal for his life begin, "Save him whose thoughts no treason ever tainted" (line 26). In the penultimate stanza Ralegh evokes the Renaissance commonplace that truth is the daughter of God and time by returning to the idea that "both God and tyme" will reveal his innocence to the queen. In the last stanza Ralegh encourages Anne to rescue him so that "I and mine" may "praise our living Queene" to whom we owe "equall, if not greater, Blisse" than we received from "her wee had." Ralegh thus challenges Anne to vie with Elizabeth in favoring him and his family. The poem resembles a verse letter more than the emotional outpouring of the "Cynthia" stanzas from which it was derived. Its direct appeal was no doubt more appropriate to Ralegh's relationship with Anne, who did intervene on his behalf despite her own failing health at the time. She did her best to emulate Elizabeth, but unfortunately for Ralegh she lacked that queen's sovereign power. He was brought to the King's Bench at Westminster on 28 October, consigned to death upon the treason verdict of 1603, and beheaded on the following morning.

Last Words

The cedar chest containing the "Art of Warre by Sea" and other personal manuscripts was not delivered to the Tower as Ralegh requested but seized by the government. After Ralegh's death Bess complained that she owned "noe other wrytyngs" bye her husband.[34] The only writing of his own that he must have had with him in the Tower and in the Gatehouse that last night was a collection of poetry. From this source he had adapted the petition to Queen Anne, and from the last stanza of "Nature that washt her hands" he devised his verse epitaph, Poem 25.

Ralegh transformed the despairing finality of this stanza by adding the simple couplet, "And from which earth and grave and Dust / The Lord shall raise me up I trust." A strong tradition among the manuscript titles to this poem states that Ralegh inscribed the stanza in his Bible the night before he died. The sentiment of the added verses is in complete harmony with his conversation that night as reported by Dr. Robert Townson, dean of Westminster, who was appointed to prepare Ralegh for death. Townson found his charge "the most fearlesse of death that ever was knowen."[35] The dean warned Ralegh that his contempt for death was inappropriate, and the prisoner was at pains to reassure him that his confidence sprang from his faith in God's mercy and salvation through Christ.

At his arraignment the day before Ralegh had been interrupted while speaking in his own defense. After sentence had been pronounced he asked that "I may be heard at the day of my death," and he begged for a few days' reprieve in order "to communicate with His Majesty by writing for his behoof and service."[36] When the latter request was denied, Ralegh applied his pen to the task of vindicating himself from the most recent slurs on his reputation. His main purpose, as he imparted to Townson, was "to perswade the world, that he dyed an innocent man," whereat the dean warned him that to do so would create "an oblique taxing of the justice of the realme upon him."[37] Ralegh was indeed a master of oblique criticism of all kinds, yet his last words, written and spoken, are short on satiric sting, and what little there is Ralegh directs toward minor targets.

Fearing that he might not be allowed to speak from the scaffold, Ralegh composed "a remembrance" that he "left with his Lady, written likewise that night, to acquaint the world withall, yf perhaps he should not have ben suffered to speake at his death." This may be the same document allegedly "found in Sir Walter Raleighes pockett after his Execution Written by him in the Gatehouse *the* night" before he died.[38] The speech is a testament of Christian faith of the kind that Townson described. It acknowledges his sovereign's "princely favour" in postponing the death sentence until he was prepared for it through repentance. It lists as well the reasons why neither death nor judgment are to be feared: "my sins do not affright me because I haue Christ Jesus for my Redemer / the Judg doth not astonish me because the Chiefe Judges sonne is my advocate." These few paragraphs comprise a graceful confession of Christian faith that was noticeably lacking from Ralegh's speech the following morning.

Ralegh was given full license to speak from the scaffold, for more than half an hour apparently, despite the weakness of his voice caused by lingering illness.[39] His remarks are preserved in over eighty manuscript accounts. He spoke from notes that he had drawn up for the occasion, their contents focused almost exclusively upon personal vindication. Two of the immediate charges against him he singled out as the most important. He confessed that he tried to escape to France but denied that he had pledged himself to serve the French king. Next he denied that he had slandered King James or that he had ever entertained "in all my Life, a thought of ill of his Majesty."[40] He denied a list of accusations made against him by Stukely and defended his conduct of the Guiana voyage not with regard to its plan or execution, as in the "Apology," but by emphasizing that he kept his word to return to England despite a mutiny among his men who tried to keep him from doing so. Finally, he denied that he had influenced the fall of Essex or rejoiced at his death. Here Ralegh was responding to a charge leveled the night before by Townson, who was present with him on the scaffold.

Ralegh's good cheer and dignified words won the admiration of the large crowd that had gathered to witness the execution. In retrospect, however, there is something disproportionate about the speech. Its contents seem too immediate and in places too trifling, poised against the ideals and accomplishments of the life now drawing to a close. Ralegh did not remind his audience of the threat from Spain or the international Catholic conspiracy against Protestant Europe. There is no mention of the need for English colonization, in Guiana or elsewhere. Instead, Ralegh used his last speech to justify his own actions and to refute even minor accusations, such as Stukely's claim that he took £1,600 in gold with him to Guiana.

If Ralegh consciously attempted "self-fashioning" after his return to England, his goal was a limited, personal one judging from what he wrote during those last few months. Most of his letters were designed, like the "Apology," to defend his conduct of the Guiana voyage. A few plead for his life outright, as does his verse petition to Queen Anne. He was entirely absorbed in warding off the immediate danger, and to this task he applied the eloquence and argumentative skill that he had developed over the years in writing to influence Prince Henry and satirize the government. Now he found no leisure for advocating national policies or attacking his enemies, aside from Stukely. The stanza he added to "Even such is time" and the prose testament of faith, if it is his, attest to the equally personal matter of his spiritual state just before the execution.

In the end, Ralegh's constricted vision worked with singular economy to promote his larger interests. He defended his own integrity so successfully from the scaffold that his death was transformed by popular opinion into a needless sacrifice to the king's vanity and weakness. Ralegh's posthumous reputation lent an interest and authority to his works (and to works supposedly his) that gave James and his son Charles good cause to regret the injustice of his execution.

Chapter Seven
Conclusion
Ralegh's Reputation

The story of Ralegh's posthumous literary reputation and influence is matter for a book-length study of its own. On the one hand, seventeenth-century printed editions of his authentic writings, particularly the *History, Instructions to his Son*, and the *Prerogative*, were widely read, as were the "Apology," "War with Spain," "Cause of War," and other treatises which circulated only in manuscript. Even during Ralegh's lifetime, however, a canon of bogus works had begun to accumulate under his name, and this process rapidly accelerated after his death. Within a few decades dozens of poems and some half-dozen prose works were widely disseminated as written by Sir Walter Ralegh. The influence and repute of these real and mythical Raleghs is illustrated by John Milton's response to them. Milton was familiar with Ralegh's dream of Guiana and had no doubt read the *Discovery*. In book 11 of *Paradise Lost* he refers to "*Guiana*, whose great City *Geryon's* Sons / Call *El Dorado*" (lines 410–11). For details in book 1 about the earthly Paradise, such as the fig leaves with which Adam and Eve clothed themselves, he drew upon Ralegh's conclusions in the *History*.[1] Meanwhile, in 1658 he took it upon himself to publish the spurious *Cabinet-Council* from a manuscript "many years in my hands," alleging that it was his duty to offer the public "the work of so eminent an Author."

Ralegh's place in the literature of his own time is a more manageable topic, though no systematic search for references to him has yet been attempted, nor does what follows pretend to be exhaustive. Ralegh's prominence as a courtier and public official elicited numerous informal poems that circulated almost exclusively in manuscript. Some of them responded to his own verses, while others attacked him for a variety of reasons. Heneage and the queen wrote answering verses to specific poems by Ralegh, while his friend, Henry Noel, probably wrote the earliest poem about him, "The foe to the stommacke, and the word of disgrace / Shewes the gentlemans name with the bold face." About 1590 the earl of Essex attacked Ralegh in verses that are linked with Poem 10, Ralegh's second commendatory poem for the

Faerie Queene. It is just possible too that Essex is responsible for one or two of the four poetic responses to "The Lie"; the controversy over this work even led to one poem that defended Ralegh.[2] The most extensive outpouring of satiric attacks on Ralegh, however, resulted from Essex's disgrace and execution. In his *Ralegh*, Appendix N, Lefranc analyzes some fifteen attacks on Ralegh written and circulated between about 1599 and 1604. Six of these are verses about or attributed to their victim in which Lefranc identifies four principal accusations: Ralegh is charged with atheism, Machiavellian policy, contributing to Essex's downfall, and nurturing personal and public vices. These charges were supplemented in a number of Elizabethan and Jacobean works of a more literary nature, and in a variety of genres.

Sir John Harington, who was at first on good terms with Ralegh, gravitated during the 1590s toward the Essex circle. Harington also became Ralegh's most prolific satirist. In fifteen of his epigrams, as in one by Sir John Davies, Ralegh is attacked under the pseudonym, Paulus.[3] Paulus is characterized as a wealthy man who is ever greedy for more. He is the victim of an imprudent marriage, and his scoffing, flippant attitude betrays a grave insensitivity to the feelings of others. Davies attributes much of Paulus's wealth to his "lawfull mart," and Harington too refers to his "writ of Mart," the letters of mart or marque issued to Ralegh in December 1594.[4] Both satirists also accuse Ralegh of stealing, with Davies clinching his case against Paulus by connecting his thefts with his unfortunate marriage: "But on the lande a little gulfe there is, / Wherein he drowneth all that wealth of his."

Harington also pokes fun at Ralegh's efforts to keep the marriage a secret by noting "that Pawlus hath a wife, / Yet was he never maried all his life" (Epigram 410). He accuses him as well of atheism and of heresies (Epigrams 110, 122, 329), of greed in his promotion of tobacco as a panacea (Epigram 134), and of a sexual encounter with "Galla," a proud, loose woman who figures in another half-dozen of Harington's epigrams.[5] The most interesting charges, however, concern Ralegh's bearing and the impression he made upon others. Harington dwells on Paulus's pride (Epigrams 22, 126) and his irreverent, sarcastic attitude: "his scoffing fashion" (Epigram 61), his tendency "to speake in mocke" (Epigram 56), and, in direct address to Ralegh, "You that will lose a friend, to coine a iest [jest]" (Epigram 79). Ralegh's pride was singled out as his particular fault almost from his first appearance at court. Harington's satire reveals that irony and biting sarcasm characterized Ralegh's speech as well as his prose style.

The failure of Ralegh's Guiana venture to yield immediate riches, coupled with his extravagant public claims for the region, laid the entire project open to satiric exploitation. In Epigram 61 Harington quips that Paulus undertakes voyages with "hellish paines, yet doth not finde / That blisse, in which he frames his wise felicitie." This is general and mild criticism compared with Joseph Hall's portrayal of Fortunio, who may or may not be Ralegh. Fortunio is, at any rate, one who "his farme hath sold, / And gads to Guiane land to fish for gold." Failing that, he turns to piracy on the return voyage but seizes nothing more valuable than a Polish pinnace.[6] Hall takes explicit aim at Ralegh and the *Discovery* in Satire 6 when he derides a gullible "brainsicke youth" who believes all far-fetched travelers' tales of "the Indian deepe," of "massy heapes of golden mines," and "Of head-lesse men; of sauage Cannibals" (lines 63–64, 70). These headless men were well known in Europe long before Ralegh published his account of them. But his prominence and the popularity of his book reinforced the currency of such tales and helped transform them into the Elizabethan equivalent of the "fish story."[7] Shakespeare may have had Ralegh's work specifically in mind when he made Othello speak of "The Anthropophagi, and men whose heads / Do grow beneath their shoulders." And in *The Tempest* Gonzalo refers to "men / Whose heads stood in their breasts."[8]

Henry Peacham likewise poked fun at Ralegh's claims for Guiana in Epigram 4 of *The More the Merrier* (1608), which concerns "Vainglorious Otho, Court and Artists scorne." The epithet recalls a satiric reply to Poem 16, "The Lie," beginning "Courte's skorne, state's disgracinge," in which Ralegh was referred to as "Artes' injury."[9] Otho is an unusual name, but connected with Ralegh through his mother's first husband, Otho Gilbert, and through Ralegh's half brother Sir Humphrey Gilbert, who named a son Otho. Peacham writes of Otho's "last voiage sauing one," which dates the epigram's composition to the months between the Cadiz and "Islands" voyages in 1596–97. He accuses Ralegh of finding fame's trumpet with which, "of his trauels he hath told more lies, / Then *Mandeuile* could for his heart deuise."

The fad for verse satire and epigram during the last decade of Elizabeth's reign sent scores of writers searching for likely targets. Ralegh's defamation in these works is thus to some extent predictable; these satires tend to exaggerate the truth, nor do they always reflect the satirists' innermost convictions. In his epigrams Harington accused Ralegh of unorthodox religious views, yet at the time of his arrest for treason in 1603 Sir John wrote the Bishop of Bath and Wells to deny that Ralegh "hathe evyll desygn in pointe of faithe or relygion. As he hathe ofte discoursede to me wyth moch lernynge, wysdom, and freedome, I knowe he dothe somewhat dyffer in opynyon from some others; but I thynke alsoe his hearte is welle fixed in everye honeste thynge . . . In relygion, he hathe showne (in pryvate talke) great depthe and goode readynge . . . In good trothe, I pitie his state."[10] Ralegh's carefully reasoned and stoutly upheld religious beliefs were well adapted to Harington's satiric purposes, yet he readily conceded the hyperbole in his attacks when Ralegh's life was called in question.

Although Shakespeare winked at anthropophagi and headless men, Ralegh figures less prominently in the drama of his age than was formerly supposed. The theory that Shakespeare modeled Armado upon Ralegh in *Love's Labours' Lost* has been largely repudiated, and with it the notion that a "School of Night" centered around Ralegh and his friends was an object of satiric attack in that play.[11] Efforts to identify Ralegh as the source for Iago, or the inspiration behind Marlowe's Tamburlaine, are similarly unpromising.[12] It is far more likely that the subversive Proditur in Thomas Middleton's *The Phoenix* represents Ralegh,[13] but this may be his most definite negative portrayal in contemporary drama. In *The White Devil* John Webster derides the injustice of King James's seizure of Sherborne by comparing whores to "those brittle evidences of law / Which forfeit all a wretched man's estate / For leaving out one syllable." In his *Fair Maid of the West* Thomas Heywood paid tribute to Ralegh's successful landing in the Azores in 1597 through a Spanish prisoner who says of Fayal, "Since English Raleigh won and spoiled it first, / The town's re-edified, and fort new built."[14]

Ralegh's literary defenders were in fact more numerous and distinguished than his detractors. George Chapman prefixed a verse encomium of the Guiana project to Lawrence Keymis's *A Relation of the Second Voyage to Guiana* (1596). In the "Certaine Satyres" appended to his *Metamorphosis of Pigmalions Image* (1598) John Marston attacked Hall for criticizing the "gallant spirit" who dared to "saile vnto the rich *Guiana*" for his country's benefit.[15] John Donne's epigram on "Cales and Guyana" makes a witty but not necessarily derisive observation about using the spoils of the Cales (Cadiz) raid to finance the Guiana venture. At about the same time his verse letter "To Mr R. W." laments that

> Guyanaes harvest is nip'd in the spring,
> I feare . . .
> ....
> Oh, slownes is our punishment and sinne.
> Perchance, these Spanish businesse being done,
> Which as the Earth betweene the Moone and Sun
> Eclipse the light which Guyana would give,
> Our discontinu'd hopes we shall retrive.[16]

At court Queen Elizabeth heard herself described as "the Lady Oriana . . ./ dight all in the treasures of Guiana," in John Wilbye's madrigal for the *Triumphs of Oriana* (1601).[17] Ralegh's dream sparked a good deal of enthusiasm in some quarters, to offset the satiric derision in others.

Spenser's support of Ralegh's projects and the representation of his patron in the *Faerie Queene* have been widely studied and need only brief summation here. In book 3, canto 5, Spenser not only celebrated Ralegh's exploits in the Irish wars and his devotion to the queen, but he also endorsed Ralegh's claims for tobacco by naming it among the herbs used by Belphoebe/ Elizabeth to cure the wound of Timias/Ralegh. Spenser is equally solicitous of Ralegh's enterprise and reputation in book 4. In canto 11 he chides his countrymen for their failure to exploit Guiana: "And shame on you, O men, which boast your strong / And valiant hearts, . . . /Yet quaile in conquest of that land of gold." In the allegory of book 4 he treats Ralegh's loss of favor in the Timias-Amoret-Belphoebe action of cantos 7–8, and even resolves their conflict with a reconciliation between Belphoebe and Timias that anticipates as it encourages the reconciliation between Elizabeth and Ralegh in 1597.[18]

In book 6 Spenser portrays Timias as a victim of slander who is attacked by three related manifestations of this vice in the brothers Despetto, Decetto, and Defetto. In contrast with his triumph over the three brothers who ambushed him in book 3, Timias is hard pressed by these assailants and must be rescued from them by Prince Arthur. Thus Spenser's allegory parallels Ralegh's misfortunes and vulnerability during the mid-nineties, suggesting that his decline has resulted from slanderous reports that he could not cope with successfully.

In this same episode Timias meets and accompanies another victim of slander, Sir Calepine's lady, Serena. In canto 6 a hermit explains to Serena and Timias that they can avoid the wounds of slander by avoiding occasions that breed malicious gossip such as secret meetings and the indulgence of their desires and "loose delight" (14.6). It would be interesting to know if this is Spenser's version of the same illicit liaison that Harington treated in the epigram concerning Paulus and Galla. Ralegh's only known extramarital affair, however, involved one "Alice Goold," who bore him an illegitimate daughter, apparently at the time of his military service in Ireland during 1580–81.[19]

Generally speaking, Ralegh was more favorably dealt with by the writers of his age than otherwise. Most of the criticism occurs in epigrams and satiric verse that exploited minor or even imaginary weaknesses in their victims. In a rather less literary vein are the verse slanders that circulated only in manuscript, most of them connected with the Ralegh-Essex rivalry. Among

Ralegh's defenders, Marston, Chapman, Heywood, and Donne are authors he is not known to have patronized; Donne was, in fact, a follower of Essex, and while he may have served aboard Ralegh's ship in either the Cadiz or "Islands" voyages, the suggestion is entirely speculative.

Ralegh's Contribution to English Literature

Poetry. Ralegh's verse offers a cross-section study of the broader evolution of Elizabethan poetry from mid-century plain style to the technically graceful, personally expressive, and witty modes perfected by Shakespeare, Jonson, and Donne. It is faint praise to claim that Ralegh's "drab" poetics, as represented by "Sweet ar the thoughts," "Callinge to minde," and "Farewell falce Love," are as pleasing in their kind as any the age produced. In these early poems he is at his most derivative in style and conceptual imagination. He was far more original, however, in adapting such standard poetic fare to his life as a courtier, and he was among the first to address love poetry to the queen in an effort to gain, or regain, her favor.

Ralegh's finest poetic achievement occurred as he moved from the style of these early poems to the emotional phrasing that began to infiltrate his verse by the late 1580s. "Farewell falce Love," for example, is a mechanical renunciation of love in which the emotion that elicited the poem is almost entirely stifled by the self-conscious rhetoric. Ralegh's main concern was to devise as many derogatory, alliterative analogies as possible. As a means of courtly display, the poem's interest focuses on this array of correctly phrased comparisons, not on the poet's thoughts or feelings. A few years later, however, Ralegh addressed "Fortune" to the queen. Its plaintive tone and expression of a sincere, personal loss create a totally different effect from Poem 4. The fact that the sentiments in this lyric are exaggerated is beside the point. The abruptly shifting passions of the Cynthia poems are even more hyperbolic. What counts is Ralegh's creation of a poetic voice that conveys emotion in a convincing manner. This was the special poetic pleasure that Sidney advocated in the *Defence*, yet in only a few of the songs and sonnets from *Astrophil and Stella* does Sidney surpass Ralegh in the intensity of his expression.

Ralegh's later canonical verse retains the well-modulated tones of his own voice. It is derisive and assertive in "The prayse of meaner wits," cynical in "The Lie," fearfully insistent in the petition to Queen Anne (Poem 23). In addition, his characteristic love of irony and sarcasm placed him among the first to experiment with the witty, irreverent style that was being brought to a high level of polish in the late 1590s, preeminently by John Donne. Ralegh created none of the far-fetched comparisons typical of the metaphysical style nor the grotesque exaggerations often termed "mannerist." Yet "Nature" and "What is our life" point out unmistakably the new directions English verse was taking at the close of the century. As with many of Donne's "Songs and Sonnets," Poem 17 begins with a Petrarchan, essentially medieval subject, in this case the origin of the lady's incomparable beauty and its vulnerability to time. But Ralegh defeats, then reverses the traditional expectations, bringing the poem to its depressing conclusion that time will obliterate even our memories from the face of the earth. Not only is the meaning and impact of this work wholly at odds with the lyric tradition on which it builds, but its progressive development of ideas creates a movement quite unlike the predictable, linear growth of "Farewell falce Love," or even the more imaginative but still conventional turns of "Callinge to minde."

A similar reversal, couched in an equally sombre tone, prevents "What is our life" from becoming merely a trite Petrarchan conceit on the similarity of man's life to a play. The convention is upended by Ralegh's assertion in the last line that the play does not end with the grave, which is only another interlude before the Last Judgment. The grim finality of both poems contrasts with the lighter tone of bemused sarcasm that characterizes most of Donne's lyrics and those of his school. Peter Ure notes that Ralegh injects an almost tragic seriousness, oddly enough, into his first commendatory sonnet for the *Faerie Queene* (Poem 9); Ure sees in this not a fin-de-siècle malaise but Ralegh's preservation of "the sententious mournfulness of the 1570s."[20] The reversals that elicit this tone in Poems 17 and 18, however, owe little or nothing to the moralizing of mid-century gnomic verse. Ralegh imparted a grim, even pessimistic aura to such earlier poems as "Fortune" and "Like truthless dreams," without deflating a conventional pose. It is the reversal of traditional expectations that gives many metaphysical lyrics their distinctive wittiness. Yet the elements that make up these lyrics are often in themselves more or less conventional. "Nature," as we have seen, combines the carpe diem and memento mori traditions, but in so extreme a divergence from the norm that it may well be termed a mannerist poem.

Prose.   In contrast with his assimilation of new trends in English verse, Ralegh nurtured an increasingly old-fashioned Ciceronian prose style throughout his career. He continued the older humanist tradition in prose, as did Milton, despite the early seventeenth-century preference for the shorter cadences of the Senecan style.[21] In so doing, Ralegh adhered to whatever formal training in style he had received at Oxford and the Inns of Chancery and Court, where Cicero's periodic structure served as the chief model, especially for dialectic and persuasive oratory. And aside from the "Cadiz" letter, the Guiana "Journal," and dominant narrative portions of

The History of the World, Ralegh's prose works are consistently thesis-oriented and persuasive.

Ralegh's concentration on argumentative prose sets him apart from most of his contemporary writers in a number of ways. Francis Bacon and Sir William Cornwallis, for example, popularized the essay as a late Renaissance English genre, yet most of Ralegh's prose is very different in tone and purpose from their expository, essentially reflective compositions. Although he frequently attacks Jesuits and the Catholic Church, his contexts are almost always secular instead of doctrinal. His concentration on political, economic, and strategic affairs thus differentiates his work from the mass of religious disputation that dominated the argumentative writing of his time. His prose was designed for the most part to influence national policy. It is often laced with satire and bolstered with the results of his own careful research. It foreshadows the great outpouring of prose debate that accompanied the Puritan revolution, such as the "Leveller" tracts in which Ralegh is occasionally quoted.[22]

Collectively, Ralegh's works comprise a body of policy statements that would make a fitting legacy for a privy councillor. They are unequaled by any other writer of the age in polish and in the significance of the issues that they address. This is all the more remarkable when we recall that more than a half-dozen of these works date from the Jacobean imprisonment, when Ralegh held no office nor even a legal identity.

In both domestic and foreign affairs Ralegh's policies generally charted England's proper destiny, especially with regard to overseas expansion and the cooperative rule of Parliament with a limited as opposed to absolute monarchy.[23] On the other hand, his fears that Spain would become invincible by seizing Guiana (*Discovery*) or the Netherlands ("War with Spain") were unrealistic, nor was Guiana in fact a particularly promising site for English colonization. In hindsight Ralegh appears equally paranoid in his fears of an assault on England by a combination of powers, whether led by James of Scotland, as outlined in the "Succession" tract, or the king of Poland, as explained in the "Jesuit" dialogue. Elsewhere, Ralegh's vision was prophetic, if not immediately influential.

The cornerstone of Ralegh's offensive strategy was the founding of a colonial empire to rival Spain's. He shared with other Elizabethans in the formulation of this plan, but he was nevertheless original in advocating that England replace Spain in the New World rather than merely plunder that empire's wealth.[24] An important component of this plan was Ralegh's equally innovative policy of humane dealings with the natives in order to build prosperous colonies and to gain their support as allies in evicting Spain from other New World holdings. He explained these ideas most fully in "Of the Voyage for Guiana," and described their implementation in the *Discovery* and "Journal."

The dynamics of Ralegh's international strategy relied on a strong English navy. He correctly perceived that "whosoever commands the sea commands the trade; whosoever commands the trade of the world commands the riches of the world, and consequently the world itself" ("Invention," 325). It was a principle he had cited as early as the "War by Sea" outline (ca. 1608), and it crops up as well in the "Jesuit" dialogue (sig. E6v, 1611). Ralegh saw that naval power was vital to England not only for defense from the threat of Catholic armadas but as the basic technology for transforming England into a world power through trade and colonization. Both the "Observations" and "Art of Warre by Sea" are devoted to maritime affairs. In addition, his repeated warnings against exporting English ordnance, his stress on the nurturing of "forcible trades" by British merchants, and on insuring access to naval stores from the Baltic appear in works that are otherwise unrelated to overseas expansion.

Ralegh's awareness of the importance of navies to both trade and international politics led to a special regard for the Netherlands in his writings. With Spain and England, the United Provinces had become the third great maritime power in Europe, and Ralegh saw that they thus controlled the balance of power. As early as the "War with Spain" discourse he was insisting that Dutch independence was vital to England's security. In the "Marriage" tract he proposed an Anglo-Dutch alliance, and he praised Dutch naval power and ability in the "Invention." This industrious, Protestant nation was a natural ally of its cross-channel neighbor; had these common interests been cultivated as Ralegh suggested, both countries might have avoided the conflict that erupted between them later in the century.

Ralegh's philosophy of governance developed and found expression primarily in response to James's conduct on the throne. Ralegh believed in the legitimacy of kingship as ordained by God, but he realized as the early Stuarts never did that Englishmen would no longer submit to despotism. His attacks on tyranny in the *History* and *Prerogative* are balanced by positive recommendations of how kings should govern. Above all, Ralegh stressed in the "Seat of Government," in the *Prerogative*, and throughout the *History* the decidedly anti-Machiavellian doctrine that kings flourish when they are loved by their subjects.[25] He had seen Elizabeth rule with little less absolutism than James, yet with far more acceptance and cooperation because she convinced her subjects of her devotion to them. His thinking on these matters was apparently rooted in his larger philosophical commitment to humane and merciful dealings with others, which derived in turn from his basic Christian beliefs. This commitment explains, for example, his condemnation of Alexander the Great, who was one of the "Nine Worthies" and among the most widely admired figures of antiquity. But Ralegh repeatedly charged him with cruelty, just as he condemned the Carthagenians, Philip of Macedon, and Henry VIII for the same vice. On the other hand he described the Theban commander Epaminondas as "the worthiest man that ever was bred in that nation of Greece" (3:12; *Works* 5: 273). Ralegh praised his justice, sincerity, temperance, and wisdom, but above all the fact that he loved his people. Accordingly, Ralegh's theoretical and practical commitment to fair dealings with native populations was a logical corollary of his humane philosophy of rule.

His prose works frequently endorse, as they collectively illustrate, his faith in the power of reason to arrive at the truth. In the *History*, "Instructions," and the "Seat of Government" he recommended adherence to reason and the independent analysis of evidence. For Ralegh, of course, the pursuit of this ideal took on a strongly pragmatic and empirical bent as shown by his chemical experiments, his concern about accurate maps, and with accurate chronology as a prerequisite to discovering historical truth. A unique quality of most of his prose is this practical, reasoned approach to the significant issues of his age.

Ralegh's pragmatic orientation helps account for the intent and distribution of most of his works in prose and verse. He undoubtedly nurtured a genuine appreciation of poetry, yet he applied most of his own poetry to utilitarian purposes: commending books by his friends, praising, cajoling, and seeking reconciliation with Queen Elizabeth, or begging Queen Anne to save his life. The fact that his most ambitious poetry (and the bulk of it from the standpoint of sheer quantity) was composed when he was out of favor brings out a related pattern in his career as a writer. Ralegh used his pen when other means of action were denied to him. Not only is most of his verse connected with crises in his life; he wrote most of his prose as an outsider as well.

The concentration of power in the sovereign throughout Ralegh's lifetime made the kinds of carefully argued tracts that he produced largely superfluous for privy councillors and other courtiers who enjoyed direct access to the monarch. This explains why Ralegh's only prose work before his Elizabethan disgrace was the *Revenge* pamphlet, which was elicited by his personal involvement with the expedition and his loyalty to Sir Richard Grenville. Until 1592 he was able to influence the queen in person. In the decade following, however, he composed at least eight works in prose on national and international affairs, including the original state of the "Observations" and the lost

"War in the West Indies" tract. The volume of his argumentative writing is to a significant extent a function of his distance from the center of power.

Similarly, during the years of confinement in the Tower he was not only cut off from court and sovereign but unable to act on his own, as he had done in 1595 by sailing to Guiana. He was reduced to serving his country only through his writings, but in addition to this patriotic impulse he hoped as well to secure his release from prison. In such works as the revised "Observations," the "Seat of Government," the *History*, "Art of Warre by Sea," and perhaps the marriage tracts, he wrote with the practical aim of winning Prince Henry's favor, as he increasingly despaired of the king's. Ralegh's disillusionment with James, as sovereign and as redeemer of his personal fortunes, led him to criticize the king with growing boldness. In the "Jesuit" and *History* he emphasized examples of incompetent, immoral rule. The *Prerogative* falls just short of a frontal assault on the king. Here, Ralegh was no doubt motivated by a certainty that he knew how James should govern coupled with his impatient resentment of James's refusal to pardon him. In any event, the *Prerogative* is the work of a disaffected outsider.

Ralegh's concentration upon immediate, concrete problems deprived some of his works of universal or lasting interest as imperial Spain and wooden ships passed from the scene. Although we can still admire the argumentative skill displayed in these works, Ralegh's most enduring achievements in prose center upon narrative and satire. Much of the spell cast by the *Discovery*, for example, depends on the narrative of his explorations, and it is no small tribute to his writing ability that this treatise inspired a series of European ventures in the area out of all proportion to its economic potential. The *Revenge* tract is a masterpiece of heroic prose, while the "Cadiz" letter and many narrative passages in the *History*, such as the "long march" from Xenophon and Hannibal's battles in Italy, are told with compelling vigor. The issues underlying the "Jesuit" dialogue are no longer relevant, yet Ralegh deserves credit for the satiric dimension he imparted to this conversation, including its shifting levels of irony, innuendo, and diatribe. In the *Prerogative* he primarily exploited another satiric device, incrimination by analogy, of the kind he had so often leveled at James within the *History*. Again, his precarious footing as royal prisoner and convicted traitor forced Ralegh to disguise his criticism of the Stuart regime through a variety of literary devices.

Overall, Ralegh earns his place in English letters by virtue of the cumulative weight of his writings as well as their quality. In prose, he is an able historian, propagandist, promoter, strategist, and satirist. As an accomplished lyric poet he turned out amorous complaints, philosophical reflections, sharp satire, and elegies for Sidney and for himself. He is a poet of the second magnitude during one of the most brilliant ages of English lyric verse. His American and Irish plantations failed, as did his efforts to acquire Guiana for England, to gain a seat on the Privy Council, and to win credit and favor with King James. In striving toward these goals, meeting failure, and responding to ostracism, Ralegh produced the works in verse and prose that assure him a more lasting reputation than he likely could have gained from success in these worldly ventures.

Notes and References

Chapter One

1. Sir John Pope Hennessy, *Sir Walter Raleigh in Ireland* (London: Kegan, Paul, Trench, 1883), 31.
2. Anthony à Wood, *Athenae Oxonienses,* ed. Philip Bliss (1815; reprint, New York: Burt Franklin, 1967), 2: col. 235.
3. Pierre Lefranc, "Un Inédit de Ralegh sur la Conduite de la Guerre," *Études Anglaises* 8 (1955):195–96 (Short Title Catalogue 15316, [1587], sig. #2).
4. Cecil S. Emden, *Oriel Papers* (Oxford: Clarendon Press, 1948), 14; Louis A. Knafla, "The Matriculation Revolution and Education at the Inns of Court in Renaissance England," in *Tudor Men and Institutions,* ed. Arthur J. Slavin (Baton Rouge: Louisiana State University Press, 1972), 243.
5. See my "'Companion Poems' in the Ralegh Canon," *English Literary Renaissance* 13 (1983):262–65.
6. Edward Edwards, *Life of Sir Walter Ralegh* (London: Macmillan, 1868), 2:22; D. C. Peck, "Raleigh, Sidney, Oxford, and the Catholics, 1579," *Notes and Queries* 223 (1978):427–30.
7. Edwards, *Life,* 2:17, 25 August 1581; Pierre Lefranc, *Sir Walter Ralegh Écrivain* (Paris: Librairie Armand Colin, 1968), 28–29.
8. *Illustrations of British History, Biography, and Manners,* ed. Edmund Lodge, 2d ed. (1838; reprint, Westmead: Gregg International, 1969), 2:186; A. M. C. Latham, "A Birth Date for Sir Walter Ralegh," *Études Anglaises* 9 (1956): 245. The Spanish ambassador reported that an Irish captain, perhaps Ralegh, "came to the Queen" on 3 December to announce the victory at Smerwick (*Calendar of Letters and State Papers Relating to English Affairs Preserved Principally in the Archives of Simancas* [London, 1892–99], 3:69).
9. Latham, "A Birth Date," 245.
10. The parallels are analyzed in James P. Bednarz, "Ralegh in Spenser's Historical Allegory," *Spenser Studies* 4 (1984):52–57.
11. Sir Robert Naunton, *Fragmenta Regalia or Observations of Queen Elizabeth, Her Times and Favorites,* ed. John S. Cerovski (Cranbury, N.J.: Associated University Presses, 1985), 73.
12. Hennessy, *Sir Walter,* 31; "Invention of Ships," *Works,* 8:330.
13. A. L. Rowse, *Tudor Cornwall,* 2d ed. (New York: Charles Scribner's Sons, 1959), 62. Ralegh's grant of the stewardship of the Duchy passed the signet 31 August 1585 (Public Record Office, Signet Office 3/1, fol. 37v). The appointment as lieutenant of Cornwall by 1587 is documented in Gladys Scott Thomson's *Lord Lieutenants in the Sixteenth Century* (London: Longmans, Green & Co., 1923), 50.

14. *Calendar of State Papers Domestic Addenda, 1580–1625,* 28/55; CSPD 169/35–36; Sir Simonds D'Ewes, *The Journals of All the Parliaments during the Reign of Queen Elizabeth* (1682; reprint, Shannon, Ireland: Irish University Press, 1973), 341.

15. Willard M. Wallace, *Sir Walter Raleigh* (Princeton: Princeton University Press, 1959), 54; British Library Add. MS. 6177, ff. 109–9v.

16. *Calendar of Letters and State Papers . . . Simancas,* 4:205 and n.

17. Wallace, *Raleigh,* 62. Ralegh is named in both poems in James Lea's *An Answer to the Untruthes,* 1589, sigs. H1v, H3v (STC 17132), in the first of which he is described as "not the least, nor used lesse in armes." A similar but not identical list naming Ralegh occurs in Richard Hakluyt's *Principal Navigations* (Glasgow: MacLehose & Sons, 1903–5), 4:217.

18. Edwards, *Life,* 2:46–48; *List and Analysis of State Papers Foreign Series, Elizabeth I,* 4:135, 300, 315; BL Lansdowne MS. 115/95; MS. 143, f. 180.

19. Cambridge University Library MS. Dd.5.75, f. 32.

20. D'Ewes, *Journals of Parliaments,* 646; Public Record Office, State Papers 9/55, #2; PRO Signet Office 3/1, ff. 64, 110.

21. Cecil to Heneage, 21 September 1592, CSPD 243/17.

22. Thomas Birch, *Memoirs of the Reign of Queen Elizabeth* (1754; reprint, New York: AMS Press, 1970), 1:56.

23. Captain Martin Frobisher to Lord Willoughby, 30 July 1587, Historical Manuscripts Commission Ancaster, 49.

24. Wallace, *Raleigh,* 66; BL Add. MS. 6177, f. 2v.

25. PRO Signet Office 3/1, f. 294; Exchequer 403/2559, f. 326.

26. Edwards, *Life,* chart on 1:8–9; BL Harleian MS. 1500, f. 110; Edwards, *Life,* 2:26.

27. Raphael Holinshed, *Chronicles* (1587; reprint, 1808; reprint, New York: AMS Press, 1965), 6:105. A. L. Rowse, *Ralegh and the Throckmortons* (1962; reprint, London: Reprint Society, 1964), 160–61.

28. The New Years' gift lists place Elizabeth Throckmorton among the gentlewomen in 1585 (Folger MS. Z.d.16), 1588 (BL Add. MS. 8159), and 1589 (BL Lansdowne Roll 17). The maids of honor are named in each of these lists and in the subsidy roll of 1590, PRO E 179/266/13.

29. Pierre Lefranc, "La Date du Mariage de Sir Walter Ralegh: un Document Inédit," *Études Anglaises* 9 (1956):193–211.

30. Historical Manuscripts Commission Salisbury, 4:596–97; Rutland, 1:324; Lodge, *Illustrations,* 2:479–80.

31. D'Ewes, *Journals of Parliaments,* 517.

32. Ernest Strathmann, *Sir Walter Ralegh* (New York: Columbia University Press), 145–47. See John W. Shirley, *Thomas Harriot: A Biography* (Oxford: Clarendon Press, 1983), 196–98; Edwards, *Life,* 2:91.

33. CSPD 250/46.

34. David B. Quinn and A. N. Ryan, *England's Sea Empire, 1550–1642*

(London: Allen & Unwin, 1983), 120; Historical Manuscripts Commission De L'Isle and Dudley, 2:218.

35. HMC Salisbury, 9:335–36; a copy of the queen's letter of thanks to Ralegh on this occasion occurs in BL Add. MS. 34224, f. 30.

36. HMC Salisbury, 10:439–40.

37. PRO Lord Chamberlain 2/4 (4), ff. 19, 45v. Some degree of favor is implicit in Lady Ralegh's complaint to Cecil (ca. 1602) that Lady Kildare had dealt unkindly with her to the queen (BL Add. MS. 6177, f. 93). Unkind dealing could scarcely have deepened Elizabeth's resentment in the months following her discovery of the secret marriage.

38. *Correspondence of King James VI of Scotland with Sir Robert Cecil and Others in England,* ed. John Bruce, Camden Society Publications, 1st ser., vol. 78 (1861; reprint, New York: AMS Press, 1968), 18–19, 67.

39. Ibid., 82–83; Linda Levy Peck, *Northampton: Patronage and Policy at the Court of James I* (London: Allen & Unwin, 1982), 21–22.

40. "A Brief Relation of Sir Walter Raleigh's Troubles" (1669), in *The Harleian Miscellany* (London, 1810), 4:389.

41. *Cobbett's Complete Collection of State Trials,* ed. Thomas B. Howell (London, 1809), 2: col. 7.

42. Hester, *A hundred and foureteene Experiments and Cures* (STC 19180); *Catalogvs Arborum, Fruticum Ac plantarum Tam Indigenarum, quam Exoticarum in horto Johannis Gerardi* (STC 11749).

43. J. H. Adamson and H. F. Folland, *The Shepherd of the Ocean, an Account of Sir Walter Ralegh and His Times* (London: Bodley Head, 1969), 416.

44. Ibid., 373; BL Add. MS. 6177, f. 194.

45. Historical Manuscripts Commission Third Report, Marquis of Bath MSS, 185.

46. J. W. Williamson, *The Myth of the Conqueror, Prince Henry Stuart: A Study of 17th-Century Personation* (New York: AMS Press, 1978), 49.

47. *The Letters of John Chamberlain,* ed. Norman Egbert McClure (Philadelphia: American Philosophical Society, 1939), 2:67.

48. Ibid., 2:179.

49. Shirley, *Thomas Harriot,* 447–48; McClure, *Chamberlain Letters,* 2:175–76; R. H. Bowers, "Ralegh's Last Speech: The 'Elms' Document," *Review of English Studies* 2 (1951):215.

50. Thomas Lorkin to Sir Thomas Puckering, quoted in V. T. Harlow, *Ralegh's Last Voyage* (London: Argonaut Press, 1932), 313–14.

Chapter Two

1. *Aubrey's Brief Lives,* ed. Oliver Lawson Dick (1949; reprint, Ann Arbor: University of Michigan Press, 1962), 260; McClure, *Chamberlain Letters,* 2:179.

2. I analyze these possibilities and print the relevant lines from Whetstone's poem in "'Companion Poems,'" 262–65.

3. C. S. Lewis coined the term "drab" to describe mid-century style in his *English Literature in the Sixteenth Century Excluding Drama* (1954; reprint, Oxford, Clarendon Press, 1968), 64; D. L. Peterson prefers the term, "plain style" coined by Yvor Winters in *The English Lyric from Wyatt to Donne* (Princeton: Princeton University Press, 1967).

4. *Miscellaneous Prose of Sir Philip Sidney,* ed. Katherine Duncan-Jones and Jan van Dorsten (Oxford: Clarendon Press, 1973), 117.

5. References to this poem follow the critical text in "'Companion Poems,'" 267–68.

6. *The Poems of Sir Arthur Gorges,* ed. Helen Estabrook Sandison (Oxford: Clarendon Press, 1953). What appears to be another translation of the original of "Callinge to minde" occurs in BL Add. MS. 5956, ff. 25–25v.

7. Michael Rudick, "The Poems of Sir Walter Ralegh," doctoral dissertation, Chicago, 1970, 27; hereafter cited as *Poems.*

8. As news of the Sidney-Gamage match reached court, Ralegh wrote Barbara's guardian to insist "that you suffer not my kinsewoman to be boughte and solde" without the consent of the queen and himself (*Stradling Correspondence,* ed. John Montgomery Traherne [London, 1840], 22). The queen did consent, however, and all the parties involved were soon brought to a full acceptance of the marriage.

9. HMC De L'Isle and Dudley, 2:180, 200, 419. Hilton Kelliher and Katherine Duncan-Jones suggest that Ralegh's verse influenced that of Sir Robert Sidney in "A Manuscript of Poems by Robert Sidney: Some Early Impressions," *British Library Journal* 1 (1975):118–19.

10. *Dudley Carleton to John Chamberlain, 1603–1624, Jacobean Letters,* ed. Maurice Lee (New Brunswick, N.J., Rutgers University Press, 1972), 44–45. The quotation is from Virgil's *Aeneid,* book 4, line 23, "a trace of the old flame" (Carleton to Chamberlain, 27 November 1603).

11. From Wiltshire Record Office MS. 865/500, f. 27. Other texts occur in Marsh's Library, Dublin, MS. 183, f. 30v, and BL Add. MS. 63742, f. 116 (formerly Phillipps MS. 3602). Walter Oakeshott prints a facsimile of the latter version in *The Queen and the Poet* (London: Faber & Faber, 1960), facing p. 156. I emend the copy text from these two manuscripts at line 2, "loves Joy," line 7 "owe," line 10 "mightie feares," line 17 "conqueringe," and line 21 "sin." Excerpts from the poem are attributed to Ralegh in George Puttenham's *Arte of English Poesie* (1589), which provides a terminus ad quem for the poem's composition. Although entries in the Additional MS can be dated from 1584 through 1589, they were not entered in strict chronological order. The items that bracket Ralegh's poem, however, between ff. 114v and 119 date from 1586 to New Year's 1588 at latest.

12. The text was first published in L. G. Black's "A Lost Poem by Queen Elizabeth I," *TLS,* 23 May 1968, 535, from Inner Temple MS. Petyt 538.10; another text occurs in the Wiltshire Record Office MS, and excerpts were printed in Puttenham's *Arte.*

13. See *Poems*, 30–31, for a summary of the views of Stebbing and A. L. Rowse. It should be noted that the poet only threatens such a desertion.

14. So called after the custom of poulterers to give a thirteenth egg with the purchase of a dozen. Each couplet in this form has six accents in the first line but seven in the second for a total of thirteen.

15. For the text of the earl's poem and a discussion of its possible context see my edition of Essex's verse in *Studies in Philology* 77:43–44, 84–88.

16. *Poems*, 31–32, notes the allusion to 11.5 in "Cynthia" 14.347–51, thus fixing the date before 1592. The St. Michael's College Tenbury MSS. 1162–67 is set to music, while that in BL Add. MS. 57555, f. 172v, is transcribed in Ralegh's autograph.

17. The other participants were Sir Robert Carey and a Mr. "Chidley," presumably John Chudleigh of Ashton, Devonshire, who sailed with Gilbert on his final voyage and was connected with Ralegh; he apparently died at sea in 1589 (see P. W. Hasler's *The House of Commons, 1558–1603* [London: Her Majesty's Stationery Office, 1981], 1:608). The entertainment is mentioned by its author, Thomas Churchyard, in his *Challenge* (1593), sig. *2; see E. K. Chambers, *The Elizabethan Stage* (Oxford: Clarendon Press, 1923), 3:267–68, for the suggestion that it was performed at Shrovetide, that is, 26–28 February 1587. Lefranc, in *Ralegh*, opts for a similar occasion in 1602 (p. 101).

18. Thomas Heywood, *Troia Britanica, or Great Britaines Troy*, 1609, sig. L5; William Browne, *Brittania's Pastorals*, 1616, sig. N1v.

19. CSPD 238/164, 22 May 1591.

20. Samuel Purchas, *Hakluytus Posthumus or Purchas His Pilgrimes* (1625; reprint, New York: 1965), 20:104–5. Grenville's motives and the historical facts are ably surveyed in John H. Stibbs's "Raleigh's Account of Grenville's Fight at the Azores in 1591," *North Carolina Historical Review* 27 (1950):20–31.

21. Ralegh noted in his *Guiana* narrative that he buried Whiddon at Trinidad "to my great griefe . . . beeing a man most honest and valiant."

22. John Strype, *Annals of the Reformation* (1840; reprint, New York: Burt Franklin, n.d.), 4:107–8; *A Transcipt of the Registers of the Company of Stationers of London*, ed. Edward Arber (1875; reprint, Gloucester, Mass.: Peter Smith, 1967), 2:282.

23. The most detailed analysis of Ralegh's prose style is in chapter 14 of Lefranc's *Ralegh*, 525–66, which draws many of its examples from the *Revenge* tract.

24. No doubt the English translation of las Casas, *The Spanish Colonie, or Briefe Chronicle of the Acts and Gestes of the Spaniardes* (1583).

Chapter Three

1. Philip Edwards concludes that the "Cynthia" series is "one vast paradox" (*Sir Walter Ralegh* [London: Longmans, Green, 1953], 123). Joyce Horner terms it a "private poem, hastily and impulsively written" ("The Large Landscape: A Study of Certain Images in Ralegh," *Essays in Criticism* 5 [1955]:198–99). With Edwards

and Horner, Donald Davie assigns the poem to the crisis of 1592 and stresses the ambiguity pervading these verses in "A Reading of 'The Ocean's Love to Cynthia,'" *Elizabethan Poetry,* ed. John Russell Brown and Bernard Harris (London: Edward Arnold, 1960), 2:70–89. In "The Date of Raleigh's '21th: and Last Booke of the Ocean to Scinthia,'" *RES* 21 (1970):143–58, Katherine Duncan-Jones reads this "infinitely ambiguous and complex poem" as a nostalgic reminiscence of Elizabeth's reign composed by Ralegh after her death and during his imprisonment by King James. A. D. Cousins alludes to a "conventional dating" of the poem at 1589 (91n), arguing that Ralegh's lack of favor in that year led him to question the order and harmony of the "Tudor aesthetic" ("The Coming of Mannerism: The Later Ralegh and the Early Donne," *ELR* 9 [1979]:86–107). Michael L. Johnson analyzes the poem without regard to its context in "Some Problems of Unity in Sir Walter Ralegh's *The Ocean's Love to Cynthia,*" *Studies in English Literature* 14 (1974):17–30. He finds "rejection from court" to be the poem's central theme, conveyed in a tone of "unrelieved grief," its generic effect that of a "winter pastoral." Robert E. Stillman interprets the work as Ralegh's unsuccessful effort to move from one set of symbols to another in order to adapt to the change in his relationship with the queen ("'Words Cannot knyt': Language and Desire in Ralegh's *The Ocean to Synthia,*" *SEL* 27 [1987]:35–51). Lefranc, in *Ralegh,* places the Hatfield poems in 1593 or 1594 and sees in their distracted, discontinuous style affinities with Browning's dramatic monologues and those of T. S. Eliot and Ezra Pound (108, 158–59).

2. Stacy M. Clanton's paleographic study of Ralegh's numerals effectively caps the modern trend to read them "21th:" and "22" ("The 'Number' of Sir Walter Ralegh's *Booke of the Ocean to Scinthia,*" *SP* 82 [1985]:200–211).

3. *The Works of Edmund Spenser, a Variorum Edition* (Baltimore: Johns Hopkins Press, 1932, 1934), 1:168, 3:2, 196. Gabriel Harvey's description of "Sir Walter Raleighs Cynthia" as a "fine and sweet" invention comes at least eight years after publication of Spenser's similar allusions to the poem (*Gabriel Harvey's Marginalia,* ed. G. C. Moore Smith [Stratford-Upon-Avon, 1913], 232–33).

4. Spenser, *Works,* 7:11, lines 164–70.

5. Lefranc, *Ralegh,* 130–32. Lefranc concludes that Ralegh composed less of the "Cynthia" series than Spenser implied.

6. Katherine Koller, "Spenser and Ralegh," *ELH* 1 (1934):53–54.

7. Lefranc contends that poems from the supposed "Ralegh group" in the *Phoenix Nest* along with such canonical poems as 8 and 11 belonged to this earlier "Cynthia" (*Ralegh,* 117–124). However, the similarities he notes between these poems and the Hatfield "Cynthia" are commonplaces of Elizabethan love poetry, which do not necessarily establish authorial links between them.

8. The cancels occur after lines 144 and 449. Other examples of unrhymed lines in the poem include 116, 118, 132–33, 159, 273, 331, 364, 404, and 479.

9. Pierre Lefranc, "Une Nouvelle Version de la 'Petition to Queen Anne' de Sir Walter Ralegh," *Annales de la Faculté des Lettres et Sciences Humaines de Nice* 34 (1978):65–66.

10. BL Cotton MS. Caligula E.8, f. 324; *Tudor Royal Proclamations,* ed. Paul L. Hughes and James F. Larkin (New Haven and London: Yale University Press, 1969), no. 746.

11. The language and attitudes of the "Cynthia" poems appear frequently in Ralegh's prose during 1592–93. Shortly after his arrest he minimized his marriage in a letter to Cecil that is filled with the rhapsodic diction of the Hatfield poems: "Once amiss, hath bereaved me of all . . . the loves, the sythes, the sorrows, the desires, can they not way down one frail misfortune?" (Edwards, *Life,* 2:52). The "withred leves" of 14.21 and 470 crop up in Ralegh's letter to the Countess of Shrewsbury in which he bemoans his disgrace and "the withered leves of an unprosperous and blasted fortune" (HMC 6th Report, Appendix, p. 456, March 8, no year, calendared in 1593), and see the discussion of the "Succession" tract below.

12. See John Nichols, *The Progresses and Public Processions of Queen Elizabeth* (1823; reprint, New York: AMS Press, n.d.), 3:596, for an account of Cecil's writing poetry for the queen's amusement, Gabriel Harvey's reference to his poetry in the *Marginalia,* ed. Smith, 231, and Chamberlain's assurance that Cecil was pleased to receive a present of verses (*Chamberlain Letters,* ed. McClure, 1:163). Cecil's death in 1612 provides a practical terminus ad quem for composition of the "Cynthia" poems and their deposition in the Hatfield collection.

13. Lefranc, *Ralegh,* terms this period "le sommet de sa carrière" (124).

14. Johnson, in "Some Problems," 19–20, agrees with Horner that Ralegh wrote in haste; Davie, in "A Reading," 77–78, praises the impulsive tenor of the poem but believes that Ralegh would have clarified it in revision. See Lefranc, *Ralegh,* 135–37, 158–59, 506–7.

15. Johnson, "Some Problems," 18.

16. Elkin Calhoun Wilson, *England's Eliza* (1939; reprint, New York: Octagon Books, 1966), 312.

17. See Horner, "The Large Landscape," 199–207, and Lefranc, *Ralegh,* 108, 155; Cousins, in "Coming of Mannerism," 92–94, argues that the moon and sea images are the most powerful in the poem.

18. Similarly, the references to her beauty—e.g., at lines 183, 376, 450, or to her "princely forme" (line 40)—cannot be platonized without severely wrenching their context.

19. This reading may shed some light on the curious claim that his error, his love for Elizabeth Throckmorton, "never was forthought / or ever could proceed from sence of Lovinge" (lines 338–39). If his true love in the platonic sense is reserved for the queen, then some lesser passion, a "frayle effect of mortall livinge" (line 445), accounted for his marriage. Even so, Duncan-Jones ("The Date," 152), is right in doubting Lefranc's belief that Ralegh clearly distinguishes between his love for the queen and love for his wife.

20. *Old Arcadia,* Poem 17, *Poems of Sir Philip Sidney,* ed. William A. Ringler, Jr. (Oxford: Clarendon Press, 1962), 39.

21. Lefranc dates the tract precisely to 23 February 1593 on grounds of its ap-

parent response to Peter Wentworth's examination on that very day by the Privy
Council for his attempt to open debate on the succession question. Ralegh's speech in
the House of Commons is summarized in D'Ewes, *Journals of Parliaments,* 484.

22. PRO SP 12/250/46; Signet Office 3/1, f. 500.

23. Lefranc, *Ralegh,* 51.

24. HMC Salisbury 8:365; De L'Isle and Dudley, 2:200.

25. Harlow, *Last Voyage,* 4–9.

26. See especially his description of the interior near the Caroli Falls, in *Discovery,* 442–43, and 427, 453.

27. Copies of Pliny, Thevet, and Mandeville are cited among the books that
Ralegh kept with him in the Tower, ca. 1606–8; see Walter Oakshott, "Sir Walter
Raleigh's Library," *Library,* 5th ser., 23 (1968):285–327, items 300, 486, 382,
395. Ralegh reaffirms his faith in Mandeville in *The History of the World,* 4:2, and
Works, 5:373.

28. CSPD 254/67.

29. The letter to Gorges was discovered and published by Lefranc, "Ralegh in
1596 and 1603: Three Unprinted Letters in the Huntington Library," *HLQ* 29
(1966):340–45. Ralegh's brief account of the battle in his letter to Cecil (Edwards,
Life, 2:135–36), suggests that he may have learned by 1596 that Sir Robert Cecil
was an unreliable intermediary for communicating with the queen and court.

30. Ralegh mentions the wound but not its source, a detail from the account
of the battle in CSPD 259/114.

31. The expedition was not a total loss for Ralegh, however. Commissioners
sent to Plymouth to control the distribution of plunder valued that taken by Ralegh
and other officers at nearly £13,000 (CSPD 259/95).

32. Lefranc, *Ralegh,* 34.

33. Lefranc, *Ralegh,* 34, proposed the 3 November meeting as the most likely
occasion for the submission of the earl's questions and the responses to them. This
hypothesis is confirmed first by details in Essex's "Articles," such as the king of
Spain's twenty ships commanded by the Adelantado of Castile, which appear in a report
forwarded to him in mid-October by Sir Robert Sidney (Birch, *Memoirs,*
2:174–75). Second, on 9 November one of the earl's secretaries wrote to Lord
Willoughby, a member of the war council, to inform him that the "counterpoint" by
Lord Burgh and Ralegh "pleas'd more their own conceits than the sovereign's ear"
(2:197). This is surely an allusion to Ralegh's "Opinion," which, with Lord Burgh's
and the others, was published late in the eighteenth century.

34. Howell, *Cobbett's State Trials,* 2: col. 21.

35. The text of Poem 16 in Huntington Library MS. HM 198, vol. 1, f. 1, is
dated 1595. A reply beginning "Courte's skorne, state's disgracinge" was transcribed
on the verso of this leaf, presumably at about the same time. For the possibility that
this poem and the one beginning "Go Eccho of the minde" were written by Essex see
my *Poems of . . . Essex,* 106–8. Lefranc's supposition that Dr. Richard Latewar wrote
"The Lie" is countered by Karl Josef Höltgen, "Richard Latewar, Elizabethan Poet

and Divine," *Anglia* 89 (1971):417–38. Höltgen's transcription of a stanza-by-stanza verse response to "The Lie" in Bodleian MS. Rawlinson poet. 212 shows that Latewar was responsible only for the response.

36. Lefranc, *Ralegh*, 87.
37. *Poems*, 40.
38. BL Add. MS. 5752, f. 99.
39. HMC De L'Isle and Dudley, 2:285–86. See McClure, *Chamberlain Letters*, 1:31.

Chapter Four

1. The Elizabethan state of the text is identified in Suzanne Gossett's "A New History for Ralegh's *Notes on the Navy*," *Modern Philology* 84 (1987):12–26.
2. First published by John Payne Collier, "Walter Raleigh: Additional Papers," *Notes and Queries*, 3d. ser. (12 March 1864):208. The authenticity of this document was confirmed by Pierre Lefranc's discovery of Ralegh's holograph copy in the Public Record Office (Beal, *Index*, vol. 1, part 2, Ralegh #571).
3. Chamberlain to Carleton, 29 February 1600, *Chamberlain Letters*, ed. McClure, 1:89. The case was turned over to the Admiralty Court where it was still in contention and a matter of concern to the Privy Council as late as September. See J. R. Dasent, *Acts of the Privy Council, 1599–1600*, vol. 31 (London, 1905), 424, 660–61.
4. "Instructions to his Son," 21. The correspondence is cited in Philip Edwards, *Ralegh*, 73.
5. See *Poems*, 57–59, for discussion of the attributions and complicated textual transmission of these poems.
6. Edwards, *Life*, 1:364–65; his suggestion that Ralegh may have given "War with Spain" to the king on this occasion has been converted into fact by a number of Ralegh's biographers.
7. Howell, *Cobbett's State Trials*, 2: col. 12; an independent account of the trial in PRO SP 12/278, ff. 202–202v, cites Ralegh's charge that Philip retained only five of his twenty-five million, which tallies exactly with the figures in the tract. Here Ralegh is quoted as saying that he "latelye wrote a treatise to the king."
8. Agnes M. C. Latham, "Sir Walter Ralegh's *Instructions to his Son*," in *Elizabethan and Jacobean Studies Presented to Frank Percy Wilson* (Oxford: Clarendon Press, 1959), 199–218. The new paragraphs, omitted from all the printed texts, are transcribed from BL Add. MS. 22587 on pp. 207–8; an interpolation in chapter 1 of the tract, also missing from the prints, appears on pp. 206–7.
9. Latham, "Ralegh's *Instructions*," 210.
10. Howell, *Cobbett's State Trials*, 2: col. 21. Burghley's "Certain Precepts" are published with Ralegh's "Instructions" in Louis B. Wright's *Advice to a Son* (Ithaca: Cornell University Press, 1962), 9–13. Sidney's letter is reprinted in Malcolm William Wallace's *The Life of Sir Philip Sidney* (1915; reprint, New York: Octagon Books, 1967), 68–70. Both works are considered in relation to the "Instructions" in Richard

Helgerson's *The Elizabethan Prodigals* (Berkeley: University of California Press, 1976), 19–39. Helgerson notes (19), that Ralegh's closing admonition that God will confound godless works like "drops of rain on the sandy ground" (32), is taken word for word from Robert Greene's *Mourning Garment* (1590).

11. Wright cites an eighteenth-century transcript of Burghley's tract that dates it to 1586 but that expands the initials "E." and "R." in one interesting passage: "I advise thee not to affect nor neglect popularity too much. Seek not to be Essex and shun to be Ralegh" (*Advice to a Son*, 13n). The names must be interpolations, however, if the "Precepts" date from 1586, for Essex did not become a public figure until he came to court in 1587, and his reputation as a popular extrovert, in contrast with Ralegh's aloof hauteur, was largely a product of the 1590s.

12. Latham, "Ralegh's *Instructions*," 212–13.

13. See Wallace, *Raleigh* 150–51, 196, and Stephen Jay Greenblatt's *Sir Walter Ralegh, the Renaissance Man and His Roles* (New Haven: Yale University Press, 1973), chapters 2 and 4.

14. Latham, *Poems*, 140.

15. Rudick, *Poems*, 45.

16. Ralegh's tendency to view life as a tragedy is documented in Michael Rudick's "The Text of Ralegh's Lyric, 'What is our Life?,'" *Studies in Philology* 83 (1986):81. Rudick arrives at a critical text on p. 87 based on the same copytext used in his dissertation but with one additional emendation based upon the readings of five of the best manuscripts of the poem.

17. Ibid., 79.

18. Gossett, "A New History," 24. Lefranc dates Ralegh's letter to Henry (Edwards, *Life*, 2:330–32), before 20 October 1608, when the keel was laid for the *Prince Royal*, the ship specially designed and built for Henry's use (257). See Gossett, "A New History," 14, 21. Gossett notes, however, that it is uncertain that the prince ever received the revised "Observations."

19. "Observations," 349. I rely on Gossett, 21–24, for the summary of Ralegh's revisions.

20. Lefranc, *Ralegh*, 596–97, cites Ralegh's allusions to the "Art of War" and suggests that the "Invention of Ships" might have belonged to it. In appendix G Lefranc lists Ralegh's three references to Machiavelli's *Art of War* (#3, 5, 18).

21. "War by Sea," 600. Cf. Lefranc, *Ralegh*, 189–90, and the catalog of maxims that Ralegh derived from Machiavelli in appendix G, 626–29.

22. *Works*, 8:538–39. After the reprieve of 1603 Cecil found a discourse on government in a trunk full of Ralegh's papers. But since he also found a copy of the king of Spain's will among them, it is clear that not all of these documents were from Ralegh's hand nor did Ralegh have evident cause to write the "Seat of Government" during Elizabeth's reign (BL Add. MS 6177, fol. 183). Lefranc notes that Ralegh's refusal in the "Seat of Government" to define the limits of a ruler's authority followed the central principle of Machiavelli's political thought, especially in the *Prince*, which likewise deals with the retention of power through wise policy (*Ralegh*, 627).

In urging that the prince gain his subjects' love, however, Ralegh contradicts Machiavelli's belief that it is better for a prince to be feared.

23. Lefranc places the composition of the "Match" between March and December 1611. References in the "Marriage" discourse to the contract of a royal marriage between Spain and France (*Works*, 8:247, 252) apparently refer to the arrangements for a double marriage involving offspring of Henry IV and Philip III that were formally ratified on 12 August 1612. Thus the "Marriage" treatise belongs to late August through early November 1612.

24. Parsons's book appeared in 1594 with a dedication to the earl of Essex. Its subject must have been doubly bitter to Ralegh looking back on it in 1612, for he had been convicted of working to place the Infanta on the throne of England. He may also have known that Parsons, under the pseudonym John Philopatris, wrote *An Advertisement* (1592) that contained the infamous charge that Ralegh sponsored a "school of atheism."

25. Book 4:2; *Works*, 5:325; Lefranc, *Ralegh*, 641.

26. BL Cotton Vitellius MS. C.16, vol. 2, f. 529. The discourse was first assigned to "Sr Arthure Gorge," then changed to Ralegh in a hand identical or at least contemporary with that of the original scribe.

Chapter Five

1. The Recusant mentions a letter from the Jesuit dated 1 July 1609. Perhaps Ralegh wrote or revised this work over a period of years. The first eight years of James's reign (cited on sig. F2) ended in March 1611, while the assertion that the Poles have not yet taken Smollensk (sig. F1) dates the work before June 1611 when that city fell to them, plus the few days or weeks it would have taken for the news to reach England.

2. Lefranc, *Ralegh*, 60–62, analyzes a number of other correspondences between this dialogue and Ralegh's canonical works.

3. Ralegh claimed at his trial to have collected nearly all of the libels written against Queen Elizabeth (Howell, *Cobbett's State Trials*, 2: col. 21). Certainly the "Commonwealth," properly entitled *The Copy of a Letter Written by a Master of Art of Cambridge* (1584), must have belonged to any such collection. Not only does it mention Ralegh by name, but its condemnation of the Elizabethan regime and its lengthy debate over the succession combine to make it the most infamous of the Elizabethan libels.

4. Sig. E6. Ralegh is known to have opposed Buckhurst on at least one occasion, for he excused his journey to greet his newly proclaimed sovereign in April 1603 on grounds that he needed a letter from James ordering Buckhurst to stop the "'waste of woods and parks'" in Cornwall (Edwards, *Life*, 1:362–63).

5. Sir John Ferne was cited in 1608 for exporting iron and brass cannon "contrary to his Majesty's commission" (CSPD Addenda, James I, 39/65). Ralegh's disapproval of Ferne was not implacable, however, for Sir John took a prominent part in the Guiana expedition of 1617–18. Edwards notes that Ralegh's privileges in the

Tower were abridged after an interview with privy councillors Salisbury (Cecil) and Northampton in July 1611 (1:502–3). The cause is more likely to have been their discovery of this dialogue rather than the marriage tracts, as Edwards speculates.

6. John Racin, *Sir Walter Ralegh as Historian: An Analysis of the History of the World* (Salzburg: Universität Salzburg, 1974), 7, 11–12.

7. F. Smith Fussner, *The Historical Revolution, English Historical Writing and Thought, 1580–1640* (New York: Columbia University Press, 1962), 194.

8. Racin classifies books 1 and 2 as Old Testament and 3–5 as classical. C. A. Patrides terms them, respectively, Jewish and Greco-Roman in the introduction to his edition of the *History* (Philadelphia: Temple University Press, 1971), 25.

9. *Conversations with William Drummond of Hawthornden,* ed. G. B. Harrison (London: Barnes & Noble, 1966), 9.

10. Wallace, *Raleigh,* 249.

11. Patrides, in *History,* asserts, "The research and the writing were almost entirely his own," for the work's unity argues Ralegh's "total control" of the project (23–24). Racin discounts Ralegh's dependence on others (20–26). Fussner (*Historical Revolution,* 192) claims that the *History* is "Ralegh's throughout in style and spirit."

12. Lefranc (*Ralegh,* 643–45) devotes appendix K to listing the textual errors that suggest that Ralegh dictated the *History* to a scribe or scribes. It would be difficult, however, to fix the dictation at this stage of textual transmission given the common printing-house practice of reading copy aloud to compositors.

13. *Aubrey's Brief Lives,* 254; Edwards, *Life,* 2:498; Cecil to Sir George Harvey, lieutenant of the Tower, 20 December 1603, BL Add. MS. 6177, fol. 183.

14. See Oakshott, "Raleigh's Library," 285–327, for an analysis of the manuscript and transcript of the book list.

15. Strathmann, *Ralegh,* 197.

16. Book 2.23; *Works,* 4:685; Racin, *Ralegh as Historian,* 120–21.

17. Fussner, *Historical Revolution,* 203–4.

18. Racin, *Ralegh as Historian,* 126–46, and part 5, "The Purpose of Historiography," 197–206. Racin errs in affirming (92) that Ralegh dropped his emphasis on providence in books 3–5. Patrides (*History,* 36) suggests that Ralegh refers less often to God's intervention in these books because he had sufficiently primed the reader to recognize it in books 1 and 2. Nevertheless, at least a score of explicit references to the operation of divine providence occur with fairly even distribution in the last three books.

19. Fussner, *Historical Revolution,* 197.

20. Lefranc, *Ralegh,* 304.

21. Francis Osborne, *Memoirs,* cited in Lefranc, *Ralegh,* 275; *Letters of King James VI & I,* ed. G. P. V. Akrigg (Berkeley: University of California Press, 1984), 338.

22. Lefranc, *Ralegh,* 321–27.

23. Racin, *Ralegh as Historian,* 107–9.

24. Book 5:5; *Works,* 7:652; Lefranc, *Ralegh,* 325; Patrides, *History,* 18–19. The possibility that these two advisors might represent James's dependence on Cecil, now lord Salisbury, and Henry, earl of Northampton, cannot be discounted.

25. Book 5:6; *Works,* 7:896; the quotation is from *The True Lawe of Free Monarchies,* ed. Craigie, 81.

26. Lefranc, *Ralegh,* 326n.

27. *The True Lawe,* ed. Craigie, 71, 76–77.

28. Lefranc, *Ralegh,* 327–28.

29. This structure is analyzed by Racin, *Ralegh as Historian,* 80–88.

30. See Milton's "On the Morning of Christ's Nativity" and C. A. Patrides, "The Cessation of the Oracles: The History of a Legend," *Modern Language Review* 60 (1965):500–7.

31. Patrides, *History,* 36.

32. Book 4:1; *Works,* 5:280. The comparison recalls an epic simile from Poem 14, lines 225–27, describing a stream that does "all unawares in sunder teare / the forsed bounds and raginge runn att large / in th'auncient channells as the[y] wounted weare."

33. Ralegh borrowed from Golding's translation of Ovid's *Metamorphoses* in book 1:1; *Works,* 2:10; and from his translation of Phillippe de Mornay's *Trewnesse of the Christian Religion* in book 2.26; *Works,* 4:742. The excerpt from *Philotas* (4:2; *Works,* 5:357) may have held special interest for Ralegh beyond its resemblance to his own circumstances, for Daniel was investigated by the Privy Council in 1605 owing to correspondences between his play and the earl of Essex's rebellion and execution.

34. Racin, *Ralegh as Historian,* 66–68.

35. Louise Brown Osborn, *The Life, Letters, and Writings of John Hoskyns* (New Haven: Yale University Press, 1937), 38–44.

36. McClure, *Chamberlain Letters,* 1:542, 568; Lefranc, *Ralegh,* 205–6.

37. Lefranc, *Ralegh,* 206.

38. Ralegh comments on the cruelty of Agathocles, "So devilish is the nature of man, when reason, that should be his guide, is become a slave to his brutish affections" (5:1; *Works,* 6:73). Racin examines this aspect of Ralegh's thesis (*Raleigh as Historian,* 126–27, 164–65).

39. D'Ewes, *Journals of Parliaments,* 632–33.

Chapter Six

1. Ralegh mentions the idea in the "War by Sea" fragments, develops it in the "Marriage" tract, and touches on it again in the "Jesuit" dialogue.

2. Lefranc, *Ralegh,* 597.

3. STC 20579, entered in the Stationers' Register on 12 February 1615.

4. Lefranc, *Ralegh,* 56, 194.

5. Ibid., 641.

6. Ibid., 56n.

7. For the subordination of religious to secular authority see "Of the Voyage for Guyana," 142; "Jesuit," sig. C5; the *History*, 1:8; *Works*, 2:346.

8. Harlow, *Last Voyage*, 22.

9. Ibid., 109.

10. Ibid., 115.

11. Edwards, *Life*, 2:392–94; E. A. Strathmann, "Ralegh Plans His Last Voyage," *Mariner's Mirror* 50 (1964):265; Harlow, *Last Voyage*, 24.

12. Harlow, *Last Voyage*, 108–9.

13. Ibid., 115; Strathmann, "Ralegh Plans," 265–66.

14. Strathmann, "Ralegh Plans," 264; letters to Queen Anne and Viscount Haddington, Edwards, *Life*, 2:333, 393.

15. Harlow, *Last Voyage*, 119.

16. Helen E. Sandison, "Ralegh's Orders Once More," *Mariner's Mirror* 20 (1934):323–30. Sandison argues that Sir Arthur Gorges collaborated with Ralegh on the "Orders" in light of the manuscript copy of them that Gorges dedicated in 1619 to Villiers, now Lord Admiral Buckingham.

17. When Captain Alley arrived in London from Guiana he refuted this lie, and the Privy Council sent Bayley to the Gatehouse (*Chamberlain Letters*, ed. McClure, 2:104, 131).

18. Edwards, *Life*, 2:349.

19. Harlow, *Last Voyage*, 49, and see the letter to Lady Ralegh, Edwards, *Life*, 2:348.

20. Harlow, *Last Voyage*, 49, 245.

21. *Chamberlain Letters*, 2:163.

22. Agnes M. C. Latham, "Sir Walter Ralegh's Gold Mine: New Light on the Last Guiana Voyage," *Essays and Studies* 4 (1951):95.

23. 22 March 1618, Harlow, *Last Voyage*, 243.

24. Ralegh mentions this massacre in his letter to Lord Carew, which was appended to the printed "Apology," and in his appeal to James of 24 September (Harlow, *Last Voyage*, 277).

25. *Chamberlain Letters*, ed. McClure, 2:167.

26. Ibid.

27. Harlow, *Last Voyage*, 277–78.

28. Lefranc, "Une Nouvelle Version," 64–65. Latham, in *Poems*, 151, likewise argues for the composition of Poems 22 and 23 in 1603.

29. Somerset Record Office, MS. DD/M I, Box 18, FL IV, 88. Abbreviations in the manuscript have been expanded and i/j, u/v normalized. The punctuation has been modernized and stanza numbers added.

30. Lefranc, "Une Nouvelle Version," 65.

31. *Chamberlain Letters*, ed. McClure, 2:178; *Works*, 8:772–73.

32. Edwards, *Life*, 2:494–95. Ralegh denied the latter charge in some detail at his execution, while admitting that he planned to escape to France.

33. Latham, *Poems*, 151; Harlow, *Last Voyage*, 276–77, 285.

34. Lefranc, *Ralegh*, 596, citing Wilson's letter to James, 2 November 1618; Edwards, *Life*, 2:499.

35. *Works*, 8:781.

36. Harlow, *Last Voyage*, 304, 311.

37. *Works*, 8:781–82.

38. *Chamberlain Letters*, ed. McClure, 2:179; BL Harleian MS. 3787, fol. 182; Beal, *Index*, notes a second copy in All Soul's College, Oxford, MS. 155, fols. 144v-5.

39. *Chamberlain Letters*, ed. McClure, 2:176; the Spanish agent Ulloa heard that the speech lasted some three quarters of an hour (Harlow, *Last Voyage*, 314).

40. Harlow, *Last Voyage*, 308. Another account reports that Ralegh said, "I neuer thought such ill of him in my heart" (Bowers, "Ralegh's last Speech," 213).

Chapter Seven

1. Sir Charles Firth, "Sir Walter Raleigh's *History of the World*," *Essays Historical and Literary* (Oxford: Clarendon Press, 1938), 52.

2. See my *Poems of . . . Essex*, 106–8, and Agnes M. C. Latham, *Poems of Sir Walter Ralegh* (London: Routledge & Kegan Paul, 1951), 137–38.

3. G. C. Moore Smith first suggested the identification in Harington's epigrams in "Sir Walter Raleigh as Seen by Sir John Harington," *TLS* 10 March 1927, 160. V. T. Harlow, "Harington's Epigrams," *TLS* 14 July 1927, 488, termed the identification "conclusive." The connection with Davies's Paulus was proposed in Carolyn J. Bishop's "Raleigh Satirized by Harington and Davies," *RES* 22 (1972): 52–56. Davies's modern editor, Robert Krueger, judges the Ralegh-Paulus equation "uncertain" (*The Poems of Sir John Davies* [Oxford: Clarendon Press, 1975], 381).

4. *Davies*, ed. Krueger, Epigram 41; Harington, Epigram 126, in *Letters and Epigrams of Sir John Harington*, ed. Norman McClure (Philadelphia: University of Pennsylvania Press, 1930).

5. For the Galla-Paulus epigram see R. H. Miller's "Unpublished Poems by Sir John Harington," *ELR* 13 (1983):154–5.

6. *Virgidemiarum*, 1598, in *The Collected Poems of Joseph Hall*, ed. A. Davenport (Liverpool; Liverpool University Press, 1949), book 4, satire 3, lines 29–30, 35. Sidney H. Atkins, "'Fortunio' and 'Raymundus,'" *TLS* 3 October 1935, 612, suggested that Fortunio was Lawrence Keymis while Ralegh was depicted as Raymundus, whose alchemical experiments are described next in Hall's satire. The theory was extended in Waldo F. McNeir's "Hall's 'Fortunio' and 'Raymundus' Once More," *Notes and Queries* 204 (1959):255–57. However, Ralegh was not known to have practiced the kind of alchemy that attempted to change base metals into gold. Other problems with these identifications are noted by Davenport (210).

7. Thomas B. Stroup traces the genesis of these tales in "Shakespeare's Use of a Travel-Book Commonplace," *Philological Quarterly* 17 (1938):351–58.

8. *Othello*, I.iii.144–45; *The Tempest*, III.iii.46–47, from *The Riverside Shakespeare*, ed. G. B. Evans (Boston: Houghton Mifflin, 1974).

9. Peacham, STC 19067; *Poems of . . . Essex*, 60.

10. McClure, *Letters . . . of Harington*, 108–9.

11. The fullest expression of this theory is Muriel C. Bradbrook's *The School of Night: A Study in the Literary Relationships of Sir Walter Raleigh* (Cambridge: Cambridge University Press, 1936). Strathmann, in *Ralegh*, argues for a less sensational interpretation of the meager evidence for any such "school," based upon a more thorough study of the Elizabethan intellectual context (262–71).

12. Paulette Michel-Michot, "Sir Walter Raleigh as a Source for the Character of Iago," *English Studies* 50 (1969):85–89; Eleanor Grace Clark, *Ralegh and Marlowe, A Study in Elizabethan Fustian* (1941; reprint, New York: Fordham University Press, 1965).

13. William Power, "'The Phoenix,' Raleigh, and King James," *Notes and Queries* 203 (1958):57–61.

14. D. P. V. Akrigg, "Webster and Raleigh," *Notes and Queries* 193 (1948): 427–28; Thomas Heywood, *Fair Maid of the West*, Part 1, ed. Robert K. Turner, (Lincoln: University of Nebraska Press, 1967), IV.iv.31–32.

15. *Poems of John Marston*, ed. Arnold Davenport (Liverpool: Liverpool University Press, 1961), 84.

16. John Donne, *The Satires, Epigrams and Verse Letters*, ed. W. Milgate (Oxford: Clarendon Press, 1967), 65.

17. E. H. Fellowes, *English Madrigal Verse*, 3d ed., ed. Frederick W. Sternfeld and David Greer (Oxford: Clarendon Press, 1967), 163.

18. The allegory is examined in greater detail in Michael O'Connell's *Mirror and Veil, the Historical Dimension of Spenser's Faerie Queene* (Chapel Hill: University of North Carolina Press, 1977), 107–24. See James P. Bednarz, "Raleigh in Spenser's Historical Allegory," *Spenser Studies* 4 (1984):60–65.

19. Ralegh mentions his daughter in the will he drew up in 1597 and in his letter to Bess after the arrest of 1603 (Agnes M. C. Latham, "Sir Walter Ralegh's Farewell Letter to his Wife in 1603: A Question of Authenticity," *Essays and Studies* 25 [1940]:40). See Latham's "Sir Walter Ralegh's Will," *RES* 22 (1971):132–33, for Ralegh's reference to "my poore daughter." The girl was apparently of marriageable age by the turn of the century, for about 1601 Ralegh matched her with Daniel Dumaresq, whose wardship he acquired after becoming governor of Jersey.

20. Peter Ure, "The Poetry of Sir Walter Ralegh," in *Elizabethan and Jacobean Drama*, ed. J. C. Maxwell (Liverpool: Liverpool University Press, 1974), 244. A. D. Cousins argues for a mannerist strain in "Cynthia" (Poem 14) and in "The Lie" on grounds of their emphasis on disorder in opposition to the concept of art as an organizing and unifying endeavor ("The Coming of Mannerism," 91–97).

21. Ian A. Gordon, *The Movement of English Prose* (Bloomington: Indiana University Press, 1966), 105–6.

22. Christopher Hill, *The Intellectual Origins of the English Revolution* (Oxford: Clarendon Press, 1965), 210.

23. See Hill, *Intellectual Origins,* chapter 4, for a detailed analysis of the extent to which Ralegh's political and economic thought developed ahead of his time.

24. David Beers Quinn, *Ralegh and the British Empire* (New York: Macmillan, 1949), cited in Hill, *English Revolution,* 157.

25. *History,* 4:576, 5:508, 6:76–77, 330–33; 7:643.

Selected Bibliography

PRIMARY WORKS

Poetry

Listed in the approximate order of composition with cross-references to the numbers in the editions of Rudick and Latham.

		Rudick	Latham
1.	"Swete were the sauce"	I	I
2.	"Sweete ar the thoughtes"	1	II
3.	"Callinge to minde"	V	IX
4.	"Farewell falce Love"	II	V
5.	"The word of deniall"	4	XXVII
6.	"Fortune hath taken thee away"		
7.	"To praise thy life"	III	IV
8.	"Like truthless dreams"	VIII	XII
9.	"Me thought I saw the grave"	VI	XIII
10.	"The prayse of meaner wits"	VII	XIV
11.	"Now we have present made"	IX	
12.	"If Synthia be a Queene"	X	XXII
13.	"My boddy in the walls captived"	XI	XXIII
14.	"Sufficeth it to yow"	XII	XXIV
15.	"My dayes delights"	XIII	XXV
16.	"Goe soule, the bodies guest"	XIV	XXVI
17.	"Nature that washt her hands"	XV	XX
18.	"What is our life?"	XVII	XXXI
19.	"One fire than other burnes"	XVIII	p. 67
20.	"Had *Lucan* hid the truth"	XIX	XXXV
21.	"My daye's delight"		
22.	"My dayes delight"	XX	XXXVII

23.	"O had Truth Power"	XXI	XXXVIII
24.	"My broken pipes"	XXII	XXXIX
25.	"Even such is tyme"	XXIII	XL

Poems Possibly by Ralegh

i.	"Lady farewell"	2	III
ii.	"Conceipt begotten by the eyes"	5	XVII
iii.	"Passions are likened best"	6	XVIII (lines 1–6 only)
iv.	"Three thinges there be"	7	XXIX

Prose

Listed in the approximate order of composition. Short titles in parentheses indicate the abbreviations by which these works are cited in this study.

(*Revenge*) *A Report of the Truth of the fight about the Iles of Acores, this last Sommer. Betwixt the Revenge, . . . And an Armada of the King of Spain* (1591). In *Sir Walter Raleigh, Selected Prose and Poetry.* Edited by Agnes M. C. Latham, 72–87. London: Routledge & Kegan Paul, 1965.

(*"Succession"*) Untitled tract on the succession to the crown (1592–93). Edited by Pierre Lefranc. "Un Inédit de Ralegh Sur La Succession." *Études Anglaises* 13 (1960):42–46.

(*Discovery*) *The Discoverie of the Large, Rich, and Bewtiful Empyre of Guiana* (1595). *The Works of Sir Walter Ralegh*, 1829; reprint, New York: Burt Franklin, [1965], 8:379–476.

"Of the Voyage for Guyana" (1595–96). In *The Discoverie of the large and bewtiful Empire of Guiana.* Edited by V. T. Harlow, 138–49. London: Argonaut Press, 1928.

(*"Cadiz"*) "Narrative of the Action in Cadiz Harbour" (July–August 1596). *Works,* 8:667–674.

(*"Opinion"*) "The Opinion of Sir Walter Ralegh upon the same Articles" (November 1596). *Works,* 8:675–681.

(*"Offensive"*) Untitled tract on the conduct of an offensive war against Spain (1596–97). Pierre Lefranc, "Un inédit de Ralegh sur la conduite de la Guerre (1596–97)." *Études Anglaises* 8 (1955):204–11.

(*"Observations"*) "Observations and Notes Concerning the Royal Navy and Sea Service" (1597–98; revised ca. 1608). *Works,* 8:335–350.

(*"War with Spain"*) "A Discourse Touching a War with Spain, and of the Protecting of the Netherlands" (1602–3). *Works,* 8:299–316.

"Instructions to his Son" (1603–5). In *Advice to a Son, Precepts of Lord Burghley, Sir Walter Raleigh, and Francis Osborne.* Edited by Louis B. Wright, 19–32. Ithaca: Cornell University Press, 1962.

"On the Seat of Government" (1604–16). *Works,* 8:538–40.

(*"War by Sea"*) "Of the Art of Warre by Sea" (1608–9?). Fragments edited by Pierre Lefranc in *Sir Walter Ralegh Ecrivain,* 597–601. Paris: Librairie Armand Colin, 1968.

(*"Jesuit"*) "A Dialogue between a Jesuit and a Recusant" (1611–12). *An Abridgment of Sir Walter Raleigh's History of the World in Five Books.* London, 1700. The tract is mispaginated in both the 1700 and 1702 editions; my references are to the second signation, sigs. C4-F3v. No modern edition.

The History of the World (1614). *Works,* vols. 2–7. Cited first by Ralegh's book and chapter numbers, then by volume and page from the *Works.*

(*"Prerogative"*) The Prerogative of Parliaments in England (1615). *Works,* 8:151–221.

(*"Invention of Ships"*) "A Discourse of the Invention of Ships, Anchors, Compass, &c." (1618). *Works,* 8:317–334.

(*"Cause of War"*) "A Discourse of the Original and Fundamental Cause of Natural, Arbitrary, Necessary, and Unnatural War" (1614–16), *Works,* 8:253–297.

(*"Journal"*) "Sir Walter Ralegh's Journal of his Second Voyage to Guiana" (1617–18). In *The Discovery of the Large, Rich, and Beautiful Empire of Guiana.* Edited by Sir Robert H. Schomburgk, 177–208. Hakluyt Society Publications, 1st ser., no. 3. London: Hakluyt Society, 1848.

(*"Apology"*) "Apology for his Voyage to Guiana" (July 1618). *Works,* 8:479–507.

Works Possibly by Ralegh

(*"Match"*) "A Discourse Touching a Match Propounded by the Savoyan Between the Lady Elizabeth and the Prince of Piedmont" (1611). *Works,* 8:223–36.

(*"Marriage"*) "A Discourse Touching a Marriage between Prince Henry of England, and a Daughter of Savoy" (1612). *Works,* 8:237–52.

"Orders to be observed by the Commanders of the Fleet" (3 May 1617). *Works,* 8:382–88.

"A Speech found in Sir Walter Rawleighes pockett after his Execution Written by him in the Gatehouse *the* night befores [*sic*] dea[th]." BL Harleian MS. 3787, fol. 182.

SECONDARY WORKS

Bibliographies

Armitage, Christopher M. *Sir Walter Ralegh, an Annotated Bibliography.* Chapel Hill: University of North Carolina Press, 1987. Topical arrangement, with less detailed annotations than Mills (1986) but more complete coverage.

Brushfield, T. N. *A Bibliography of Sir Walter Ralegh Knt.* 1908. Reprint. New

York: Burt Franklin, 1968. Still useful for its coverage of primary sources and nineteenth-century scholarship on Ralegh.

Mills, Jerry Leath. "Recent Studies in Ralegh." *English Literary Renaissance* 15 (1985):225–44. Well-annotated survey of mid-twentieth-century Ralegh scholarship.

_____. *Sir Walter Ralegh: A Reference Guide.* Boston: G. K. Hall, 1986. Chronological annotated survey of Ralegh scholarship, 1901–84.

Books and Parts of Books

Adamson, J. H., and H. F. Folland. *The Shepherd of the Ocean, an Account of Sir Walter Ralegh and His Times.* London: Bodley Head, 1969. A readable, comprehensive biography covering Ralegh's life, times, and works.

Beal, Peter. *Index of English Literary Manuscripts.* Vol. 1, 1450–1625, part 1. London: Mansell, 1980. Locates manuscript copies of Ralegh's authentic and doubtful works in verse and prose. Introduction deals with books and papers owned by Ralegh, his letters, and the apocrypha.

Davie, Donald. "A Reading of 'The Ocean's Love to Cynthia.'" In *Elizabethan Poetry*, edited by John Russell Brown and Bernard Harris, 70–89. Stratford-Upon-Avon Studies, no. 2. London: Edward Arnold, 1960. Interprets the "Cynthia" as a revised but unfinished tribute to the queen's power over Ralegh's will.

Edwards, Edward. *The Life of Sir Walter Ralegh.* 2 vols. London: Macmillan, 1868. Remains an essential work on Ralegh for its well-documented life with texts of his letters and related papers.

Edwards, Philip. *Sir Walter Ralegh.* London: Longmans, Green, 1953. Appreciative survey of the poetry and prose with emphasis on the "Cynthia" poems and *History of the World.*

Firth, Sir Charles. "Sir Walter Raleigh's *History of the World.*" In *Essays Historical and Literary*, 34–60. Oxford: Clarendon Press, 1938. Discusses the composition and seventeenth-century influence of the *History.*

Fussner, F. Smith. *The Historical Revolution, English Historical Writing and Thought 1580–1640.* New York: Columbia University Press, 1962. Chapter 7, "Sir Walter Ralegh and Universal History," analyzes the philosophical background and didactic purpose of the *History.*

Greenblatt, Stephen J. *Sir Walter Ralegh: The Renaissance Man and His Roles.* New Haven: Yale University Press, 1973. Interprets Ralegh's writings, speech, and actions as the conscious creation of a "fashioned" life.

Harlow, V. T. *Ralegh's Last Voyage.* London: Argonaut Press, 1932. Offers a wealth of contemporary documents concerning the second Guiana voyage and its aftermath.

Hill, Christopher. *The Intellectual Origins of the English Revolution.* Oxford: Clarendon Press, 1965. Chapter 4 portrays Ralegh as far ahead of his times in his understanding of science, political theory, and economics.

Latham, Agnes M. C. "Sir Walter Ralegh's *Instructions to his Son*." In *Elizabethan and Jacobean Studies Presented to Frank Percy Wilson*, 199–218. Oxford: Clarendon Press, 1959. Supplements the printed texts of Ralegh's *Instructions* with material from BL Add. MS. 22587.

Lefranc, Pierre. *Sir Walter Ralegh Écrivain*. Paris: Librairie Armand Colin, 1968. Comprehensive survey of Ralegh's canon and text, with analysis of his intellectual and cultural background, including sources, influences, and new texts by or relevant to Ralegh.

Patrides, C. A., ed. *Sir Walter Ralegh, The History of the World*. Philadelphia: Temple University Press, 1971. An abridged edition with an introduction stressing Ralegh's providential theory of history.

Racin, John. *Sir Walter Ralegh as Historian: An Analysis of the History of the World*. Salzburg, Austria: Institut für Englische Sprache and Literatur, Universität Salzburg, 1974. Covers the composition, publication history, philosophical and theological background of Ralegh's *History*.

Strathmann, Ernest A. *Sir Walter Ralegh, a Study in Elizabethan Skepticism*. New York: Columbia University Press, 1951. Analyzes Ralegh's intellectual makeup in its Renaissance context and affirms his Christian orientation as opposed to the accusations of atheism.

Tennenhouse, Leonard. "Sir Walter Ralegh and the Literature of Clientage." In *Patronage in the Renaissance*, edited by Guy Fitch Lytle and Stephen Orgel, 235–58. Princeton: Princeton University Press, 1981. Interprets Ralegh's quest for patronage through his poetry under Queen Elizabeth and King James.

Ure, Peter. "The Poetry of Sir Walter Ralegh." In *Elizabethan and Jacobean Drama: Critical Essays,* edited by J. C. Maxwell, 237–47. New York: Barnes & Noble, 1974. Sensitive analysis of the melancholy and tragic strain in Ralegh's Elizabethan verse.

Wallace, Willard M. *Sir Walter Raleigh*. Princeton: Princeton University Press, 1959. Scholarly coverage of Ralegh's career and writings.

Articles

Bednarz, James P. "Ralegh in Spenser's Historical Allegory." *Spenser Studies* 4 (1984):49–70. Traces Ralegh's most likely appearances throughout the allegory of the *Faerie Queene*.

Bishop, Carolyn J. "Raleigh Satirized by Harington and Davies." *Review of English Studies* 23, n.s. (1972):52–56. Equates Ralegh with Paulus in the epigrams of both poets.

Clanton, Stacy M. "The 'Number' of Sir Walter Ralegh's *Booke of the Ocean to Scinthia.*" *Studies in Philology* 82 (1985):200–11. Compares other numerals in Ralegh's hand to show that the Hatfield MS numbers the "Cynthia" books 21 and 22.

Cousins, A. D. "The Coming of Mannerism: The Later Ralegh and the Early Donne." *English Literary Renaissance* 9 (1979):86–107. Argues that Ralegh's disillusion with the "Tudor aesthetic" caused him to write in the new mannerist style.

Duncan-Jones, Katherine. "The Date of Ralegh's '21th: and Last Booke of the Ocean to Scinthia.'" *Review of English Studies* 21, n.s. (1970):143–58. Interprets the "Cynthia" as an elegy for the queen rather than a plea for restoration to favor.

Edwards, Philip W. "Who Wrote *The Passionate Man's Pilgrimage?*" *English Literary Renaisance* 4 (1974):83–97. Argues that the poem belongs to a Catholic literary tradition and could not be Ralegh's.

Gossett, Suzanne. "A New History for Ralegh's *Notes on the Navy.*" *Modern Philology* 85 (1987):12–26. Restores the Elizabethan state of the "Observations" from a version of the text in Folger MS J.a.1.

Horner, Joyce. "The Large Landscape: A Study of Certain Images in Ralegh." *Essays in Criticism* 5 (1955):197–213. Reads the "Cynthia" as an emotional lament filled with nature imagery, but failing to sustain its "Cynthia and the sea" motif or its pastoralism.

Johnson, Michael L. "Some Problems of Unity in Sir Walter Ralegh's *The Ocean's Love to Cynthia.*" *Studies in English Literature* 14 (1974):17–30. Reads the poem as an impulsive and poorly organized expression of grief on the theme of Ralegh's banishment from court.

Latham, Agnes M. C. "Sir Walter Ralegh's Farewell Letter to his Wife in 1603: A Question of Authenticity." *Essays and Studies* 25 (1940):39–58. Argues for the authenticity of the letter transcribed in a manuscript at All Souls College, Oxford.

————. "Sir Walter Ralegh's Will." *Review of English Studies* 22, n.s. (1971): 129–36. The will of July 1597 mentions Ralegh's daughter by Alice Goold who is also referred to in the letter of 1603 (Latham, 1940).

Lefranc, Pierre. "Une Nouvelle Version de la 'Petition to Queen Anne' de Sir Walter Ralegh." *Annales de la Faculté des Lettres et Sciences Humaines de Nice* 34 (1978):57–67. Presents a seventy-eight-line text of the "Petition" (Poem 21) with evidence that the poem was written during the imprisonment of 1603 rather than that of 1618.

Luciani, Vincent. "Ralegh's 'Discourses on the Savoyan Matches' and Machiavelli's 'Istorie Fiorentine.'" *Italica* 29 (1952):103–7. Traces three direct borrowings from Machiavelli in the "Marriage" tract.

May, Steven W. "Companion Poems in the Ralegh Canon." *English Literary Renaissance* 13 (1983):260–73. Shows that "Sweete ar the thoughtes" echoes a poem by George Whetstone, and that Sir Thomas Heneage wrote answering verses to "Farewell falce Love."

Oakeshott, Walter, "Sir Walter Ralegh's Library." *Library* 23, 5th ser. (1968):285–327. Provides an annotated list of the books from Ralegh's library in the Tower as recorded in BL Add. MS. 57555.

Power, William. "'The Phoenix,' Raleigh, and King James." *Notes and Queries* 203

(1958):57–61. Identifies Ralegh as Proditur in Thomas Middleton's *The Phoenix*.

Rudick, Michael. "The 'Ralegh Group' in *The Phoenix Nest*." *Studies in Bibliography* 24 (1971):131–37. Gives Ralegh only two of the sixteen lyrics claimed for him without further attribution by previous scholars.

———. "The Text of Ralegh's Lyric, 'What is Our Life?'" *Studies in Philology* 83 (1986):76–87. Analyzes variant readings in early texts of the poem to arrive at a critical text.

Stibbs, John H. "Raleigh and Holinshed." *Modern Language Review* 44 (1949): 543–44. Finds that Ralegh's historical background in the *Prerogative* derives from Holinshed's *Chronicle*.

———. "Raleigh's Account of Grenville's Fight at the Azores in 1591." *North Carolina Historical Review* 27 (1950):20–31. Compares Ralegh's account in the *Revenge* pamphlet with two independent contemporary records of the battle.

Stillman, Robert E. "'Words Cannot knyt': Language and Desire in Ralegh's *The Ocean to Synthia*." *Studies in English Literature* 27 (1987):35–51. Interprets the poem as Ralegh's unsuccessful effort to transmute the symbols he used to represent his relationship with the queen after his disgrace.

Strathmann, E. A. "Ralegh Plans his Last Voyage." *Mariner's Mirror* 50 (1964): 261–70. Prints the unique text of Ralegh's proposal for the second Guiana voyage from Folger MS G.b.10.

Williams, Arnold. "Commentaries on Genesis as a Basis for Hexaemeral Material in the Literature of the Late Renaissance." *Studies in Philology* 34 (1937):191–208. Ralegh relied on Pererius's *Commentariorum* for much of his scholarly analysis of *Genesis* in the *History*.

Index